HISTORIC TEXTS AND INTERPRETERS IN BIBLICAL SCHOLARSHIP

THEOLOGY AS HERMENEUTICS

Rudolf Bultmann's Interpretation of the History of Jesus

John Painter

The Almond Press · 1987

For my friend John Cumpsty

Published by Almond Press
Almond Press is an imprint of
Sheffield Academic Press
The University of Sheffield
343 Fulwood Road
Sheffield S10 3BP
England

Typeset by Sheffield Academic Press
and
printed in Great Britain
by Billings & Sons Ltd
Worcester

British Library Cataloguing in Publication Data

Painter, John
Theology as hermeneutics : Bultmann's interpretation of the history of Jesus.—
(Historic text and interpreters in Biblical scholarship, ISSN 0263-1199; 4)
1. Bultmann, Rudolf
I. Title II. Series
230'.092'4 BX4827.B78

ISBN 1-85075-050-5
ISBN 1-85075-051-3Pbk

CONTENTS

Preface

My interest in the work of Rudolf Bultmann goes back to my days as an undergraduate student. I was soon to learn that what Bultmann has to say himself is often misrepresented in the secondary literature. In my present role as a teacher I find that my students are faced with the same problems. In many ways they are the reason for this book. A course on *Contemporary Christian Thought* gave me the opportunity to develop the basic outline of the book in a small section of that course devoted to Bultmann. An Outside Studies Program in 1980 enabled me to complete the research and a first draft of the manuscript. Returning to teaching and administrative duties prevented the completion of the book until 1983. My aim was then to have the book published in 1984 to mark the centenary of Bultmann's birth on the 20th of August. Finding an English publisher for such a project proved to be a problem. Bultmann was out of fashion. That this was the case even beyond the shores of Great Britain became apparent in Bultmann's centenary year. One purpose of this book is to argue that Bultmann's work is both important and relevant today.

My manuscript was submitted to Fortress Press in 1983 with a view to publication in Bultmann's centenary year. After a long delay Fortress indicated that they had decided, on balance, that they would prefer to publish a volume of Bultmann's own essays, *New Testament and Mythology*, and the essays from the Wellesley Symposium, *Bultmann in Retrospect and Prospect*. While awaiting the page proofs of *Theology as Hermeneutics*, the Wellesley essays came into my hands. The essay by Schubert Ogden on Bultmann's christology is important. It makes a number of emphases in agreement with my own presentation:

1. Criticisms of Bultmann's christology are generally inadequate, being based on a caricature of his position (see pp. 38, 49, 57f.).

2. The historical Jesus and his preaching are the indispensable presupposition of the kerygma. The distinction between the person and personality of Jesus is crucial (see pp. 52ff. and compare my critique of Roberts, pp. 178f.–212, especially pp. 200ff. below).

3. There is a difference between the first believers and believers today in that the witness of the first believers remains normative, hence the role of New Testament theology.

I am glad to find new support from Ogden's work as I regard him to be one of the more perceptive interpreters of Bultmann, as my treatment of his earlier work shows. There is one important assertion, made in his earlier work (*Point*, p. 111), which is influencing current views, with which I must take issue. There Ogden argued that Bultmann asserted nothing could be said of the 'empirical-historical' Jesus, appealing for evidence to Bultmann's *Jesus*, pp. 14–16 (pp. 16–19 in my edition). This is a mistaken view and inconsistent with Ogden's own recognition of the essential link between the historical Jesus and the kerygma. It could be that Ogden attributed to Bultmann a view which Bultmann criticized in Barth's view of the resurrection (seee below pp. 81ff.); that there are certain events that we know have happened but which cannot be established using historical methods. But if they cannot be established in this way, as Bultmann asked Barth, how can we know that they have happened? Bultmann certainly did not hold this view.

His reconstruction of the teaching of Jesus is based on the critical methodology worked out and demonstrated in *The History of the Synoptic Tradition*. His method was to trace the history of the Synoptic tradition back to its oldest layer. Even this could not be assumed to be authentic to Jesus as it had been transmitted in the witness of the believing community. Hence Bultmann developed criteria for recognizing what was authentic within the oldest tradition. Norman Perrin (*Rediscovering the Teaching of Jesus*, pp. 40, 43) has recognized that the criteria of 'dissimilarity' and 'coherence' were originally developed by Bultmann in his pioneering work. The aim of this work was to establish what could be said, with some degree of probability, about the historical Jesus. Of the reconstruction on the basis of these methods Bultmann wrote:

> By tradition Jesus is named as the bearer of the message, according to overwhelming probability he really was (*Jesus*, p. 18 my edition).

If Ogden concluded that 'overwhelming probability' does not put us in touch with the 'empirical-historical' Jesus, he has misunderstood the status of the understanding which results from historical reconstuction. Knowledge of the past is established with a greater or lesser degree of probability. In the case of Jesus as the bearer of the message so reconstructed, Bultmann argued that this has been established as the 'overwhelming probability'. It was, however, his view that such an understanding could not establish what faith proclaimed in the kerygma, and that the certainty of faith goes beyond the probability of historical reconstruction. These qualifications should not be allowed to obscure the fact that Bultmann asserted the necessity of the historical Jesus for faith, and beyond that, outlined the details of knowledge which we have of Jesus and his teaching. That is, the historian can know, as overwhelmingly probable, more about the historical Jesus than the believer needs to know. The believer has the assurance of the correctness of the connection between the Jesus of history and the Christ of the kerygma, as a matter of faith. The appearance of the collection of essays seems an appropriate time to comment on this matter, which is discussed at length in what follows.

Since this manuscript was completed E.P. Sanders' *Jesus and Judaism* (Fortress Press, 1985) has been published. In this book Sanders has continued the line of criticism begun in *Paul and Palestinian Judaism* (see pp. 107-11 below). In response to criticism Sanders now acknowledges that Bultmann has interpreted Jesus in the context of Judaism, not Christianity (p. 361 n. 27). But he does not consider the treatment adequate. How could one who, as Sanders argued, stands in the succession of Bousset and Billerbeck (*Jesus and Judaism*, p. 29) understand Judaism adequately? Naturally there is room to debate, on the basis of evidence and sound historical methods, how Jesus is to be understood in relation to the Gospel tradition. But it is not in such terms that Sanders criticizes Bultmann's understanding. Of critical importance is the question of whether Jesus like Paul was critical of Jewish legalism. From Sanders' perspective Jewish legalism was virtually non-existent in the first century. The question is, has Sanders portrayed Judaism as 'a pale reflection of Protestant Christianity'? From a Jewish point of view, what is wrong with legalism, as long as the term is free of pejorative connotations? This question is forcefully put by P.S. Alexander in his review of Sanders' *Jesus and Judaism* in the *Journal of Jewish Studies*, Vol. XXXVII, No. 1 (Spring, 1986), pp. 103-106 especially point 3, p. 105.

One final word is appropriate. This book on Bultmann has been written by someone working in the area of New Testament Studies and especially in Johannine studies, not by a professional systematic theologian. Like Bultmann the author is a contemporary Christian who must think of what the New Testament means for us today and not merely what it meant as a document of the past. It seems to me that sharing this perspective is an important qualification for understanding Bultmann rather than a limitation.

In the writing of a book there are many who contribute in indirect ways. La Trobe University gave me study leave in 1980 and the secretarial staff in the Department of History and especially Sharon James in the Division of Religious Studies have worked on various stages of the manuscript. Michael Kellock worked out the program to enable the manuscript to be transferred from our Word Processing equipment to a set of discs for typesetting. Kingsley Barrett and John Rogerson recommended the book for inclusion in this series. I am grateful to them all for their help.

The book was essentially finished in 1983. Only minor adjustments have been made since then, most of these to conform the manuscript to the style of the series in which it now appears. I acknowledge with thanks the precise assistance given by the editorial staff of the Sheffield Academic Press.

ABBREVIATIONS

Full details of all works referred to are given in the bibliography.

1. **Works by Bultmann**

'AR'	'Autobiographical Reflections', in Kegley, pp. xix-xxv and *EF* pp. 283-288.
'CHD'	'C. H. Dodd, The Interpretation of the Fourth Gospel', in *NTS* I, 1954, pp. 77-91; ET in *HDB* 27, 1963.
'DJNF'	'Das Johannesevangelium in der neuesten Forschung'
EF	*Existence and Faith*
EPT	*Essays Philosophical and Theological*
Exegetica	
FC	*Form Criticism*
FU	*Faith and Understanding*
GJ	*The Gospel of John*, ET of *EJ*
GV	*Glauben und Verstehen* (4 vols.)
'GTPC'	'General Truths and Christian Proclamation', in *History and Hermeneutic*, ed. by R.W. Funk, pp. 153-62.
HE	*History and Eschatology*
HST	*History of the Synoptic Tradition*
JCM	*Jesus Christ and Mythology*
Jesus	
JR	*Journal of Religion*, 1962, also in *NTI*, ed. by R. Batey, pp. 35-44.
K&M	*Kerygma and Myth* (2 vols.), being extracts from *KuM*
KuM	*Kerygma und Mythos*, ed. by H.W. Bartsch
Letters	*Karl Barth Rudolf Bultmann Letters 1922-1966*
M&C	*Myth and Christianity*
'OTPD'	'On the Problem of Demythologizing', in Batey, pp. 35-44.
PC	*Primitive Christianity in its Contemporary Setting*

'PCKHJ'	'The Primitive Christian Kerygma and the Historical Jesus' in *HJKC* (see below)
'Reply'	in Kegley, pp. 257-87.
'RHG'	Review of *Honest to God*, in *The Honest to God Debate*, ed. by J.A.T. Robinson and D.L. Edwards, pp. 134-38.
'SOTCF'	'The Significance of the Old Testament for Christian Faith', in Anderson, pp. 8-35.
ThNT	*Theology of the New Testament* (2 vols.)
'TIGMM'	'The Idea of God and Modern Man', in *World Come of Age* ed. by R. Gregor Smith, pp. 256-74.
'TLYN'	'To Love your Neighbour', in *Scottish Periodical* I, 1947, pp. 42-56.
TWB	*This World and the Beyond*

2. **Other Works**

ABR	*Australian Biblical Review*
AET	*An Existentialist Theology*, Macquarrie
Anderson	*The Old Testament and Christian Faith*
AR	*Archiv für Religionswissenschaft*
Barth	*Romans*
Barth, *CD*	*Church Dogmatics*
Barth, *KD*	Being the German original of *Church Dogmatics*
Bousset	*Kyrios Christos*
Braaten	*History and Hermeneutics*
B&T	*Being and Time*, Heidegger
BTB	*Biblical Theology Bulletin*
CBQ	*Catholic Biblical Quarterly*
ChrW	*Die Christliche Welt*
Edwards	*Reason and Religion*
ExpTim	*Expository Times*
Fuller	*The Formation of the Resurrection Narratives*
Frankfort	*Before Philosophy*
HJKC	*The Historical Jesus and the Kerygmatic Christ*, ed. by C.E. Braaten & R.A. Harrisville
HTR	*Harvard Theological Review*
HZ	*Historische Zeitschrift*
JHI	*Journal of the History of Ideas*

Johnson	*The Origins of Demythologizing*
JR	*Journal of Religion*
JTC	*Journal for Theology and the Church*
JTSA	*Journal of Theology for Southern Africa*
Kähler	*The So-called Historical Jesus and the Historic Biblical Christ*
Kegley	*The Theology of Rudolf Bultmann*
Küng, *God*	*Does God Exist?*
Küng, *Christian*	*On Being a Christian*
Macquarrie, *Scope*	*The Scope of Demythologizing*
Malet	*The Thought of Rudolf Bultmann*
Nicholls	*Systematic and Philosophical Theology*
NTI	*New Testament Interpretation*, ed. Marshall
NTI, Batey	*New Testament Issues*, ed. Batey
NTS	*New Testament Studies*
Oden	*Radical Obedience*
Ogden, *CWM*	*Christ Without Myth*
Ogden, *TRG*	*The Reality of God*
Ogden, 'OR'	'On Revelation', in *Our Common History*, ed. by Deschner, Howe and Penzel
Ogden, *Point*	*The Point of Christology*
Palmer	*Hermeneutics*
Pannenberg	*Revelation as History*
Perrin	*The Resurrection Narratives: A New Approach*
PICG	*Proceedings of the International Colloquium on Gnosticism*, ed. by Geo Widengren
RGG	*Die Religion in Geschichte und Gegenwart*
RHPh	*Revue d'Historie et de Philosophie Religieuses*
RM	*Review of Metaphysics*
Roberts	*Rudolf Bultmann's Theology*
Robinson, *TBDT*	*The Beginnings of Dialectical Theology*
Robinson, *NQHJ*	*A New Quest of the Historical Jesus*
Robinson, *Theology*	*Theology as History*
Robinson, *NH*	*The New Hermeneutic*
Robinson, 'TPHD'	'The Pre-history of Demythologizing', in *Interpretation*
RSR	*Religious Studies Review*
Sanders	*Paul and Palestinian Judaism*
Schillebeeckx	*Jesus: An Experiment in Christology*
Schmithals	*An Introduction to the Theology of Rudolf Bultmann*

SJT	*Scottish Journal of Theology*
Smith	*The Composition and Order of the Fourth Gospel*
TBCP	*The Beginnings of Christian Philosophy*
TDNT	*Theological Dictionary of the New Testament*
ThBl	*Theologische Blätter*
Thiselton	*Two Horizons*
ThLZ	*Theologische Literaturzeitung*
ThR	*Theologische Rundschau*
ThT	*Theology Today*
Tracy, *TAI*	*The Analogical Imagination*
Young	*History and Existentialist Theology*
Young, *Creator*	*Creator, Creation and Faith*
ZKG	*Zeitschrift für Kirchengeschichte*
ZNW	*Zeitschrift für die neutestamentliche Wissenschaft*
ZTK	*Zeitschrift für Theologie und Kirche*
Zuurdeeg	*An Analytical Philosophy of Religion*
ZZ	*Zwischen den Zeiten*

Introduction

Rudolf Bultmann was born on the 20th August 1884 and died on the 30th July 1976, the last of the great European theologians born in the 1880s. His studies were undertaken at Tübingen, Berlin, and Marburg where his most notable teachers were Hermann Gunkel, Adolf Harnack, Wilhelm Herrmann, Adolf Jülicher, Karl Müller and Johannes Weiss. Marburg became his *alma mater* and he returned there as Professor of New Testament in 1921, remaining there until his retirement in 1951, having declined various other offers. He was a foundation member of the Confessing Church (from 1934) and an opponent of the *Third Reich*. His opposition was expressed in his academic work, in essays from the period, and in his actions in relation to the Jewish question ('AR', Kegley, p. xxi). He was not only concerned with the independence of the Church but more especially with human dignity and freedom. The biographical details recently published by the Jewish philosopher Hans Jonas throw significant light on this aspect of Bultmann's life.[1] Only because Bultmann cared sufficiently and dared to support Jonas was Jonas' great work on Gnosticism published. Here we find evidence that, for Bultmann, Christian values are human values, but experienced with an urgency and clarity not always evident elsewhere.

Bultmann's thought has not fared well in England. Perhaps what was perceived as his historical scepticism is the basis of this situation. Nor did the demythologizing debate help his reputation. The situation has been exacerbated by the absence of any standard collection of his works, not to mention that there is no standard translation of his writings. Those works that have been translated do not follow a standard translation practice. His great commentary on the Fourth Gospel had three translators, each of whom appears to have gone his own way to some extent. Hence there is no standard translation of such crucial terms as *Dasein*, *Sein*, *Existenz*; *existentiell*, *existential*; *Geschichte*, *geschichtlich*, *historisch*; etc. Translations have contributed to the problem of understanding Bultmann in English.

Misunderstandings have also arisen because Bultmann tends to state his position bluntly, often failing to define his terms carefully, e.g. 'myth', 'symbol', 'analogy'. Because of this what he has written is open to misunderstanding, though ambiguities in one essay can often be clarified by reference to another. It is not unusual to read that Bultmann denies any knowledge of the historical Jesus[2] or that he rejects the resurrection of Jesus. Both assertions are wrong and obscure the issues that are at stake in the debate.

The issues raised by Bultmann's work remain central to the contemporary debate and this dialogue with Bultmann is carried on in that context. Our concern is with his presuppositions and methods. English readers owe a great debt to John Macquarrie.[3] However, he expounds Bultmann's thought step by step on the basis of Heidegger. Perhaps because of Bultmann's admission of his debt to Heidegger this line of interpretation is common, e.g. Barth, Buri, Ogden, Roberts, (Roberts, p. 17). But Bultmann's existentialist interpretation antedates his relation to Heidegger and was a consequence of his reading of Kierkegaard and the influence of his teacher Wilhelm Herrmann.[4]

The influence of Herrmann on Bultmann was important. But not as a mediator of Marburg Neo-Kantianism merged with nineteenth century Lutheranism,[5] as is sometimes suggested. The Neo-Kantian influence was supposedly manifest in a dualism between fact and meaning, existence and world (see Albrecht Ritschl, *Theologie und Metaphysik*, pp. 9, 34). There are points of contact with Bultmann's distinction between history and nature. But value is perceived in both. It is also doubtful that Herrmann should be seen simply as a Ritschlian as James Richmond has argued (pp. 41f., 296ff.). Rather his thought should be seen as a correction to Ritschl's theology, as H.R. Mackintosh has argued (p. 180). Given that Bultmann's criticism that the liberal theology spoke only of man was a criticism of the Ritschlians, Mackintosh might well be right, as this does not seem to be Bultmann's view of Herrmann.

Bultmann's theology developed out of the context of the liberal theology of the nineteenth and early twentieth centuries. That context was not simple. Bultmann had as little sympathy as Barth for the Kantian moralism which found expression in some of the Ritschlians. But in Herrmann there was a Ritschlian with a concern to state the meaning of the revelation in Jesus Christ in harmony with the New Testament (Mackintosh, p. 180). Herrmann's relation to the tradition of Schleiermacher also needs to be recognized. Bultmann saw Schleiermacher standing in the tradition which stretched from Jeremiah to Kierkegaard (*Letters*, p. 6).[6]

Bultmann's relation to Schleiermacher is yet to be clarified. There are strong points of contact if Schleiermacher's 'feeling of absolute dependence' is understood as existential awareness (*GJ*, p. 44 n. 2), though this would only constitute a 'preunderstanding' for Bultmann. Both also reject the view of miracles as divine interventions in the world but allow for the perception of God's acts *in* history and nature. But this does not constitute a *Weltbild* for Bultmann, which would make the world luminous with God's activity. Rather the hidden acts of God break through the barrier that hides them, from time to time, challenging the believer to obey God in a specific situation.

Two important and related themes have emerged in this discussion of Bultmann's context in liberal theology. The first concerns man in his awareness of 'need' and the second concerns the revelation communicated in the New Testament. If we add to this the recognition of the History of Religions school that the thought of the New Testament was expressed in the language and imagery (mythology) of Judaism and Hellenism we have recognized that what remained fundamental for Bultmann was already to be found in certain tendencies in 'liberal theology'. Those tendencies found a distinctive association and development in Bultmann's writings. They provide the clue to his approach to theology as hermeneutics. An understanding of the existence of man gives a direction to the enterprise. But the matter to be interpreted is the revelation in relation to man. From this context it is possible to see how and why Bultmann identified with 'the new theological movement' to which Barth first gave clear voice in his *Romans*, and especially the 'manifesto' (p. 10) in which Barth outlined his system based on the recognition of 'the infinite qualitative distinction', and of the relation between God and man constituted by the revelation.

Here we are at the heart of Bultmann's hermeneutical theology. Understanding the Word is only possible by understanding the believer who has been encountered by the Word. Theology as hermeneutics draws attention to the hermeneutical circle. The aspect of the circle with which we are here concerned is the relation between the past and present, the Word and the believer. The past is only accessible through the present and the Word through the believer. This indicates Bultmann's solution, with its stress on understanding, which stretches back to Schleiermacher through Wilhelm Dilthey and not without some contribution from Heidegger. Heidegger's contribution should be recognized in the clarifying of the idea of 'pre-understanding', so important for Bultmann, and his provision of more precise existentialist categories/conceptuality. However Bultmann's concern 'for conceptual clarity' is not something he learned from Heidegger. This is apparent in his 1922 review of Barth's *Romans* and in his letter of 25 May 1922 where in the space of a short letter he, three times, talks of clarifying concepts.

> I cannot give up the obligation of conceptual clarity on this account.[7]

Clarification of concepts also involved clarification of problems and questions. Hence his approach to theology could be described as a *problematic* approach.[8]

Bultmann's theology, whatever he influences, is distinctively his own. It arose from the tensions in the theology of his teachers and he made use of whatever would contribute to his own constructive approach. Because of this Bultmann could acknowledge his debt to many people, to Barth, Gogarten, Heidegger, etc. But whatever he took over became distinctively his own and in the context of the contemporary crisis for theology in the field of epistemology he has attempted *to develop a basis* in terms of which God can be known and spoken of. His aim was to interpret what it means to know and speak of God. In so doing he has defended the value of man and his responsibility in love for the neighbour and the world. In this regard his theology stands in the tradition of Irenaeus, Origen and Schleiermacher who have defended the freedom and responsibility of man on the basis of kerygma. At the same time he has taken seriously those boundaries which limit human freedom which Heidegger spoke of in terms of 'thrownness' and 'facticity'. His understanding of the kerygma is a significant theological discussion and defence of revelation in the present crisis of knowledge and relativization of values. That is not to say that there are no problems to be overcome, even in terms of his own theology. Quite late in his life he recognized that the debate was not concluded[9] and in principle he saw theology as the perpetual hermeneutical task.

In this study it is argued that Bultmann's theology is best

understood from the perspective of his work as a New Testament exegete. Naturally this involved recognizing the critical problems involved in interpreting the New Testament in the twentieth century. Nevertheless, it was Bultmann's aim to grasp the understanding of faith which has come to expression there. That this was his aim and achievement is confirmed by two groups of writings largely ignored by Bultmann's theological critics, in addition to his exegetical works. The first is the Barth Bultmann correspondence and the second is Bultmann's replies to his critics in the Kegley volume. In the latter Bultmann has repudiated criticisms which have become almost standard in the literature on Bultmann.

Perhaps the most pressing problems which arise from his work can be spoken of in terms of the relation between history and theology. How much of the life and teaching of Jesus is *necessary* for the kerygma? How far is the miraculous, in particular the resurrection of Jesus as a physical event, an integral part of the kerygma? Is this element really incompatible with Bultmann's theology or is it only the interpretation which seeks to make the miraculous a guarantee, a proof, that is incompatible? What if the miraculous is interpreted as a mode of revelation which, in spite of its remarkable character, remained ambiguous? After all, what would the resurrection of a dead man actually prove?

Bultmann's theology also raises christological questions in a critical way. His exposition of the existential basis of christology is persuasive. Nonetheless, his insistance that the revelation in the Christ event is unique and exclusive presses for an interpretation beyond functionalism. How is it that God's act occurs in and through this one man alone? Was and is this a sufficient ground for the New Testament writers to go beyond speaking of what he achieved and to speak of him as the pre-existent divine Son or Word? While such statements are *projections* on the basis of existential evidence, are they justified and should they be understood symbolically rather than mythologically? If they are understood mythologically then they are to be interpreted in terms of the existential ground which gave rise to them, that is, knowing Christ's 'benefits'. But does not Bultmann's insistence that these benefits are known *only* through the Christ event suggest that something must be said about the one who alone brings such 'benefits'? Schubert Ogden has drawn back from this problem by asserting that God has acted decisively in Jesus, but not uniquely. Hence the problem of the *necessity* of christology falls somewhat into the background for him.[10] Bultmann refused to move this way. Hence the christological problem is more sharply defined in his work.

The stance that Bultmann takes on christology is also significant for the discussion of the relation between Christianity and the religions of the world. Bultmann has a distinctive contribution to make in this area. He takes the New Testament claim to communicate the revelation of God seriously without degrading human life and the search for goodness and happiness which is alive in the world generally. Yet here again Bultmann is in conflict with the views of Schubert Ogden.[11] The differences which exist between these two are worthy of debate, not only in terms of theoretical theological value but in terms of understanding the Church's mission in the world. Bultmann saw that the distinctive role of the Church in the world was to be the bearer of the Word, both in preaching and action. He also called attention to the responsibility for the world which Christians share with all men.

It should come as no surprise that the central thrust of Bultmann's theology is concerned with 'knowledge'. The fundamental question is not about whatever is but *how we know*. Obviously we can only speak with validity of what we know. Theology deals with the knowledge inherent in faith, that knowledge, its origin, object and consequences. Today the grounds of all knowledge are questioned in the light of our understanding of perception. The world and human life in it can no longer be appealed to as unambiguous evidence for the existence and reality of God. In sharp focus the problems to be overcome if faith in God is to be possible seem insurmountable. Indeed, 'we can only believe in God in spite of experience' (*JCM*, p. 84). Here we find no optimistic view about the goodness of the world or the purpose of God demonstrably evident in it. Bultmann had no such illusions as are possible within the shelter of our affluent Western world. If such a perspective could once have been attributed simply to the impact of two world wars, the present threat of a nuclear holocaust suggests that the perspective is more permanent and is a consequence of the way man, who seeks to take possession of the world, in fact falls prey to it (*JCM*, p. 40). This is also true of modern man who makes use of science (technology) in order to take control of the world. Bultmann did not share the optimism of some who perceived in science the solution to the human predicament. For Bultmann the problem lies with man himself.

Such a view of man could perhaps be called Lutheran, if the distinctive nature of Bultmann's Lutheranism is recognized.[12] Certainly he often appealed to Luther and like him he understood christology in relation to soteriology. He was indebted to Lutheran scholars, Melanchthon, Kierkegaard and Herrmann, behind whom stood Tholuck and Ritschl, who were Lutherans. Like Luther Bultmann gave special place to the theology of Paul and John. It is not always recognized that Bultmann's great preoccupation was with John, Gospel and letters, a work that was central for him from 1923 until the publication of *Die drei Johannesbriefe* in 1967.[13]

Lutheranism is also characterized in terms of the formulae *sola gratia*, *sola scriptura*, *sola Christi*, *sola fidei*. Bultmann's distinctiveness is clear when seen in relation to these terms. Grace is the divine initiative in the Word, to which man responds. Scripture is understood in terms of the kerygma and Christ is the Christ of the kerygma. Faith is the response to the call of God in the kerygma, which overcomes the scandal of the cross and leads to a life of love for the neighbour and responsibility for the world.

Because theology is the interpretation of the 'classic' text of Christianity, the New Testament (see Tracy, *TA1*, p. 68) in which the kerygma is embodied, the question is, does the theological aspect of hermeneutics influence the way the New Testament is interpreted? Bultmann is clear that the historian's presuppositions should not include his conclusions. But does he not presuppose God? Does he not presuppose faith? It is a *partial* answer to say that the choice was not his, as an interpreter of the New Testament, except in his decision to interpret the New Testament. Belief in God and his act in Christ are given in the historical evidence Bultmann sought to understand. Whether what the New Testament writers believed is true is another question. Bultmann was himself a believer. His own beliefs were consistent with *his understanding* of the beliefs of the New Testament writers, especially Paul and John. Whether his own understanding is historically adequate is another matter. It needs to be tested in two ways; in terms of an historical understanding of the New Testament and from the perspective of a critical judgment of what is true.

It is argued in this study that Bultmann's attempt to establish the existential basis of theological knowledge is sound. Because of this our study opens with a chapter on his relation to existentialism. There it is argued that whatever is known has an existential and relational basis.

The existential, relational aspect is best seen in historical relationships. Bultmann's understanding of history is the next area of focus. It is argued that faith has its basis in the history of Jesus and continues because Jesus is effectively risen in the kerygma which evokes faith down through the ages.

The central problem for Bultmann's theology is the subject of the third chapter — his understanding of God, emphasizing his transcendence. The idea of transcendence is complex, involving invisibility; absolute qualitative difference from the world; and a rejection of the idea that God does/can intervene in the natural and historical causality of the world. Hence the idea of God is bound up with an idea of the world which Bultmann associates with the modern scientific *Weltbild*. Here there is some justice in the criticism that Bultmann has allowed a philosophical understanding of God and the world to mould his critical interpretation. But God's actions, as particular 'interventions' which are evident *as God's actions*, are not easy to find. By what criteria would we recognize them as God's actions? Further, Bultmann did not absolutize any *Weltbild* but insisted on the critical use of the analogy of present experience as the only way to separate fact from fancy in accounts from the past. In other words, recognizing Bultmann's over-statement concerning causality and his interpretation of transcendence to exclude miracles does not solve the problems. Further, Bultmann did argue that it is possible for *faith* to perceive God's act in otherwise ordinary historical events.

Given this understanding of transcendence, God's action in the world and any knowledge of such an action seem to become logically impossible. Hence Bultmann's use of image/symbol, analogy, and encounter become logical problems. These problems are made more complex by his failure to provide adequate discussion of these terms as a basis of his own use. The same criticism has often been made concerning his treatment of myth, to which the other themes are related. Some attempt is made to clarify these questions in chapters 3-5. Whether the problems related to his understanding of God are fatal for his position cannot be determined at this stage, though there is room for clarification in various directions, as Schubert Ogden has shown.[14]

The central theme in Bultmann's theology is faith and understanding, the subject of chapter 5. His dominant concern is for man as free and responsible before God, in love for the neighbour, and urgent concern for the world. Such freedom and responsibility could be described as 'radical obedience', reminding us that Bultmann's theology was expressed with the intention of living a Christian life in the world. His theology was intentionally tied to the New Testament and the kerygma and faith expressed there. More than most other theologians he saw these texts as the foundation documents of faith, the critical study of which was to provide a test for true faith and an adequate proclamation of the kerygma. For this reason it is argued that the most adequate description of his approach is *Theology as Hermeneutics*. To do theology is to interpret the New Testament. But to interpret the New Testament, the foundation documents of faith, we must understand the questions that arise in our own existence in the world and hear what the New Testament has to say in its own way to our questions. Surprisingly, for one who emphasized the positive role of the modern scientific *Weltbild* in exposing myth, Bultmann did not take a stand with those who set their hopes on the progress of the world through science. However correct science might be in its basic assumptions of order and causality, in the hands of men, science, like the Law, becomes an instrument of tyranny. Only in the kerygma, preserved and communicated through the New Testament, did Bultmann see any hope for the liberation of man. This could only be achieved through perpetual hermeneutical work, otherwise a fossilized kerygma would itself become an instrument of tyranny.

Chapter One

Existentialism and the Theology of Rudolf Bultmann

Synopsis

A preliminary discussion of 'theology as hermeneutics'. Theology is the interpretation of the classical texts of the Christian faith in which an understanding of human existence and the interpretation of the New Testament are mutually illuminated. Throughout this chapter the evidence for influences on Bultmann's thought, especially Heidegger and Marburg Lutheran Neo-Kantianism, will be examined. While it is hoped that these relationships will be clarified, the main aim is to show what kind of theological knowledge is possible for man and how such knowledge comes about. In so doing it is hoped that language that claims more than man can possibly know, for example, how God created the world, will be clarified. Such language is not meaningless but speaks of what is known in a language shaped by the conceptual framework of a bygone era. However, once the conceptual framework has become obsolete the language may actually obscure the knowledge of which it was once an expression.

Evocative Epigram

> Since the Fall we have been essentially equal in our capacity to recognize good and evil . . . (However) nobody can remain content with the mere knowledge of good and evil in itself, but must endeavour as well to act in accordance with it. The strength to do so, however, is not likewise given him . . . (Therefore) man is filled with fear; he prefers to annul his knowledge of good and evil . . . ; yet the accomplished cannot be annulled, but only confused. It was for this purpose that our rationalizations were created. The whole world is full of them, indeed the whole visible world is perhaps nothing more than the rationalization of a man who wants to find peace for a moment . . .
>
> FRANZ KAFKA: *Reflections* (no. 82)[1]

Chapter One

EXISTENTIALISM AND THE THEOLOGY OF RUDOLF BULTMANN

1. Theology as Hermeneutics

Hermeneutical theology or *theology as hermeneutics* might well be the most adequate characterization of Bultmann's theological enterprise, drawing attention to the complex of ideas at the heart of his theology. For him the motivation for the historical enterprise is to be found in the possibility of new self-understanding provided by the texts from the past. Theology, from this perspective, is the understanding of existence (*Existenz*) given to faith, in response to the revelation. The thesis of this book is surprisingly simple. It is that, according to Bultmann, the way to do theology is to interpret the New Testament, that theology is the interpretation of the New Testament. Erich Dinkler recognized this in his 'Foreword' to Bultmann's commentary on *Second Corinthians*, p. 7 where he wrote that

> in the last analysis for Bultmann the exegetical-interpretative work is basic to his theological statement.

Such a position might seem naively biblicist. However, for those who know Bultmann the complexities will be obvious, and they will be nervously aware that this short statement covers a perilous minefield. Let the person who walks here beware. First, only the New Testament is mentioned. What is the relation of Christian faith and theology to the Old Testament? Second, Christian theology has to do with the *interpretation* of the New Testament, not with the New Testament *per se*. What is involved in such interpretation?

The title, *Theology as Hermeneutics*, is consciously developed in distinction from *Revelation as History*, ed. by W. Pannenberg, and *Theology as History*, ed. by J.M. Robinson, not as a rejection of history but to place the emphasis on the *understanding* which occurs in history through history (see *FU*, pp. 150, 154; *Th.N.T.* II, p. 251).

But theology is not the understanding which occurs in history through history generally. It is the understanding which occurs in history through the history of Jesus. It is the essential role of the history of Jesus which gives to the New Testament its exclusive and unique role in the interpretation which is Christian theology. The task of interpretation is carried forward by Bultmann on the basis of his work of historical reconstruction in which he sought to outline the developing understanding which arose from the history of Jesus. That developing understanding is to be found in the New Testament. Understanding is not only concerned with Jesus and God but involves the way the believer comes to understand himself and everything else as a consequence of the faith which the history of Jesus evoked. Hermeneutics is the process of understanding by which man comes to understand himself in terms of his relationships, whether authentically in terms of love as an expression of the divine revelation, or inauthentically in the rejection of the revelation.

The obvious starting point for a discussion of Bultmann's theology is his presuppositions. A good case can be made for beginning with his understanding of human being. There can be no doubt that this plays a significant role in his hermeneutical theology and that some understanding of human being is *selfconsciously* presupposed. It is not necessary to demonstrate the reality of existence after the fashion of Descartes: '*cogito ergo sum*' (I think, therefore I am). It is self-evident, not only that man exists, but also that his existence is *in the world, with others*. What this involves will need to be examined in some detail in order to ascertain his relation to 'Existentialism'.[2] That he has a positive relation is indicated by his characteristic vocabulary, not to mention his well-known 'dependence on Martin Heidegger'. Robert C. Roberts acknowledges his Heideggerian approach to Bultmann and justifies this on the basis of Bultmann's repeated appeal to Heidegger (Roberts, p. 16).

2. **Dependence on Heidegger?**

Bultmann made no secret of his significant relation to Martin Heidegger in their years together at Marburg (1922-1928) (see 'AR', in *EF*, p. 288 and Kegley, p. xxiv). This ready admission of indebtedness to Heidegger gave rise to the tendency to interpret Bultmann in terms of Heidegger which has become widespread and finds expression in the works of Barth, Burie, Macquarrie, Ogden and Roberts. Macquarrie (*AET*) interprets Bultmann, step by step, on the basis of his exposition of Heidegger. He notes that the New Testament often justifies or permits Bultmann's dependence on Heidegger, and that Bultmann modifies Heidegger at certain points. But his approach suggests that Bultmann's theology was *systematically dependent* on Heidegger. Through his book this view has become common (see Johnson, p. 19 n. 2). For a number of reasons this must be called into question.

First, Bultmann was not reluctant to acknowledge what he learned from others. In the same paragraph in which he mentions his relation to Heidegger he writes of his debt to Barth and also mentions his teachers Johannes Weiss, Wilhelm Herrmann, Adolf Harnack, Herman Gunkel, Karl Müller, Adolf Jülicher, Wilhelm Heitmüller ('AR', in *EF*, p. 288; Kegley, p. xx). This is quite an extensive catalogue of indebtedness. Because neither Barth nor Bultmann has made any secret of the differences which separate them it is unlikely that anyone *now* would attempt to interpret Bultmann in terms of Barth. But it was the similarity of their positions that made it necessary to draw attention to the differences.[3] Bultmann also mentions his debt to Friedrich Gogarten (*EF*, p. 102).

These and other indications of indebtedness raise questions about how seriously they should be taken because in them it becomes apparent that Bultmann was ready, perhaps too ready, to acknowledge his indebtedness. At the very least we see that a singular influence on Bultmann may not be attributed to Heidegger. A.C. Thiselton draws attention to ten different influences on Bultmann, which could be increased had thinkers such as Kierkegaard been added to the list. Hence he rejects the view that the influence of Heidegger was simple and singular. He grouped the individual scholars who influenced Bultmann into schools of thought: Existentialism, Liberal Theology, nineteenth-century Lutheran Neo-Kantianism, the History of Religions School and Dialectical Theology. Having done this he raises the question concerning Bultmann's own contribution. Was the net result of this 'synthesis' '*a* view' (position) or a combination of 'ultimately incompatible standpoints'? Johnson argues that Bultmann's theology is 'for the most part' '*a* view' but this appears to be rejected by Thiselton (pp. 206ff., 232f., 284f.). The position argued here is that Bultmann's theology is at least a creative synthesis and quite possibly much more than this because of the contributions he made to the synthesis. Indeed, it is argued that he took from others only what clarified his own emerging understanding.

Second, in his 'Autobiographical Reflections', Bultmann indicated that it was through Heidegger that he became acquainted with the work of 'existentialist philosophy', which became decisively significant for him. This comment indicates a broader indebtedness than Heidegger alone. It suggests that account should also be taken of the works of Søren Kierkegaard, amongst others. But are we to understand that Bultmann was not acquainted with Kierkegaard until his discussion with Heidegger? Surely this is not possible in the light of his relation to the 'new movement' of which Karl Barth was at first the foremost spokesman. Barth's *Der Römerbrief* appeared in 1919 and a second edition in 1922. In the Preface to the second edition there is a passage which has the ring of a 'manifesto' (*Romans*, p. 10). The stress on '*relationality*' in this passage is crucial for an understanding of Bultmann as is the stress on 'the infinite qualitative distinction' between God and man. On the importance of this theme for Bultmann see Ogden in *EF*, p. 14 and Nicholls, p. 155. While Barth was to move from this position and consciously attempted to eradicate 'existentialist' presuppositions from his theology, the statement remains an accurate 'manifesto' of Bultmann's theological enterprise. It is significant also that Barth specifically mentions Kierkegaard. Discussion with Heidegger clarified and furthered Bultmann's understanding of 'existentialism' rather than setting him off in a new direction. Bultmann also indicated that Wilhelm Herrmann introduced him to the ideas of history and the historicity (*Geschichtlichkeit*) of man which he was later to encounter in Heidegger (Thiselton, pp. 207f.).

Third, we need to note what it was that Bultmann says he found significant in existentialist philosophy.

> I found in it the conceptuality in which it is possible to speak adequately of human existence and therefore also of the existence of the believer (*EF*, p. 288; see also *JCM*, p. 45; Kegley, p. 275).

This 'conceptuality' was analysed systematically by Heidegger. In making use of this Bultmann denies that he is dependent on Heidegger's philosophy as such (see his Preface to Malet, pp. 1f.; and his 'Reply' in Kegley, p. 259). Therefore it is not surprising that when Bultmann is interpreted in terms of Heidegger he is criticized as inconsistent and distorting Heidegger, as he is by Roberts (pp. 12f., 16f.). Such an approach and conclusions are recognized as wrong by Johnson, (pp. 17f.).[4] Bultmann's repeated denial that his theology is dependent on Heidegger's philosophy could not be more explicit.

Such denials are frequent in his published works and also appear in his private correspondence. 'In fact I base no theology on Heidegger's philosophy.' What is more, Heidegger concurs: 'Bultmann builds no theology upon my philosophy' (Malet, p. 333). The necessity for this repeated denial is to be found in the persistence of the view that Bultmann was in fact dependent on Heidegger's philosophy. It is not impossible that both Heidegger and Bultmann were wrong about this but it is surely unlikely.

In what follows it should become clear that they were not mistaken. Bultmann indicates that he learned from Heidegger 'not *what* theology has to say, but how it has to say it' ('Reply', in Kegley, p. 276). More to the point is the question of whether the 'conceptuality' or 'terminology' (*Begrifflichkeit*) of 'existentialism' is adequate for the task of interpreting 'the New Testament and the Christian faith'. Here it is necessary to clarify what is involved in Bultmann's use of *Begrifflichkeit*. This word indicates not only 'terminology' in the sense of vocabulary but also the *conceptual framework* to which the terminology belongs.[5] Does theology, like the natural sciences, have to do with 'objects' or does the subject matter demand a different 'conceptual framework' with its appropriate vocabulary? Bultmann affirms the latter and has worked hard to demonstrate the consequent distortion resulting from the failure to make this distinction (*FU*, pp. 262ff.). The basis for this point of view is to be seen in the way he understands theology.

> ... Christian faith is the answer to the word of the transcendent God that encounters man and that theology has to deal with this word and the man who has been encountered by it.[6]

The theme of theology is 'existence (*Existenz*) in faith' and the 'conceptuality', including both vocabulary and frame of reference, must be appropriate to man (*Dasein*) who is encountered by the Word of God. For even when man speaks of his encounter with the Word of God, as he does in the New Testament, he does so as a man. Bultmann bases his case on the observation that the New Testament expresses, more or less consistently, an understanding of human existence for which the appropriate interpretation is existentialist and the goal of this interpretation is to grasp the understanding of existence which finds expression there. This is not merely to reconstruct an understanding of the past, though this is involved. Rather the interpreter discovers the meaning of believing existence in his own situation (see 'Reply', in Kegley, pp. 258f.; *Th.N.T.* II, p. 251).

The existential understanding of the New Testament is the understanding given in faith, or more precisely, the understanding which is 'a factor in the structure of faith, namely faith in so far as it understands itself' (*GJ*, p. 435). This understanding is the goal of Bultmann's *existentialist* interpretation in which he has made use of Heidegger's *ontological* analysis.[7] That analysis provides the categories which Bultmann finds appropriate for the description of human being as such and consequently appropriate also for the description of believing existence. In one sense it is remarkable that philosophy independently says 'the same thing as the New Testament' (*K&M* I, p. 24). However it should really be expected because both the philosopher and the New Testament deal with actual human being and 'the *man of faith* is in any case *a man*' (*EF*, p. 94). Further, while this philosophy is working independently of the New Testament, Bultmann argues that Christian faith has contributed significantly to its development as Heidegger's existentialist analysis was influenced by Paul, Augustine, Luther and Kierkegaard ('Reply', in Kegley, p. 260). Perhaps Bultmann should himself be added to this list. Heidegger's *Being and Time* was written during his time of collaboration with Bultmann at Marburg (see Johnson, p. 175 n. 1). This 'existentialist analysis' is 'ontological analysis', that is, analysis of the being of man as man. Such analysis takes account of the nature of human life with all its possibilities. In other words, it provides the categories (*Begrifflichkeit*) by means of which it is possible to understand human being regardless of the form it actually takes in specific human lives simply because the categories are appropriate to the description of human being as such.

From this discussion it becomes apparent that the distinction between philosophy and theology is not clear cut. In Bultmann's terms, philosophy deals with human being *ontologically*, with all of its possibilities, while theology treats the same subject *ontically*, that is *Existenz* specifically and actually. Philosophy has the task of clarifying the concepts (*Begrifflichkeit*) in which theology expresses its understanding of believing existence and everything else from this perspective. The conceptuality of ontological analysis needs to take account of the actual experiences of life if it is to be developed adequately. An adequate existentialist analysis will provide the conceptuality to understand any actual experience simply because it is a human experience. Bultmann appeals to a common 'human structure' which is what existentialist analysis seeks to understand.

Though Bultmann has named Kierkegaard as an influence on Heidegger, he suggests that Heidegger's ontological analysis (*Daseins-analyse*) can be enriched by Kierkegaard's specifically Christian understanding (*Daseinsverständnis*). Bultmann's conceptuality was derived from Heidegger but the actual understanding which he sought to express with this conceptuality was derived more from Kierkegaard's Christian understanding of man (see *EF*, pp. 101, 288; *JCM*, pp. 45, 56; Malet, p. 2). Thus, for Bultmann, the idea of enriching Heidegger's ontological analysis, his conceptual clarification of the description of the possibilities of human existence, with 'Kierkegaard's explicitly Christian understanding of man' (*Dasein*) is not hypothetical. It is an indication of the task he has himself undertaken. In his exposition categories such as 'fallenness', 'authenticity' and 'inauthenticity' take on specific significance in the light of the faith which arises from the kerygma.

While Bultmann made use of Heidegger's ontological analysis, his understanding of human being should be seen in close relation to Kierkegaard. Kierkegaard stressed that the reality of human being was intensely subjective and from this point of view the uniqueness of each person comes to light. This understanding is present in Kierkegaard but is given a precise analytical means of description by Heidegger. In this understanding Bultmann found what he considered to be the New Testament understanding. The analysis of Heidegger does no more nor less than make it possible to give conceptual clarity to this understanding. 'Existentialism' takes account of man as a unique subject. Each man is a unique subject. With Heidegger this does not produce such fragmentation that speaking of mankind becomes nonsense. His ontological analysis deals with the possibilities of existence for man as man and enquires concerning the formal structures of human being (*Dasein*) (*EF*, pp. 94, 101). The unity of mankind arises from the structure of *Dasein* shared by all men who live in the same world in relation to objects and to other men (*EPT*, p. 243). However, this analysis of human being is not an anthropology, nor is it a speculative philosophy. But what does Bultmann mean when he says that it is 'an analysis of the understanding of existence that is given with existence itself'? (See Bultmann's Foreword to *AET*, p. ix and also pp. 9, 70f.; *KM* II, p. 192; and 'Reply', in Kegley, p. 274.)

3. Understanding Human Being (Dasein)[8]

Existenz refers to the specifically historical character of *Dasein* which involves an 'understanding of existence that is given with existence itself'. What Bultmann means is not precisely clear. His thought has been construed in terms of Heidegger's view of 'primordial' self-understanding prior to rationalizing conceptual thinking (Thiselton, pp. 197ff.). According to this view, uninterpreted existentialist conceptuality is given with existence itself. But this position can only be maintained by asserting that Bultmann changed his position, as Johnson does (p. 214 n. 2). Johnson not only asserts that Bultmann changed his position, but that he inconsistently vacillated between the two explicitly mutually exclusive views. Bultmann clearly continues to speak of the understanding of existence given with existence itself, of understanding which belongs to life. But this is *not* identified with existentialist *conceptuality* even if this conceptuality is more appropriate than some other forms when dealing with human existence.

Bultmann's position is clarified in the 'Epilogue' of his *Theology of the New Testament*, vol. II, pp. 237-41. Here Bultmann expresses clearly his view that thought and concepts are historically conditioned. This is true for the texts of the New Testament as well as the interpreter of the New Testament. From the perspective of a critical understanding of present conceptuality, the interpreter attempts to understand the historical process of the past. Thus interpretation cannot be done once and for all. In each new age 'faith, fed by its origin, understandingly masters its constantly new historical situation'. This faith is itself a response to the kerygma which is always expressed in a particular theological interpretation moulded by a particular understanding of existence. He goes on to make the distinction between existential self-understanding and existentialist interpretation. Johnson appears to have confused the two. What is given in existence is not existentialist interpretation with its conceptuality but existential self-understanding. How this is conceptualized is not the issue. The *content* of the existential self-understanding is *not* determined. According to Bultmann it may be authentic or inauthentic. Nor is this determined by existentialist conceptuality but by response to the kerygma.

When Bultmann speaks of the understanding of existence given with existence itself he is referring to the formal structures of *Dasein* which involve the possibility of understanding. To be human is to search for understanding, to have some self-understanding. What that will be is the possibility which each person is to choose, or to put this another way, in his choices man chooses himself, chooses what he is to be. Hence this understanding does not involve an anthropology or *speculative* philosophy. Rather it is an understanding of existence *within existence*, a self-understanding which is known by existing. Further, human being is in the world, which is as little to be doubted as the reality of existence itself. Thus it is at once clear that this understanding of human being is not rightly understood in terms of the old problem of subjectivity and objectivity. Yet Bultmann continues to be misunderstood as if he denied the objective reality, that is, reality apart from man, of the world and God. However Bultmann asserts that what man is to be is determined by his relation to the world and to God (*Th.N.T.* II, p. 239; *EPT*, pp. 259f.).

a. **Human Being (Dasein) in the world**[9]

Human being in the world involves a perception of order in the world (*FU*, pp. 247ff.); it is existence confronted with limitation;[10] it is existence in which man discovers what he is;[11] in fact, all that man can know is given in and through his existence in the world (*EF*, pp. 62, 65f.; *FU*, p. 192 n. 4). Here we have, in summary form, a statement of the significance of Bultmann's understanding of existence. It is this understanding of existence which is the foundation of Bultmann's work as historian, exegete and theologian.

Perhaps the most important point to note is that Bultmann speaks of the world in two senses. In this he stands within the Johannine tradition where the world is seen as the created order (John 1.10) but also as the order opposed to God and the revelation (8.23; 12.31; see *FU*, pp. 166ff.; *GJ*, pp. 44f., 497). A certain amount of confusion has arisen from the failure to recognize the different shades of meaning in Bultmann's use of 'world'. The world is God's creation. No cosmological dualism is possible. But without the revelation man does not perceive the world as creation. Hence man has a false understanding of the world and a false understanding of himself as belonging to the world. Bultmann, as John, characteristically speaks of the world in terms of this false understanding. It would, however, be a gross misunderstanding to think of this in terms of a denial of the ontological reality of the created order.

While it has already been asserted that, for Bultmann, man's existence in the world is presupposed, it has become common to assert that, for him, the reality of the world is a 'throw-away truth' and that the world is a construct of reason. In support of this R.A.

Johnson (pp. 31f., 44-50, 80, 167) argues that the language of *being* (*Sein*) is not used in relation to the role of objectifying reason, 'Objectification ... is stripped of any positive ontological significance', that the reality of the world is a 'throw-away truth' and that Bultmann has 'sundered in a radical way the connection between reason and Being'. As a consequence of this attitude, it is argued, he pays no attention to empirical data because the world is objectified by reason rather than being ontologically real. This view ignores what Bultmann says about the role of the modern scientific *Weltbild*.

> It is impossible to use the electric light and the wireless and to avail ourselves of modern medical and surgical discoveries, and at the same time to believe in the New Testament world of spirits and miracles (*K&M*, I, p. 5).

Bultmann knew that it was not *factually* impossible to hold these two things together (see *K&M*. I, p. 5 n. 1). It is, in his view, logically impossible in terms of the implications of the modern scientific *Weltbild* which he used to separate reality from fantasy. Further, the modern scientific *Weltbild* is itself open to revision on the basis of new discoveries and the principles of criticism which are part and parcel of the modern scientific method. While Bultmann's critique is open to criticism as it did not keep pace with these changes, Johnson's interpretation is based on his reconstruction of a particular fusion of Lutheran anthropology with Marburg Neo-Kantian epistemology in Bultmann's thought. Johnson is followed by A.C. Thiselton (pp. 39f., 205ff., 209ff., 245ff., 290ff.) who emphasizes a dualism of fact and value in Bultmann's thought sundering fact from interpretation. The criticism suggests that the interpretation has only an arbitrary relation to the facts of which it is an interpretation. This is a misunderstanding of Bultmann for whom event and meaning are inseparable (*HE*, p. 117; *GJ*, p. 566; *Th.N.T.*, II, pp. 237-40, 244). However, the meaning of an event is not something that is fixed. It has different meanings from different perspectives, times and places and the meaning has to be discovered afresh by each new generation. If the question is raised concerning the ultimate or complete meaning of an event Bultmann does not deny that there is such a meaning. He raises the question of how man, who stands *within the flow of history*, can achieve such ultimate knowledge which presupposes a perspective outside or beyond history.

The criticisms of Johnson and Thiselton, though expressed in different terms, are a return to the old subjectivity versus objectivity debate with Bultmann being charged with subjectivism. R.C. Roberts (pp. 249ff., 257f.) has expressed his criticism in precisely these terms. This criticism is not new. Bultmann frequently repudiated its validity and Malet (p. 3), rightly sees it as a distortion of Bultmann's position which is fundamentally relational. Johnson has given the old critique a new form and a supporting historical explanation. Plausible as his case might seem, in terms of historical explanation, it raises intractable problems in terms of understanding Bultmann's writings, which perhaps should be seen as the ultimate obstacle which cannot be negotiated in this way.

First, it is not true that Bultmann does not use the language of *being* in relation to what *we* speak of as the objective world. For example Bultmann speaks of 'the being of nature' (*Sein der Natur*)[12] Here Bultmann is concerned to elucidate what it is that distinguishes human being, as *historical being*, from the *being of nature*. There is no suggestion that one form of being is more real than the other, though it is clear that they are to be distinguished from each other and the *being* of man (*das Sein des Menschen*) is appropriately referred to as *Dasein*.

Second, it is clear that the order of the world, of nature, is not thought of as a construct imposed by reason.

> The idea of conformity to law, the idea of 'Nature', underlies explicitly or implicitly all our ideas and actions which relate to this world. It is not an 'interpretation of the world' (*Weltdeutung*), a 'world view'(*Weltanschauung*); it is not a notion about the world, either subjective or based on a conscious decision, but it is *given with our existence in the world* (sondern er ist *mit unserem Dasein in der Welt gegeben*) (*FU*, p. 248 = p. 215).

Bultmann speaks about the being (*Sein*) of nature and indicates that nature involves order. Awareness of order depends on both the structure of *Dasein* and the structure of the being (*Sein*) of nature. He goes on to say:

> We recognize as real in the World only what can be set in this context of the rule of law; and we judge assertions which cannot be accommodated to this conception as fantasies.

There is no question that the *being* of the world of nature, what is real, as distinct from fantasy, conforms to the order of nature, the awareness of which belongs to man's being (*Dasein*) in the world.

This basic awareness of order, the 'causal nexus', is distinguished from theoretical constructions which might be related in some way to it. The basic sense of order belongs to man's being in the world and what is real in the world of nature conforms to this.

Third, the distinction between what is real and what is fantasy is no 'throw-away truth' for Bultmann. It is on this basis that he has developed his critique of mythology, which is hardly a trivial aspect of his work. The modern scientific *Weltbild* is used to expose and criticize all mythological *Weltbilder*. The modern scientific *Weltbild* is superior because in it the existential awareness of order is critically and systematically developed. However, Bultmann does not give absolute status to any *Weltbild.*[13] On the contrary, all *Weltbilder* are open to criticism and revision *on the basis of* perceived order and it is part of the superiority of the modern scientific *Weltbild* that this recognition is essential to it (*JCM*, p. 38; *K&M*, I, p. 210).

This discussion of the perceived order of the world relates to the ontological status of the world, the *being* of the world. However, man's *relation* to the world is never based simply on the perception of order in the world. Man's *relation* to the world arises from the insecurity of his *being* in the world, from the *care-structure* of *Dasein* (*EF*, p. 97 n. 16 and *AET*, p. 107). Man is whatever he is in his relationships, in the way he relates. Man has a given relation to the world which, at the formal level, is parallel to his relation to God. This relation is never neutral for man is always for or against God and this is manifest in his relation to the world.

Bultmann interprets man's *anxiety* in the world as a negative awareness of transcendence, as pre-understanding of God, because it expresses the fact that man is not lord and master of his own being as he wills to be. Man is understood *ontologically* in terms of freedom because freedom is an aspect of the structure of *Dasein*. But the use of that freedom, apart from the faith which is the response to kerygma, must be described as *fallen freedom* which distorts man's relation to the world and God and can be characterized as sin, or in Paul's sense, life lived 'according to the flesh'. Man is determined by the way he lives because this leads to and arises from understanding and self-understanding. In fact, 'all man's understanding is conditioned by his understanding of himself' (*GJ*, p. 317).

The question is, will man acknowledge his *anxiety* as a sign of his fundamental insecurity in the world or will he seek to silence his anxiety and conceal his insecurity? Further, how does this awareness of anxiety relate to the perception of order in the world? While the perception of order, which is basic to science, is valid, when it becomes an existential stance taken to silence anxiety it is evidence of fallen freedom.

> By means of science men try to take possession of the world, but in fact the world gets possession of men (*JCM*, p. 40; and see *EF*, p. 210; *FU*, p. 60; *GV*, III, p. 132 and Johnson, pp. 239f.; Roberts, pp. 37f.).

This point, which has been made explicitly and clearly, has not been adequately recognized. Bultmann stresses the validity, in principle, of the modern scientific *Weltbild*, developed critically as it is on the perception of order. In this sense it is superior and makes obsolete all mythological *Weltbilder*. However, man in his fallen freedom makes use of both science and mythological *Weltbilder* in a similar fashion. The *primary* function of the mythological *Weltbilder* should not be seen in terms of primitive science. Rather they are expressions of the way mythopoeic man fixed his place, secured his existence, in the world. This is not different, in principle from the existential stance in relation to science where man seeks to gain control of the world by means of science. In both, man seeks to overcome his insecurity for himself, manifesting his fallen freedom in his denial of the claim of the '*Wholly Other*', which is the mode in which God encounters those who look for him in the world (*FU*, pp. 55f., 60f.).

> Bultmann says over and over again that men lose their souls by over attachment to the things of this world. He denounces man's self-deification, and man's deification of the world through technological and scientific mastery. Men have replaced God by their own technical skills and highly organized world; they have lost their sense of God and of the eternal.[14]

This *use* of the 'picture of the world' (*Weltbild*) needs to be clarified. The *Weltbild* which dominates our thinking comes to us through the Renaissance and the Enlightenment from Greek philosophy (*FU*, pp. 58f.). As such it is a view of the unified order of the natural world seen as a *Kosmos*.

> When this picture of the World (*Weltbild*) is completed by the inclusion of man, it is customary to call it a world-view (*Weltanschauung*) (*FU*, pp. 58f.).

Bultmann indicates that such (*Weltanschauungen*) 'world views' are highly valued, in spite of their negative evaluation (unflattering evaluation) of man, because they provide easy ready answers to ultimate questions and offer security in the face of the riddle of destiny and death (*FU*, pp. 58f.). 'World views' are an expression of man's attempt to secure his own existence. Even if God is introduced this is in order to make use of him to overcome otherwise intractable problems.

For Bultmann, the problem of the law is parallel to the problem of the modern scientific *Weltbild.* Both are formally (in principle) correct. But man, in his fallen freedom, adopts a similar relation to each and attempts to secure his existence by them. Thus, as with myth, these can become an expression of man's flight from his own being disclosed in *Angst* (*AET*, p. 65). The distinction between the perception of order, upon which the modern scientific *Weltbild* and enterprise are developed, and the existential stance, whereby man seeks to secure his existence in the world, is vital. Bultmann in no way devalues the reality of the world and its order. What he does criticize is the existential stance whereby man seeks to make use of the perception of order to obscure his anxiety and his sense of 'wonder', which lies hidden in the awareness of anxiety. Such is a betrayal of true science (*EF*, p. 210).

b. **Human Being (Dasein) with others**

> Human being is *being with the other*, and this is what makes it *historical* being in distinction from the being of nature.[15]

In the light of this statement it is difficult to see how Bultmann could be charged with individualism.[16] For him human being is defined in terms of I-Thou relationship. It is the I-Thou relationship which constitutes man's being as historical as distinct from the being of nature. Whether this stark contrast between history and nature is altogether adequate is another question. It could be that it is no more than a consequence of the human point of view, a point of view from which we cannot escape, though Bultmann recognized that man like nature, could also be treated as a mere object. If man can be treated as an object, is it possible to perceive the historicity of nature? This is not a line of questioning that Bultmann was inclined to follow. By turning to the writings of Martin Buber it becomes clear that it is not without its value. Yet it would seem that there is some validity to the distinction, even if it is not as clear-cut as Bultmann implies (*Jesus*, p. 3; 'Reply', in Kegley, pp. 266f.).

Historicity (*Geschichtlichkeit*) is constituted in decisions made in man's *being in the world in relation to others*. Here comparison with Heidegger illuminates Bultmann's position. For Heidegger, death is that which limits man's life in the face of which man resolves his life in decision (*EF*, p. 103). For Bultmann such decision is a 'resolution of despair' (*EF*, p. 105-108; and see *AET*, p. 71, 76, 80, 120). Bultmann follows Gogarten in seeing man as limited by the neighbour, the thou (*EF*, p. 103). For him 'love is the *only* possibility of authentic existence. Only in love is man historical' (*EF*, p. 105). Human being (*Dasein*) has the possibility of *historicity*, of authenticity, but this is actualized only in love. By stressing the *historicity* of man it could appear that the individual is nothing more than a 'flux of decisions', and this is precisely the charge Roberts makes (pp. 27, 33, 214f.). Against such a charge Bultmann responds that the human person is not properly understood until it is recognized that the subject of the ever-new decisions is the same ever-growing, ever-increasing, improving or denigrating *I*. While this *I* is something of a mystery there are clues to its identity in the phenomena of memory, consciousness and repentance (*HE*, p. 145; and see *Th.N.T.*, II, p. 239). The concerns with which Bultmann deals focus on the decisions through which *the person* becomes, and it is for this reason that a false impression has been created.

c. **Human Being (Dasein) as 'possibility'**

In understanding human being as 'possibility' (*Möglichkeit*) Bultmann follows Heidegger[17] and this constitutes his nearest approximation to a philosophical position in relation to the understanding of man. But it is not what Bultmann describes as a 'speculative philosophy'. It is, according to Bultmann, an understanding given in existence and firmly rooted there. The world of nature is understood in terms of the causal nexus but man is able to 'stand out' from this determinism in nature. The point is *not* the reality of the subjective over against the unreality, or 'throw away' reality, of the objective world (pace Johnson, p. 167). His perspective is the problem of genuine human freedom. Man's existence is understood as 'possibility' (*Möglichkeit*) because he can become other than he is, he is open to becoming, to the future (*FU*, p. 149, 187). What he is, his historicity (*Geschichtlichkeit*), is constituted by his 'free acts' (*freie Taten*), his 'decisions' (*Entscheidungen*) as real events (*Erlebnisse*),[18] his 'potentiality to be'. Thus the self is understood as an 'I' existing in history who becomes himself in his concrete decisions *in relation to* whatever confronts him (*EPT*, pp. 30-33).

> We believe that we understand the being of man (*das Dasein des Menschen*) more truly when we designate it as *historical* .And we understand by the *historical* nature of man's being (*des menchlichen Seins*) that his being is a *potentiality to be* (*dass sein Sein ein Sein-Können ist*). That is to say, the being of man (*das Sein des Menschen*) is removed from his own control, it is risked continually in the concrete situations of life and goes through decisions (*Entscheidungen*) in which man does not choose *something for himself*, but chooses *himself* as his *possibility* (*Möglichkeit*).[19]

This discussion concerns man in the *ontological* sense, which Bultmann distinguishes from man actually (*ontic* sense). In actual fact man is not free. He is conditioned by his past decisions, tied to his past. Man must be understood from two perspectives. Ontologically he is open to the future, free. But actually (ontically) he is determined by his own past decisions, his past life. This is the contradiction in which man finds himself unless he is set free to discover his authentic existence. For Bultmann, authentic existence (*Existenz*) is possible only in the decision of faith, in response to the Word of grace in Christ, which, paradoxically, has the character of both indicative and imperative. It is a word of acceptance and demand which actualizes the claim of the moment in which the claim of God is encountered. Thus, in faith, the ontological possibility, which properly belongs to man's existence, is actualized in the claim of the moment in which the claim of God is encountered. The decision of faith is not to be understood as a new form of self-assertion. On the contrary, it is freedom from self in love for the neighbour and the *submission* of the self to the claim of the moment which is truly free submission because, through the Word of grace, man is able to break away from his past and achieve authentic existence as a creature of God (*EPT*, p. 309; *EF*, p. 107). Freedom from the past involves turning away from the quest for security (*EPT*, p. 318).

In another sense man who gives up every false security finds genuine security (*JCM*, p. 84). But this is a 'subjective' security in faith which can have no guarantee outside itself. Not even the Word of grace is to be understood as an objective guarantee, though it is the means by which believing existence becomes actual in the world.

Because *Dasein* involves 'potentiality' or 'possibility' it is always expressed in concrete existence (*Existenz*) and is not to be understood as an essence even if it is possible to speak of the structure of *Dasein*. This structure is discovered underlying and making possible all the ways men actually *exist* in the world. Thus, for Bultmann, while *Dasein* refers ontologically to human being, *Existenz* and *Existieren* relate to the actual concrete act of existing in which man chooses himself and in so doing choose authentically or inauthentically.[20] Because authentic existence (*Existenz*) comes only in the faith which is a response to the kerygma, which frees the believer from the determinism of the past, Bultmann also refers to it as eschatological existence (*Existenz*). The freedom of the believer involves a new understanding of God, himself, and the world and this understanding is a structural element of the faith which is a response to the kerygma. The distinctions which have been made here are crucial for Bultmann's work on the Fourth Gospel.

4. **Human Being in the Fourth Gospel**

Bultmann's commentary on *The Gospel of John* provides a wealth of material concerning his understanding of human existence thus relating his understanding to the Fourth Gospel. This discussion will focus on his use of the following terms: *Dasein*, *Sein*, and *Existenz*. The page numbers of the English translation are given first followed by reference to the German in brackets.

Dasein is used on pp. 41(22), 42(23), 43(24), 45(26), 46(27), 52(32), 53(32), 66(42), 139(99), 141(100), 185(136), 590(454), 591(456), 595(459), 625(484). It is always translated 'existence' except on p. 591 where *zeitliches Dasein* is translated 'temporal sphere', obscuring the way *Dasein* consistently refers to man.

Sein is used on pp. 140(99), 141(100f.), 317(240), 321(243), 434(333), 437(334), 438(336), 608(469f.), 628(486), 629(486). While it is frequently translated 'being' it is also translated as 'life', pp. 434, 628, and 'existence', pp. 141, 608, 629.

Existenz occurs on pp. 43(24), 44(25), 58(36f.), 59(37), 60(38), 107(75), 140(99), 142(101), 191(140), 258(194), 321(243), 344(261), 381(290), 390(298), 391(298), 410(313), 436(334), 473(361), 479(365), 491(375), 589(454), 591(455), 594(458), 595(459), 598(461), 602(465), 605(467), 605(467), 606f.(468f.), 608(469f.), 613(474), 620(480), 621(480), 624(483), 628f.(486f.), 630(487) and is always translated 'existence'.

These three important terms are all translated 'existence' at times so that the reader of the commentary is left without an indication of which German word is being used. Only on pp. 590f. and 608 is there an attempt to indicate, in brackets, what is being translated. But even on these three pages this is not done consistently. Had the practice been followed throughout the commentary the reader would have been in a position to judge whether some fine distinctions were intended by Bultmann. The translators apparently were unaware of this problem or were unable to solve it. All three terms are sometimes translated 'existence'. *Sein* is generally translated 'being' which, in Bultmann's terms, when it relates to man, has the same meaning as *Dasein*, which always relates to man. But *Dasein* is translated 'existence' and is thus not readily distinguishable from *Existenz*, which is always translated 'existence'. Thus the three terms are at times confused, and where a distinction is made it is misleading.

This confusion in translation obscures crucial aspects of Bultmann's theology in its relationship to the Fourth Gospel. By *Dasein* Bultmann refers to man ontologically, involving all the possibilities of human existence. *Sein* can be used in this sense in such phrases as *das Sein des Menschen* or *menschliches Sein* which, like *Dasein*, refer to man ontologically in terms of the conditions and possibilities of human existence. But while *Dasein* always refers to man as man, *Sein* can be used of the 'being' of nature ('TLYN', p. 44). *Sein* can denote that which distinguishes the believer from the unbeliever, from an ontological point of view, while *Dasein* covers both possibilities. *Sein* can also denote the 'being' of nature as distinct from the historicity of the 'being' of *Dasein*. It is interesting and important to notice that Bultmann uses *Sein* of the believer and the unbeliever indicating that in the decision of faith the believer's 'being' is changed. According to Bultmann, only in the decision of faith can man become other than he is.

Dasein refers to human potentiality in terms of light and darkness, that is, in terms of the possibility of authentic *Existenz* or inauthentic *Existenz*. While the possibility of authentic *Existenz* was given in creation, that is, as possibility it belongs to *Dasein*, in fact, Bultmann claims, it is obtained only in the decision of faith. For this reason Bultmann refers to authentic *Existenz* as eschatological *Existenz*. What was given in creation was the possibility of the illumined state of *Existenz* (*GJ*, pp. 41-53), of true self-understanding. *Dasein* involves self-understanding but because it contains the possibility of light and darkness man can fail to find the light for which he searches and does in fact err (*GJ*, pp. 52f.). He chooses to become entangled in 'this-worldly *Sein*' and loses the 'other-worldly *Sein*' (*GJ*, p. 141).

Man's particular choices arise from his being (*Sein*). His *Existenz* is an expression of his being (*Sein*). He could only choose differently if he were changed to become other than he is. His unbelieving being (*Sein*) must become believing being (*Sein*) before authentic existence (*Existenz*) can become a reality in the world. However before this theme can be dealt with, certain expressions need further clarification. It is important to distinguish *weltliches Dasein* from *weltliche Existenz*. Here, as elsewhere, *Dasein* refers to the possibilities and conditions of human being as such. Human being is in the world with the relationships that this involves. This is a structural element of *Dasein*. However *weltliches Sein*, which is expressed in *weltliche Existenz*, refers to man in his surrender to worldliness, to his capitulation to the seduction of worldly security and pleasure which Paul referred to in terms of 'the life lived according to the flesh' (*GJ*. pp. 141, 191, 590). Such *Existenz* is opposed to the authentic or eschatological *Existenz* which is the salvation for which man (*Dasein*) actually searches, whether consciously or not (*GJ*, pp. 58-60, 258). While such *Existenz* is a possibility given to *Dasein* in creation, in fact it is only actualized with the coming of the Revealer. Without the revelation man is an unbeliever determined by his unbelieving *being* (*Sein*) (*GJ*, p. 317). He cannot change his own *being* (*GJ*, p. 140), therefore authentic *Existenz* is not a human possibility (*GJ*, p. 142). However, the Revealer puts the *being* of the unbeliever in question so that, in this situation, there is the unique possibility of a free decision for or against the revelation and in this decision man constitutes his *being* definitively as a believer or an unbeliever (*GJ*, pp. 317, 497, 44f.; *FU*, pp. 166ff.). In the encounter with the Revealer, man has the possibility of a changed *being,* of eschatological *Sein*, eschatological *Existenz*. There is believing *Sein*, believing *Existenz*, unbelieving *Sein* and unbelieving *Existenz*; there is eschatological *Sein*, eschatological *Existenz*, and worldly *Sein*, worldly *Existenz*. While believing, authentic, eschatological *Existenz* is historical *Existenz* in the world (*GJ*, pp. 606-608), it is not restricted to life in this world. There is, in eschatological *Existenz*, life beyond this worldly present, beyond death in the other worldly reality (*GJ*, pp. 595, 602).

From this survey of Bultmann's exposition of the Fourth Gospel the following seems to be clear. *Dasein* refers to the conditions and possibilities of human being as such in an ontological sense. *Sein* can also be used in this sense when it appears in such phrases as *das Sein des Menschen* or *menschliches Sein*, 'human being'. However *Sein* is normally used with a qualification which indicates the nature of the 'being' to which reference is made while *Dasein* always refers to 'human being' as such. *Sein* is not restricted in use to the description of human *being* and even when it is used of man it can be so qualified that it distinguishes people from each other so that there is believing *being* and unbelieving *being*. This ontological terminology is used in order to show that decisions and actions arise out of *being*. Believing *Existenz* is an expression of believing *Sein* and unbelieving *Existenz* is an expression of unbelieving *Sein*. Both express the possibilities inherent in *Dasein*. Otherwise they would not be possible, or in the fulfilment the individual would cease to be man. Without the revelation, Bultmann argues, man's existence is inauthentic and this is an expression of his unbelieving being. Through the coming of the revelation, the eschatological event, the unique possibility for change has occurred. The change itself is referred to as eschatological *Existenz*, which is the manifestation of eschatological *Sein*, believing *Sein*.

The hermeneutical task, which constitutes Bultmann's theological enterprise, can now be clarified. In the encounter with the text there is the possibility for man to understand himself anew as well as the text. However, according to Bultmann, only through the revelation proclaimed in the *kerygma* does a radically new understanding become actual for the believer. Such understanding is a structural element of faith and can be spoken of as authentic *Existenz* which is a manifestation of believing *Sein*. If to speak of the new life in terms of a new self-understanding seems to undervalue the Christian teaching about 'salvation' it should be recognized that self-understanding cannot be changed at will. To have a new self-understanding is to have a new life, especially if that new understanding corresponds to the reality of God's creation. It is Bultmann's claim that only in the faith which is a response to the proclamation does human self-understanding correspond to the reality of God's creation and this is authentic *Existenz*. All other self-understandings are inauthentic, false, because they do not correspond to the reality of God's creation as distinct from the 'world'. The illuminated state of *Existenz*, which is authentic, was a possibility given in creation. Faith is a return to and fulfilment of that lost possibility. Hermeneutics is concerned with understanding the possibilities of human being (*Dasein*) embodied in texts. But theology as hermeneutics asserts that only in the believing *Existenz* which is the response to the proclamation embodied in the New Testament does man turn aside from falsehood to his authentic being.

5. **Human Being (Dasein) and 'Pre-understanding'**

Without pre-understanding there would be no understanding at all. 'We know ... because it belongs to our life ... '[21] Existence provides a preliminary existential understanding of all that can be known whether that be of music, economics, politics, friendship, love etc. Naturally such pre-understanding must be conceptually clarified before it becomes actual understanding. The situation is relatively simple when texts deal with events in the world of space-time because author and interpreter live in the same world. But it is more complicated when texts deal 'not with objects and temporal events in the world'. Understanding in both cases involved 'pre-understanding' otherwise understanding would not be possible (*FU*, pp. 156ff.). In all cases pre-understanding is a preliminary, questioning, a 'not knowing kind of knowing' (*EF*, pp. 61-65; *FU*, p. 159). However where that which is to be known does not belong to the world of time and space as such the pre-understanding is to be understood *in a special negative sense*. This distinction has not been adequately recognized and will be discussed below.

Another important distinction concerns that 'understanding' which belongs to *Dasein* (human life in the world) and the pre-understanding that the exegete brings to the text. In addition to the understanding given with *Dasein* he brings actual understanding from other life situations and from the tradition in which he stands (*EF*, pp. 65f.). Thus there are two distinct *modes* of pre-understanding: that which is the result of previous understanding; and that which is inherent in *Dasein*. However, as pre-understanding, both modes are to be thought of as

> unknowing knowledge ... which has the character of a question. Unless I ask I cannot hear; for man is not a *tabula rasa*, a photographic plate. But to be able to question, I must in some fashion already know (*FU*, p. 159).

To be man (*Dasein*) is to question because *das Dasein des Menschen* (= *das Sein des Menschen*) is to be understood in terms of historicity

(*Geschichtlichkeit*) in which man becomes himself, chooses himself, in his decisions in relation to other thous and the world of nature. Because *Dasein* is potentiality or possibility, man is always searching for what he is to be. This appears to be one aspect of what Bultmann means by the structure of *Dasein* (*EF*, pp. 94, 101). *Dasein* involves self-understanding though what that self-understanding will be is left open.

There is a correlation between the structure of *Dasein* and the order of the world and it is this that makes possible the pre-understanding which is given with human life in the world. However it is only through experience and reflection that this not-knowing, questioning knowing, becomes actual knowledge. Naturally, in the process pre-understanding might be confirmed, modified, or even negated.

We have distinguished two *modes* of pre-understanding and referred to pre-understanding 'dealing with natural objects or with events in the world of space-time', which is to be distinguished from the situation when the subject is, for example, the revelation or God. In this case pre-understanding takes on a special negative sense. According to Bultmann, neither the revelation nor God is present in the structure of man's being or in the order of the world, though it is true that both the structure of man's being and the world as such raise the question of God, because *Dasein* is questioning and searching.

> I can also say that the existentialist interpretation of history attempts to answer the question that the factual history in which we are entangled poses for us ('Reply', in Kegley, p. 275).

Man's existence raises the question of meaning and it is of the essence of *Dasein* to search for an answer to this question. Pre-understanding, which gives rise to the question, is an expression of the sense of absence. This special negative sense has not been adequately noted with regard to Bultmann's use of the idea of pre-understanding in relation to the revelation and God. Yet it has been a recurring theme in his writings (*JCM*, pp. 52f.; *EPT*, pp. 257f.; *FU*, pp. 318ff.; 'Reply', in Kegley, p. 275).

Preunderstanding of God is an awareness of God, a knowledge *about* God, whether conscious or unconscious. Such awareness is rooted in the question about the meaning of existence, a question that moves all men because what it means to be human is a potentiality, a possibility to be discovered. In the face of this uncertainty fear arises as an inauthentic expression of man's insecurity, his ontological anxiety (*Angst*). Such anxiety is the fundamental affective state of man's being in the world of which fear is an inauthentic mode because, in fear, man flees from anxiety and all that it would disclose.

Anxiety belongs to the structure of being human, though it is known predominantly in man's flight from it in fear (*EF*, p. 305 n. 16). Anxiety is made known through the evidence of fear, but even more in the attempt to suppress fear. Anxiety is the 'dizziness of freedom and finitude' (Kiergegaard); or the 'facticity' of 'possibility' 'thrown' into the world (Heidegger); that is, limited freedom. There would be no flight from freedom if freedom were unlimited. But man's existence in freedom is in an alien world which he cannot master.

Anxiety reveals that man is not at home in the world, shattering illusory contentment and arousing uneasiness. Because of this fear arises in which men flee from anxiety by losing themselves in the world (*JCM*, p. 40). All of man's attempts to secure his life are flights from anxiety, whether he uses the modern scientific *Weltbild*, Jewish legalism, or myth. Such is the power of fear that even what is in itself legitimate (science, the Law) can be used to maintain the plausibility of inauthentic existence. Man is right to take responsibility for the world and to direct its development through science and technology. What is wrong is man's flight in fear from ontological anxiety and modern science can be used to aid this flight by assuring him that he has control over his own life. What then is the authentic human response? According to Bultmann it is not 'resolution in the face of anxiety' (Heidegger), which is only a 'resolution of despair' (*EF*, pp. 105, 107; *AET*, pp. 71, 76, 80, 130 n. 37).

Bultmann argues that the revelation answers man's search for the fulfilment of his 'possibility', however that is conceptualized. But the revelation contradicts all human answers. The emphasis on contradiction highlights the special negative character of preunderstanding in relation to God. Preunderstanding of other subjects such as music, economics, friendship, etc., is not necessarily contradicted by actual understanding, however much the realization of knowledge involves a transformation. The negative aspect of preunderstanding in relation to God is a consequence of the possibility of knowledge being taken to be actual knowledge so that the question is turned into an answer. The contradiction of these answers by the revelation[22] is as fundamental for Bultmann as it was for Luther or Barth. But, for Bultmann, the contradiction is also the point of contact for the revelation with man.[23]

6. **Human Being (Dasein) and Knowledge**

Human being characterizes itself in terms of understanding or knowledge and self-understanding is the foundation of all knowledge in the sense that the way man understands himself affects the way he understands everything else (*GJ*, p. 317). Apart from the faith which is a response to the revelation, man has a false self-understanding, although the *possibility* of authentic self-understanding was given in creation (*GJ*, pp. 39ff.). Without faith this remains an unfulfilled possibility. Because man's self-understanding is false, all other understanding is affected. Even technically correct knowledge, such as that upon which the modern scientific *Weltbild* is based, becomes 'tainted'. This 'deceitfulness' which obscures 'wonder' and man's anxiety is not genuine science (*EF*, p. 210). Self-understanding determines man's existential attitude to everything. Only the revelation, which is a direct attack on this false self-understanding, offers authentic self-understanding to faith. The theological significance of this existential knowledge is clear. We need now to see the epistemological consequences of grounding knowledge, including knowledge of the revelation, in human being.

Whatever is known has been derived from human being in the world and is, in principle, open to human knowledge. Naturally, in terms of history, this statement needs to be qualified by time and place. But there is no genuine knowledge which cannot be traced back to its existential origin. Sometimes, as in the case of mythology, this is obscured by the form in which the knowledge is expressed (*K&M*, II, p. 185 n. 1). The nature of the revelation can also be obscured by mythological language. This is illustrated by Colin Gunton's recent review of Edward Schillebeeckx's *Jesus: An Experiment in Christology* (*SJT* 33/2 [1980], p. 175). Gunton suggests that the religious language of faith communicates 'new information' otherwise inaccessible, gained from God, mediated through the Bible and asks if this is a 'pre-critical' way of understanding texts.

Such would indeed be a 'pre-critical' understanding of the text (see *EF*, pp. 99f.). The questioner does not consider how God gave such 'new information' to the biblical writers, information inaccessible to man through his existence. Presumably what is presupposed is the notion of revelation by means of which God communicated information in words, statements and dogmas, which related accurately facts inaccessible to man in his own existence; facts about the beginning and the end, for example. Such an explanation says nothing about the process by which such information is communicated, understood and recognized as the truth of God. This is quite a problem because what is communicated is otherwise inaccessible. The situation is not materially improved by introducing the notion of the inspiration of the Holy Spirit. How then is the Holy Spirit to be recognized?

In fact few scholars today treat the Bible as if revelation occurred in the dictation of facts in verbal form. The creation stories of Genesis are not normally read as if God had dictated how he created the Universe. Obviously such events are outside the scope of human knowledge as a whole and the only way they could be known is along the lines of verbal inspiration. But to reject this approach to the creation stories does not mean that they should be consigned to the rubbish tip in which we can find all forms of primitive science. For if these stories embody primitive science they are only so *in part*, the part which should perhaps be called the form. It is significant that the creation stories are an expression of the faith of the Exodus community. God, who was encountered in history in the Exodus, was proclaimed as creator. Perhaps the meaning of the creation stories is, on another level, to be found in what it was that gave rise to them. Why did the Biblical writers assert these things? Bultmann asserts that the existential origin of this language should be regarded as indicative of the way it is to be understood.

The kerygma can also be expressed in mythological language. For Bultmann the question is, 'Why did the Biblical writers say what they did about Jesus?' The existential origin of the language is to be verified existentially in the new life which remains a possibility for those who believe today. Revelation is not to be found in the communication of *facts* inaccessible to man but in the *actualization* of authentic existence which is given as the human possibility (*EF*, pp. 58ff.).

There is no doubt that in the Bible there are statements which, analysed linguistically, make assertions which go beyond the scope of knowledge gained through human existence. This fact is sometimes used to show that Bultmann's method is too narrow. No one denies that the existential element is present in the New Testament and theology. The question is whether the existentialist approach does justice to the New Testament and theology as a whole. Many critics have answered this question in the negative[24] and recently Bultmann has been charged with inconsistency. In dealing with the question of pre-understanding Bultmann writes:

> The historical picture is falsified only when a specific way of raising questions is put forward as the only one—when, for example, all history is reduced to economic history (*EF*, p. 29[346]).

Now it is asked, has not Bultmann himself fallen into this very trap in his exclusive line of existentialist interpretation,[25] that is, interpretation which seeks the existential significance and origin of what is said? This criticism misses the point. First, existence is not a 'sectional interest' in the life of man in the way economics is. Rather it *is* the life of man. Second, theology is not concerned with the 'sectional interests' as such but with man's life as a whole. Third, and most importantly, all knowledge is grasped in human existence and what man does not come to know in his existence he does not know. Bultmann applies this awareness critically in a way that is by no means an alternative to the task of historical reconstruction in political, economic and other terms (see *Th.N.T.*, II, p. 251). Hence Bultmann defended his understanding of 'existence' as his *canon* of criticism (*Letters*, p. 96).

The critical use of the *existential* perspective involves the assumption that the possibilities of existence today are in principle the same as always. This can be the only basis for a critical approach which does not accept meaning and truth as equivalents simply on the basis of authoritative assertion. Thus Bultmann recognizes 'mythological' language in the New Testament without affirming the truth of such statements in any straightforward sense. The language *apparently* asserts what is beyond existential knowledge. To reject this apparent meaning does not necessarily indicate that the assertions are meaningless. The valid meaning is to be found in the existential source/origin of the language, the language itself being the form and idiom of the cultural context. Existentialist interpretation is demanded by Bultmann's critical standpoint. It is a bonus for him that he can claim Paul and John as exponents of this approach (*JCM*, pp. 32f.; *HE*, p. 40). If they fall away from this standpoint Bultmann also applies 'content criticism' (*Sachkritik*) to draw attention to the inner contradiction (*Widerspruch*) (*K&M*, I, p. 11). His intention is to overcome one side of the contradiction by recognizing that it conflicts with the overall meaning of the text. It is overcome by reinterpreting it in terms of its existential origin. What, in the life of the writer or his context, gave rise to the mythological assertion?

As a critical historian Bultmann attempted not only to say what the statements in the New Testament mean, but also to assess their truth. Had there been no contradiction, allowing him to choose one or other side of the contradiction, Bultmann might have found himself interpreting the New Testament against its own intention. But, as it stands, he appeals to Paul and John as exponents of his approach. This makes his hermeneutical task less embarrassing. Indeed the case for demythologizing cannot rest *alone* on the recognition of a mythological *Weltbild* and conceptuality in the New Testament. It would be unjustifiable if this was what the writers sought to communicate because the standard of criticism 'can only be the intention of the New Testament' ('SOTCF', p. 11).

Historical-critical work demonstrates that the kerygma was first presented in the conceptual framework of Jewish apocalyptic and was reinterpreted in the conceptual framework of Hellenistic Gnosticism. Thus Bultmann argues that no *Weltbild*, apocalyptic, Gnostic, or modern scientific is definitive or essential to the message of the New Testament[26] and that the intended message of the New Testament is distinguishable from the mythological form in which it sometimes appears.

Bultmann's practice of *Sachkritik* has been widely criticized as 'partial exegesis[27] and this can be related to the criticism of turning *a* way into *the* way of interpreting. Such criticisms of Bultmann's practice do not do justice to the complexity of the problem. If Bultmann detects conflicts and contradictions in the texts within the New Testament he is not alone. While it might seem, to some, to be possible to refer to such conflicts as 'diversity', implying that no contradiction is involved, even if it is apparent, such an approach might well be a consequence of a *presupposed* unity. Bultmann recognizes conflicts between books in the New Testament and even within books. Apparent contradictions should not be treated as a unity simply because it is possible that the problem lies with us not being able to see the unity. As long as this is the case it is critically correct to recognize conflicts and contradictions in early Christianity. Is it not the task of the historian to trace the development of the contradiction? At the heart of this task is the problem of assessing the role and significance of Jesus. Almost everything turns on this. On the basis of his reconstruction Bultmann argues that the earliest church proclaimed Jesus in the framework of Jewish apocalyptic and that Hellenistic Christianity made use of the Gnostic redeemer myth. Both approaches were open to the problem of confusing the significance of Jesus with the conceptual framework.

Bultmann's position in relation to knowledge *through Dasein* has also been criticized because knowledge *through* so easily becomes knowledge *of Dasein*.[28] One reason for this is the suspicion, in the mind of the critic, that Bultmann is addressing the subject/object problem. In this the critic is mistaken. Whether on good or inadequate grounds Bultmann assumes that man's relation to the world (and to the neighbour) is a 'given' and knowledge of it is given *in human being*. It is existential knowledge. Two illustrations will perhaps demonstrate the point.

First, in his kerygmatic theology Bultmann is frequently charged with having dissolved the historical element and made it irrelevant (thus John Macquarrie, in Kegley, p. 141). Bultmann replied that he did not ignore the factual history of Jesus and that Christian faith declares the paradox that the history of Jesus is the eschatological event. Further, there would be no existentialist interpretation of history without the factual history. Such interpretation of history 'attempts to answer the questions that the factual history in which we are entangled poses for us' ('Reply', in Kegley, pp. 274f.). The interpretation of Jesus as the revealer of God through whom new life comes to man is not historically verifiable. What the factual history of Jesus does is to pose the question as to whether this might not be the case. The claim can only be verified in man's existence in faith (thus Thiselton, p. 84).

The second problem concerns God-talk. To speak of God man must speak of himself (*FU*, p. 55, etc.). But we should not understand this as speaking only of man, which was the chief problem with 'liberal theology' (*FU*, p. 29). What Bultmann has in mind is to speak of God in his relation to man and man in his relation to God. How else could man speak of God? This is to speak of God from the perspectives of an existential relation. But the problem, in this case, is more critical because God is not an *object* in the world and the way he impinges on human existence and consciousness constitutes a problem of a different order than is involved in human knowledge of the world. This has already been noted in relation to *pre-understanding*. The question is, in what way does God impinge on our existence? What is it that gives rise to God-talk?

This problem also needs to be related to the history of Jesus and the development of christology. Why did believers come to use God-talk of Jesus? Bultmann approves of Melanchthon's rejection of '*Christum cognoscere eius naturas modos incarnationis contueri*' in favour of '*Hoc est Christum cognoscere, beneficia eius cognoscere*' (*FU*, pp. 263, 279; *K&M*, II, p. 92).

There is no doubt that the early fathers intended to speak of the two 'natures' of Christ. How did they come to possess this knowledge? Simply put, they learned of it from the New Testament on the basis of what they *understood* to be involved with being God and man. Consequently the question comes into focus in terms of why the New Testament writers used God language of Jesus. It is Bultmann's contention that this occurred because the first believers found new authentic life through him. That was his uniqueness, that the authenticity of life that was possible for man and for which man was searching, actually became reality in the lives of believers. It is not only that, historically, Bultmann considers it to be highly improbable that Jesus asserted 'I am God incarnate', but also, such a claim, even if it had been made, would by itself mean nothing. There would still need to be something which made such a claim credible, providing it with a foundation of meaning. That foundation is to be found in what came about, and continues to come about, through Jesus. It is this that justifies the language of the New Testament which speaks of Jesus as God's Word, God's act, Messiah, Son of Man, Son of God - in other words, in the conceptual frameworks, both Jewish and Hellenistic, of the day. The significance of Jesus was experienced in the lives of the first believers. For them he was unique and absolute. Because of their cultural contexts, they 'projected' that significance into the past, in terms of creation, and into the future in terms of eschatology.

Such projections arose from the existential awareness of the new life through faith which had come about through the Christ event. That was the evidential base of the projections, forwards and backwards. How should these 'projections' be interpreted? Linguistically the words say that the Logos, incarnate in Jesus, brought

Creation into being, that Jesus now reigns with the Father and that he will come again as judge at the end of the age. But what is the basis for these assertions? If they arose from the awareness of the new life brought by Jesus then they need to be seen as projections and Bultmann is content to assume that such projections need to be interpreted exclusively in terms of the existential foundation. This need not necessarily follow. If authentic existence becomes a reality only through the faith which Jesus evokes it is not unreasonable to suggest that this has implications which go beyond the existential event. Bultmann is content to leave as a mystery why the eschatological event should be tied to this one man. The New Testament writers were more optimistic about saying something positive concerning that mystery, though Bultmann has reminded us that the evidence remains rooted in existential reality. If this seems like moving back to agree with those who criticize Bultmann for partial exegesis, such is not really the case. Bultmann is right in principle, though a case can be made for allowing certain extrapolations on the basis of faith. This is done in the awareness that what is actually known is existential truth. Some extrapolations, seen as projections, seem to be demanded in order to understand the implications of existential truth.[29] On the basis of the belief that God's act is known *only* in the Christ event faith concludes that Jesus is the Son of God.

7. **Conclusions**

This treatment of the existentialist theology of Rudolf Bultmann has attempted to demonstrate that, whatever Bultmann's intellectual debts might be, he is not theologically dependent on Heidegger's philosophy nor is his epistemology to be understood in terms of some synthesis of Lutheran anthropology and Marburg Neo-Kantian epistemology. Rather Bultmann stresses the 'relationality' of man in the world of nature and other 'thous'. It is relation to the 'thou' which constitutes the 'historicity' of man and the perception of order in the world of nature that opens up the possibility of life in the world as such.

The world constitutes a problem for Bultmann, not because it is 'unreal', but because, in his fallen freedom, man loses himself in the world by an inauthentic attachment to it through which he becomes enslaved. The problem which is in focus for Bultmann is the freedom of man which, in fact, is realized only in response to the kerygma.

The key to Bultmann's thought is the perspective of existence in faith, that is, the knowledge that is given in faith. The perspective of the existential *relations* of man in faith excludes the possibility of understanding man as an isolated subjective entity. Rather, the being of man (*Sein*) is discovered in relationships as believing being or unbelieving being, and such relationships are expressed in decisions in relation to the world of nature and other 'thous'.

Chapter Two

Hermeneutics and History

Synopsis

If theology is concerned with understanding the 'classical' texts of the Christian faith then the problem of understanding the past cannot be avoided. Theology also involves special problems because it has to cope with, what Bultmann calls, the 'new history', the history of the revelation. It is important to understand the relationship of the two histories. For Bultmann, the 'new history' is a part of general history and can be studied using 'normal' historical methods. However, it is recognized as 'new history' only by faith, and theology interprets this history from the perspective of the evaluation of faith. While the theologian is not necessarily a believer, it is necessary for him to interpret the texts as an expression of believing comprehension. Such comprehension can be elucidated by 'normal' historical procedures. In fact, the meaning of believing comprehension becomes clear only in an understanding of the history of its developing expressions. Because of this the task of reconstructing the history of Primitive Christian thought is vital.

Evocative Epigram

> And faith has its basis in the appearance of Jesus, which broke through the circle of intra-mundane events in order to create a new history—a history of the efficacy of the Spirit, of the proclamation of the word.
>
> . . . Jesus' life and work have come to an end as an event in world-history; the revelation which he brought will never come to an end. But in accordance with its origin, this new history will not have the character of world-history.

RUDOLF BULTMANN (*GJ*, pp. 615f.)[30]

Chapter Two

HERMENEUTICS AND HISTORY

The juxtaposition of the two terms hermeneutics and history is reminiscent of the title of Carl Braaten's important book *History and Hermeneutics* and suggestive of apparently obvious lines of thought. The reversal of order in our title is intended to throw the emphasis on hermeneutics. 'Hermeneutics' is obviously a 'technical' term. In the writings of Rudolf Bultmann, precisely because of the stress on hermeneutics, vocabulary concerning 'history' is also used with sophistication that has little in common with the popular understanding of history. Hence the title is more suggestive of problems than of clear lines of thought.

1. What is Hermeneutics?[31]

Bultmann's approach to hermeneutics is in the tradition of Schleiermacher and Dilthey with the emphasis on the process of understanding. 'Understanding' is a key note theme in all of his writings. As Karl Barth has said, 'The name of Rudolf Bultmann is inseparably linked with the idea of "understanding"' (*K&M*, II, p. 83). His predominant concern is with understanding historical phenomena. Historical phenomena are not restricted to texts but the possibility of understanding is predominantly bound up with literary documents (*EPT*, p. 234). Any discussion of hermeneutics inevitably raises the question of meaning in history or the meaning of history. It is well known that Bultmann is critical of attempts to speak of the meaning of history as a whole, as if any one could view the whole of history from some vantage point outside of history or from the end of history (*EF*, p. 295). This does not mean that historical events have no meaning. It does mean that no absolute meaning can be discerned at any time. Rather history unfolds the meaning of events (such as

Caesar's crossing of the Rubicon: its meaning for Caesar, for Rome, for the West). Here the meaning depends on perspective. There is also what Bultmann calls 'the existential encounter with history' through which 'an understanding of the possibilities of human life' is opened up. Bultmann refers to this aspect in relation to the historicity (*Geschichtlichkeit*) of man.

Through the encounter with history comes the possibility of a new self-understanding which is a consequence of encountering the other. However the encounter with history can ever only be recounted as an interpretation, a point of view (*Jesus*, p. 13).

The distinction between an historical event as an event and the text which reports such an event is also important. Naturally the event includes its meaning or importance (*HE*, p. 117); it also evokes interpretation (Kegley, p. 265), which can be viewed from different perspectives—for example, the significance of Jesus for Pontius Pilate, or Paul, or Augustine etc. The 'ripples' from such an event go on causing consequences in a chain-like fashion so that the definitive meaning can be known only when history has come to an end (*EF*, p. 295). Consequences of events are both direct and indirect. One action can set off a chain of events so that it can be demonstrated that it 'caused' those events which flowed from it. In another way events evoke interpretation. The interpretation is unthinkable without the event but it may not be the demonstrable meaning of the event as it will be the consequence of looking at the event in a particular way. That way might include presuppositions which are likely to be valid or indeed palpably false. An action has a direct consequence, for example when someone shot the President of the United States of America and he died. But the meaning and significance of that event is bound up with the way it is understood, as the act of a madman, a C.I.A. conspiracy or a Communist plot. Part of the meaning of the action is a direct consequence but the more significant aspect of its meaning depends on the framework in which the event is understood. The understanding of the event is a consequence of it and also has its own consequences. Meaning can be viewed from any point in the chain. Thus any understanding of history involves a perspective or viewpoint. This is somewhat different from the problem of understanding the meaning of a text. The meaning or importance of a particular event may prove to be of far greater significance than is evident at the time or thought by those involved, such as the action in which Martin Luther nailed his ninety-five theses to the doors of the

Castle-Church of Wittenberg. This act set in motion those events which were to lead to the Reformation with consequences as yet still unknown. Certainly it is true of Luther that he did more than he knew. Should we say the same of authors, that they have said more than they know?[32] Viewed as an event, Luther's ninety-five theses were instrumental in setting in motion events of which Luther had not even dreamt. But does this change the *meaning* of the words he wrote? It gives them a new importance, but a new meaning?

If the meaning of an historical event is to be discovered in its consequences, is this also true of literary documents? Bultmann recognized that no interpretation could ever become definitive because interpretation is always carried out in concrete historical situations (*Th.N.T.*, II, p 237; and see Tracey; *TA1*, p. 310). Thus, however perceptive Luther's interpretation of Paul might have been, it cannot become definitive because, if it did, it would block fresh insight and the new interpreter would first have to understand Luther before he could understand Paul (*FU*, p. 154). This is true because the meaning of texts is discovered anew in each new situation. Can it be that new situations reveal new meanings in the text? Obviously this *can* be the case. However, much depends on what we mean by 'meaning' and 'in' the text.

Literary works 'mean' different things to different readers at various times. The same text can be variously understood by different readers because a literary work, once produced, does have a life of its own. All sorts of meanings might be concealed in a text awaiting release through new times, places, situations and people. From this point of view it has become common to speak of texts as 'polyvalent'. What does a text mean? It could be that the author's intentions had become obscured until uncovered again by a new generation. Alternatively, new readers might discover altogether new meanings never dreamt of by the original author. Does this not suggest that it is not the texts that are 'polyvalent' in this instance, rather it is minds or understanding—in Bultmann's terms 'pre-understanding'—that affect the way texts are understood?

While there can be no doubt that texts mean different things to different readers, a good case can be made out for reserving the phrase 'the meaning *of the text*' to refer to the meaning 'intended' by the author. New situations can aid the recovery of this meaning when it has been obscured. The problem for this view is the assertion that the recovery of such meaning is impossible. But if it is impossible all that is possible is for each reader to discover his own meaning from the text, not in the text, for it is not possible for him to know what meaning is 'in' the text.

While the problems involved in the historical interpretation of texts should not be put aside lightly, surrender to them does not leave us with polyvalent texts, but with texts of which I can say only what they mean *to me*, that is, how *I* understand them. The same problems which prevent the interpreter from discovering the meaning 'intended' by the author stand in his way when he seeks to discover the way other interpreters understand the text. That there are problems and obstacles can hardly be denied. But these are more serious in theory than in fact or practice because human beings live in the same world even if they understand it differently. There is, however, no existential language free from the colouring of a cultural context which would be transparent to every age. Language as a human phenomenon is always a specific language, an expression of a particular cultural context and an expression of a specific interpretation.[33] There is no language free from interpretation because language is always used to express human understanding.

The study of texts allows for many possibilities. It is possible to search for the meaning of the author; or to set out a history of the interpretation of the text; or simply to read it evocatively, to discover what lines of thought are set in motion. There is no point in seeking to reject any of these approaches. Each of them has its place. There are some texts for which it is fruitless to search for the meaning of the author; for example, the Gilgamesh epic. Yet one can trace something of the history of the interpretation of that epic. With ritual texts, whatever the meaning is, is perhaps to be discovered by participation in the ritual. Such examples divert our attention from what, for Bultmann, is the central problem, the interpretation of the New Testament as a collection of literary documents by individual authors such as Paul and the author of the Fourth Gospel.

Bultmann's work on hermeneutics, though based on general discussions of the subject by historians and philosophers of history, is directed towards the interpretation of the New Testament as a collection of historical documents (*Th.N.T.*, II, pp. 237, 251). Any such interpretation involves coming to terms with *the two horizons* of the past and the present. The interpreter whose interest in the New Testament is strictly antiquarian should not lose sight of 'the two horizons'. Were he to do so he would inevitably fail to *reconstruct* the meaning of the text in terms of its past context and meaning and would distort it in terms of present conceptuality. He can only begin with his own contemporary understanding and conceptions. But his own understanding and conceptions must be modified by the encounter with the text, at least for the sake of the reconstruction. Bultmann's intention was to go beyond this position because he believed that historical texts are 'expressions of human life in written form' through the study of which it is possible to discover the possibilities of human life (*Dasein*) ('Hermeneutics', *EPT*, p. 234; *Th.N.T.*, II, p. 251). He approached the New Testament with the question 'How does the New Testament understand human existence?' for which his existentialist approach was appropriate ('Reply', in Kegley, pp. 258f.). His approach is appropriate to his view that the New Testament has 'something to say to the present' (*Th.N.T.*, II, p. 251). This is true of the New Testament in a special way, though all historical texts have something to say to the present in terms of the possibilities of human existence.

Bultmann's interest in the New Testament was not that of an antiquarian. But he rejected any approach which would simply interpret the New Testament in terms of contemporary ideas and questions. What the New Testament has to say to us today can only be discovered on the basis of historical reconstruction (*Th.N.T.*, II, p. 251) using appropriate historical critical methods.

> Investigation and reproduction of the context of world history only has meaning - though, to be sure, a very important meaning - to the degree that it serves the kind of interpretation which is genuinely historical. It does that in so far as it aids the reactualizing of the past (*Vergegenwärtigung*), i.e. in so far as it renders possible *translation* from a past conceptuality into that of the present. Therefore it plays a critical role so far as it critically calls into question the present onceptuality, since through the medium of the latter we would understand a document of the past wrongly or even not at all.[34]

With this quotation we encounter a number of important themes and questions. There is, first, the distinction between 'world history' (*weltgeschichtlich*) and 'genuinely historical' (*echt-geschichtlich*) where the one is related to the other in that it can serve it. Second, there is the problem of hermeneutical *translation* which is a response to the recognition of the chasm which separates the present from the past (see also *K&M*, II, pp. 186f.; *EF*, p. 292). At this point a preliminary discussion of the distinction and relation between world history and the historicity of man is appropriate. Bultmann's ultimate concern is with the latter which is actually made possible only on the basis of the kerygma of the New Testament, which can be grasped and understood only through historical reconstruction.

The historicity of man should not be confused with the task of historical reconstruction though the latter can serve the realization of it. Because of this Bultmann was firmly committed to the application and refinement of 'the (so called) historical-critical method' which he had learned from the great scholars of the nineteenth century, many of whom had been his teachers. In Bultmann's hands the method was developed systematically and applied radically in the criticism of false ideas, beliefs and practices,[35] much in the way Martin Kähler and Albert Schweitzer had criticized the 'lives of Jesus' of the nineteenth century. Like Kähler he did not consider it possible to establish faith in this way or to realize the genuine historicity of man. Faith is not a phenomenon of this world (*EF*, p. 288). It is an eschatological phenomenon. The Jesus of history is accessible via the 'historical method', but the revelation which occurred through him is not, because the history of the revelation is a new history which does not have the character of world history (*GJ*, pp. 615f.; *FU*, p. 177). Here we encounter Bultmann's distinction between the Jesus of history and the Christ of faith, developed on the basis of insights drawn from Wilhelm Herrmann and Martin Kähler for whom 'the real Christ is the preached Christ'.[36] This distinction did not lead Bultmann to disregard 'the historical-critical method'. Rather he developed it more radically than his predecessors, secure in the conviction that no criticism could touch that which had to do with faith.

The development of 'the historical-critical method' involved a concern for methodology including the ordering of questions, not placing secondary questions in a position of primary importance. Bultmann was not primarily concerned to make the Christian faith more palatable to modern man. While his attempt to 'demythologize' has been interpreted in this way, Bultmann regarded this as a misunderstanding. His intention was to remove the misunderstandings of the New Testament writings which were inevitable today if they were not translated into a conceptual form appropriate to our time. Hence his work is concerned primarily with understanding rather than apologetics (pace Barth, in *K&M*, II, pp. 118f.; see *Letters*, p. 90).

2. Hermeneutics as Translation

The idea of *hermeneutical translation* (henceforth simply translation) is very important for Bultmann's theology. In the passage already quoted he spoke of '*Translation* from a past conceptuality into that of the present'. Naturally this has special importance with reference to '*Demythologizing*' (*Letters*, p. 88). While 'myth' might be the most obvious form of 'past conceptuality' it is by no means the only one and 'translation' is not reserved exclusively for the task of bridging the gulf between past and present. Translation is involved wherever there is a conceptual gulf which can occur, not only with the passage of time, but also between cultural and 'sub-cultural' groups of the same era.

What did Bultmann mean by translation in this context? What is 'hermeneutical translation'? Bultmann has been accused of conceptual confusion in this use of 'translation'. Roberts (pp. 80f., 217ff., 221ff., 230f.; and see Thiselton, pp. 360f., 382, 406, 442) argues that translation deals with words. We translate one word by another word but the aim is to retain and communicate the same idea or conception using the new word. Hence to translate concepts is said to be a contradiction.

> There is no such thing as a different set of concepts which carry the same meaning, and thus no translation from conceptuality to conceptuality (Roberts, p. 231).

The *prima facie* case put forward in this quotation seems impregnable. If you change the concepts you change the meaning. Therefore there is no translation but a new statement saying something new. The point indeed seems to be obvious. What is it then that takes place in the New Testament? How are we to account for the diversity of presentations by different authors; or even by the same author, Paul? It is well known that Bultmann interprets the development of the New Testament from Jesus, through the earliest church, some form of Jewish Christianity; through Hellenistic Christianity, fundamentally gentile in character, of which Paul and John are the most authentic spokesmen; and on into what we call to-day 'early Catholicism'. In the Jewish context the proclamation of

Jesus as Messiah was appropriate to the existing conceptual framework. What we are speaking of is an idea, 'Messiahship', in the context of a constellation of ideas or a conceptual framework. The conceptual framework was provided by Jewish interpretations of the Old Testament tradition. The idea of Jesus as Messiah made sense in that context even if it was necessary at the same time to proclaim that the nature of Jesus' Messiahship was somewhat different from common expectations. At least there was a *'pre-understanding'* of what was meant by 'Messiah' even if that preliminary understanding was to be corrected and modified by the proclamation.

Outside the boundaries of Judaism there were two possible forms for the proclamation. The form 'Jesus is the Messiah' could be retained if at the same time the meaning of Messiah was elaborately explained. The problem with this form is that one unknown, Jesus, is identified with another, 'the Messiah', in the proclamation, 'Jesus is the Messiah'. This would amount to teaching the hearers to exchange their conceptual framework for one from Judaism in order to understand the proclamation. In all probability there were those who thought that this was the 'correct' approach. Is this perhaps *one* way to view the Judaizing controversy in earliest Christianity? According to the author of Acts Paul tried a different approach at Athens (Acts 17.6-34, esp vv. 22ff.).

There is more than a change of words to distinguish the Fourth Gospel from the Synoptics, leaving aside the differences between the first three evangelists. The presentation of Jesus in the Fourth Gospel would appear to have been shaped by a conceptual framework somewhat different from that which we find in the Synoptics. For John the understanding of the pre-existent Logos, who is from above, who enters human history as the man Jesus and returns to his heavenly abode, dominates the whole presentation. For Roberts the question must be, is it possible to speak truly of Jesus both in the terms of the Synoptics and the Fourth evangelist? Is it the same proclamation? Can the same thing be said in different conceptual frameworks or is such translation impossible? Where the conceptual framework changes is all continuity of thought broken? It is difficult to deny that there has been a significant change in conceptual frameworks from the Synoptics to John. In their differing contexts and approaches is it not possible that their meaning, given their different conceptual frameworks, is closer than is at first apparent? The same point could be made concerning the translation of the Gospel from its Palestinian roots to the Hellenistic context with Platonic presuppositions.

The letters of Paul appear to offer evidence of a fairly self-conscious attempt at hermeneutical translation. At the risk of over-simplification it might be said that Paul was working, often fighting, on two fronts—in fact this is to reduce many actual situations to two broad types. The two fronts can be described as Jewish legalism and gentile 'enthusiasm'.[37] Paul writes quite differently within the context of the conceptual framework determined by the Jewish understanding of the Law from the way he writes when working within the context of 'Gentile religious experience'. One only need contrast the vocabulary and ideas expressed in Galatians and Romans with 1 Corinthians to become aware of different conceptual frameworks determining vocabulary and ideas. This is not to suggest that Galatians and Romans represent identical contexts, though they stand together when compared with 1 Corinthians, in so far as the problem of the Law is central for both letters. From this point of view it seems apparent that problems and questions set up their own conceptual frameworks. Hence new situations, new problems, new questions involve new conceptual frameworks (*EF*, p. 296; and see Schmithals, p. 236). The words which answered one question might not be meaningful when repeated in response to a new question. But need this mean that the old question, with its answer, is irrelevant to new questions? Is no hermeneutical translation possible so that the old might throw light on the new?

According to Bultmann there are major and minor changes of conceptual framework within the New Testament itself. But the most significant change, with consequences for hermeneutical translation, is that from the mythological *Weltbild* of the New Testament to the modern scientific *Weltbild* of to-day. Here we are concerned with the problem of understanding texts from the past generally which involves the task of historical reconstruction in order to understand the conceptuality of the text from the past ('SOTCF', p. 13 n. 2; *EF*, p. 292). However there is no way that the conceptuality of the past can be recovered 'pure and simple' in the present. The historian cannot annul his present in his attempt to recover his understanding of the past. Not only is this impossible, it is undesirable, because it is only by making self-conscious use of present understanding that a genuine understanding of the past is possible at all.

3. The Hermeneutical Circle

In the tradition of Schleiermacher and Dilthey, Bultmann approached the study of history on the basis of the awareness of the hermeneutical circle. This circle involves a number of intricate relations which are described in terms of a circle because there can be no simple movement from one side to the other but each side interacts with the other. Hermeneutics which failed to recognize this complexity would almost certainly distort what it sought to understand. As Heidegger indicated, the hermeneutical circle cannot be avoided. What is decisive is to come into it in the right way (*B&T*, p. 195). The right way involves entering the circle at the right point, or perhaps better, it is to know where and how you enter.

The first relationship to be discussed is that of 'preunderstanding' and understanding. Bultmann credited Heidegger with the discovery of 'preunderstanding' and termed it a 'phenomenon', denying that it had been 'invented' (*Letters*, p. 98). To speak of it as an 'invention' is to deny its validity as the description of a phenomenon of human being. Here, this discussion will take account only of Bultmann's use of preunderstanding.

Man is not a '*tabula rasa*', a photographic plate. He does not approach the text, which is to be understood, with a blank mind. Questions arise which indicate some preliminary knowledge (*FU*, p. 159). They arise because of the structure of man's being and consciousness in relation to himself and the world. This questioning, 'not-knowing knowledge' is what, in the first instance, Bultmann calls 'preunderstanding', and says of it that it 'belongs to our life'. It is of the nature of human being (*Dasein*) to question. Man's life in the world provides the possibility of understanding texts which are the expression of life moments in writing.

While preunderstanding describes the human possibility of understanding, that possibility is always moulded by a particular tradition. All the interpreter's previous understanding is brought into relation with the text which is to be understood (*EF*, pp. 65f.). The interpreter has no alternative but to start where he is with his own understanding, inadequate as that might be. Recognition of the role of preunderstanding in the hermeneutical task is the right point of entry. Used correctly this would allow the interpreter to trace backwards along the route which brought him to his present understanding. For Bultmann this route is the way back from the present to the authors of the New Testament. Along the way back he is able to take account of the notable influences on his own understanding, such as Luther. Recognition of the influences is important if he is to be able to relate critically to them, especially as he was not content simply to repeat their formulations. That was *not* because he thought Luther's exegesis lacked real insight into Paul (*FU*, p. 154). It was because such an approach would demand an understanding of Luther as a precondition of understanding Paul and this is made complex by the different crises and conceptual frameworks of the sixteenth and twentieth centuries. For Luther it was the crisis of conscience before the judging God. Today it is the insecurity of the ego before a threatening world (*K&M*, I, pp. 210-11; II, p. 191; *JCM*, p. 84; Johnson, p. 34; Thiselton, pp. 213, 263). Hence a fresh understanding of Paul is needed today.

Clarification of preunderstanding is only part of the task on the way to understanding. Other traditions of understanding, which call the particular preunderstanding into question, have an important role to play. Bultmann sought to renew his understanding of Paul 'in discussion with Catholic exegesis' (*EF*, p. 296). Naturally, the final arbiter should be the text itself. It should be allowed to call preunderstanding into question, to modify and even reject it.

Preunderstanding, moulded by a tradition, involves conceptions, ways of thinking, which arise from an understanding of reality (*Letters*, p. 96). That understanding of reality sets the conceptual framework in the terms of its 'world view'. The interpreter can only approach the text with his own conceptuality and he should be critically aware of this. To fail to do this opens the possibility of importing an unsuitable conceptuality, which is what Bultmann accuses Barth of doing in his Dogmatics where he has

> naively adopted the older ontology from patristic and scholastic dogmatics (*Letters*, p. 38).

Such an ontology belongs to neither the New Testament nor the present day. New times, with their conceptual frameworks, preclude the possibility of understanding through the repetition of words which once expressed authentic understanding. Translation is necessary. In a new age the same truth can be spoken only by saying something new. For this reason historical exegesis cannot be achieved definitively. Gains in knowledge can be passed on as tradition (*Th.N.T.*, II, pp. 237ff.; *FU*, pp. 150-59), as the preunderstanding with which a new generation will approach the text. But for them also the old word will have new meaning in a new situation.

> Always anew it will tell him who he, man, is and he will always have to express this word in a new conceptuality (*EF*, p. 296).

A number of issues emerge from this statement. First, the new conceptuality is a new conceptual framework with its dominant categories and characteristic vocabulary.[38] We are reminded again of the problem of hermeneutical translation from one conceptual framework to another or in the context of a paradigm shift. Just as the understanding of faith was translated into the conceptual framework of neo-Platonism in the early church so it now is translated into a conceptual framework appropriate to the modern scientific *Weltbild*. The way in which the matter has been stated in the quotation suggests that the meaning does not remain exactly the same in the process of hermeneutical translation. However, unless what is said can, in some way, be distinguished from the conceptual framework in which it is expressed, that is, how it is said, the problem of hermeneutical translation from one conceptual framework to another becomes insuperable.[39]

Second, the quotation presupposes a particular objective or aim in the interpretation of the text. This aim, objective or perspective, which the interpreter brings to the text, is an aspect of preunderstanding. The perspective is set by the questions the interpreter puts to the text (*Letters*, p. 96; and see Tracy *TA1*, p. 254), questions without which the text would remain dumb. Naturally historical texts concern many different subjects. But a text can be investigated along lines which are only indirectly related to the purpose of the text, that is, the purpose of the author in writing the text. The New Testament can be studied from the point of view of geography, economics, botany, etc. Because all texts are the expression of some life moment fixed in writing all historical texts express, directly or indirectly, some understanding of human existence (*EPT*, p. 241). When this is expressed indirectly the interpreter needs to take account of the two aspects of meaning in the text, the meaning intended by the author and the understanding of existence indirectly expressed. Bultmann's aim in the study of history was to uncover the possibilities of human existence which find expression in texts (*JCM*, p. 53; *K&M*, I, p. 192; *EF*, p. 62), recognizing that this can only be done by reconstructing the meaning intended by the author. In this way the interpreter who interrogates the text is confronted by the understanding of existence in the text and his own understanding is put in question by it (*EPT*, pp. 253f; and see Schmithals, p. 232).

While existential understanding is not the direct subject of all historical texts it is Bultmann's view that this is the subject matter of the New Testament. The New Testament can be studied from different perspectives, but the interpreter approaches it in terms of its own intention when he seeks to hear what it has to say about his own existence (*EPT*, p. 259). The interpreter's questions, arising from his perspective, guide the inquiry. If the enquiry is to be valid his presuppositions must not prejudice the results by predetermining them (*K&M*, p. 191), otherwise what the text had to say would never be heard. If the New Testament speaks about the possibilities of human existence addressing those who inquire of it concerning their own existence, two questions are raised. 1. Does not the New Testament speak of God?; and 2. Does not the man who asks about his own existence prejudice what the New Testament has to say? In some ways these questions are a way of asking about the correct point of entry into the hermeneutical circle.

Barth rejected Bultmann's view that valid theological propositions are part of the Christian understanding of human existence. Relevant though theology might be to an understanding of human existence, its proper meaning is to speak of God who is other than man, and is 'not reducible to propositions about the inner life of man' (see *EPT*, pp. 259ff. and *KD*, III (2), pp. 534ff.). But this is to misinterpret Bultmann in terms of Feuerbach. For Bultmann the meaning of human existence is a consequence of man's relation to the environment, his fellow man, and God. His interpretation was intended to develop appropriate conceptuality for speaking of man in his relationality, whether with nature, man or God. To say that theological propositions are part of the Christian understanding of existence is a clue to the meaning of the preunderstanding of God.

Barth was critical of Bultmann's understanding of pre-understanding, seeing in it a betrayal of dialectical theology and a return to liberal theology. That this is a misunderstanding becomes apparent in Bultmann's insistence on the provisional nature of pre-understanding as an understanding which raises questions which find their answers in the text, and as an understanding of the purpose of the text which provides the interpreter with his objective in interpretation. Barth was especially critical of Bultmann's application of man's pre-understanding of God. For Bultmann this meant the question about God, the search for God. Because man is searching for God the revelation of God is intelligible. But the only 'point of contact' is

God's conflict with man, even in his religion. Because man is searching for God, knowingly or unwittingly, the conflict is comprehensible (*EPT*, pp. 135ff.). To raise the question of the meaning of existence is an expression of the search for God and the man who asks about his own existence has entered the hermeneutical circle at the only point possible for him if he is to hear what the New Testament says to him of God. Here our attention is turned to the role of the questions with which the interpreter approaches the text.

First, the questions cannot be suppressed and if they were the New Testament would become dumb. However, the questions might be modified or even rejected if the interpreter finds them to be inappropriate or in conflict with the text to be interpreted. This is only otherwise when preunderstanding is mistaken for final understanding. But because human being has the character of *possibility* interpretation can never, in fact, be final. It is at best relatively adequate (see Tracy, *TA1*, p. 319).

Second, if the New Testament speaks of God, should this not lead to the rejection of such questions as the interpreter might ask about his own existence? Should not the interpreter be asking about what the New Testament has to say rather than about his own existence? This way of posing the problem is reminiscent of Karl Barth's criticism of Bultmann.

Barth was critical of Bultmann's use of the notion of preunderstanding. He was particularly critical of the idea that man has a preunderstanding of God. One reason for this criticism was that he did not take account of the special negative sense of preunderstanding in relation to God. But he was generally critical of the notion and of Bultmann's use of it. That is the point of his comment, 'Apparently he (Bultmann) already knows *what* is in the New Testament' (*K&M*, II, p. 88). This misunderstanding of preunderstanding, as if it were already understanding, is related to Barth's view of Bultmann's practice of hermeneutical translation. Barth saw such translation as an apologetic device based on understanding, assumed the priority of understanding and relegated translation to the secondary task of making what is already understood intelligible to others. Hence he was puzzled when Bultmann rejected the view that he was an apologist (*K&M*, II, p. 119). Bultmann had a different and more negative attitude to apologetics than Barth. But this is not the reason he rejected this evaluation of his work. For him translation was an hermeneutical task involving interpretation and understanding (*K&M*, II, p. 186; *Letters*, p. 90). Translation is necessary if the problems involved in the two horizons are to be overcome so that the text from the past can be understood in the present.

Barth failed to grasp the difference between preunderstanding and understanding. Because of this he was critical of Bultmann while making use of the principle himself. In his commentary on *Romans* Barth says that, for genuine interpretation the exegete should concentrate on the same subject as the author (*Romans*, p. 7). Words and phrases should be understood in terms of what the whole document is speaking about (*Romans*, p. 8; *K&M*, II, pp. 87f.). Two aspects of the hermeneutical circle are presupposed here: the parts should be understood in terms of the whole, yet the whole is the sum of the parts; and a preunderstanding of what the whole is about is necessary when reading the parts.

The task of translation is made necessary by the recognition of the two horizons—the horizon of the present time of the exegete in relation to the horizon of the past time of the text—and the cultural differences which such a separation represents. Both Barth and Bultmann recognized this problem. But Barth did not propose to overcome it by translation. This is partly because he misunderstood what Bultmann meant by translation. But it is more because he did not see the need for translation. The two horizons did not pose a critical problem for him.

Two passages in Barth's *Romans* (pp. 7-8), in the Preface to the second edition, indicate that he recognized the problem of the two horizons. Referring to Luther and Calvin as exegetes he spoke of 'the walls which separate the sixteenth century from the first'. Later he referred to 'fortuitous or incidental or merely historical conceptions' which constitute barriers, 'boulders', obscuring the meaning of the text. How are these problems to be overcome so that genuine understanding would become possible? Barth outlined the following procedure: First the text must be established. Then the exegete should concentrate on the same subject as the author of the text, interpreting the parts in terms of the meaning of the whole text. This involves understanding the text in terms of its own questions and problems. In this way the exegete is to rethink and wrestle with what has been written. Such rethinking is to be done with creative energy via intuitive certainty (as with Luther) or systematically (Calvin).

Either way, Paul speaks and the exegete hears and understands. The walls which separate author and exegete become transparent, and the two horizons become so radically merged that the distinction between the author of the text and the exegete virtually ceases to exist.

Theoretically the differences between Barth and Bultmann are not as great as is often supposed. This was recognized in Bultmann's response to criticisms which he thought Barth had aimed at his own exegetical practice.

> In this question I cannot at root see any difference between your exegetical approach and mine, great though the difference may be in exegetical practice (*Letters*, pp. 4ff.).

In practice the differences were considerable. While Barth claimed that he did not ignore the historical critical methods, in his haste to hear what the text had to say to him, he gave little attention to their application. There is no evidence of his concern to deal with the problem of contemporary conceptuality nor did he attempt to reconstruct the meaning of the text in its own context in the past. Rather he argued that the differences between the past of the text and the present of the exegete virtually disappear. How this can happen is not made clear. The exegete is to understand the text in its own terms by concentrating on the subject of the text. In this way the text is made immediately and directly relevant to the man of today, or any other day for that matter. This is possible because the text (Paul's letter to the Romans) is concerned with the relation between God and man, the permanent *KRISIS* of the relation between time and eternity. On the basis of the assumption that this is a permanent situation, Barth argued that Paul was confronted by the same reality as he, the exegete was confronted (*Romans*, pp. 10ff.).

Barth has here made use of the analogy of present experience which Bultmann used widely as an hermeneutical principle. Barth assumed that what confronted him was the subject matter of Paul's discussion in Romans. Given that the common structure of human life and understanding is the basis of communication, and this is one of the levels of preunderstanding, nevertheless Barth has overlooked cultural and conceptual differences. Even if there is a permanent *KRISIS* this could be expressed in different conceptual terms. The problem is to discover whether Paul, in his own way, was talking about the same *KRISIS* which we understand in our own way. Concern for the same subject will not necessarily annul the conceptuality that the exegete brings to the text, nor does the text automatically correct false presuppositions which are brought to the text, as Barth over-optimistically hoped. The multitude of conflicting interpretations proves that to be a forlorn hope.

Bultmann's concern for correct methodology was intended to safeguard the integrity of the two horizons. Barth was attempting to merge the two horizons in the belief that nothing of fundamental significance separated them in the light of the permanent *KRISIS*. From this perspective Barth saw Bultmann's work as offering reductionist *explanations*. Barth criticized the work of Jülicher, arguing that he did not bring out the message of Romans but merely deciphered words and dismissed difficult passages by attributing them to some Pauline peculiarity, or to Judaism, or to Hellenism, 'or, in fact, to any exegetical semi-divinity of the ancient world' (*Romans*, pp. 7f.). Bultmann thought that these criticisms were also aimed at him (*Letters*, pp. 4ff.). He argued that it was both valid and important to identify the context of Paul's thought in Hellenism and Judaism. The purpose of this analysis was not to give a reductionist explanation but to illuminate the decisive questions for the text which are the key to understanding it. The language and conceptuality of the text must be understood if its meaning is to be grasped.

Both Barth and Bultmann believed that the New Testament has something to say to the present (*Th.N.T.*, II, p. 251). But Bultmann insisted that historical reconstruction is essential if a text from the past is to be understood in its own terms ('SOTCF', p. 13 n. 2; *EF*, p. 292). The purpose of such reconstruction is not explanation. It is understanding (*Letters*, pp. 4ff.). Reconstruction is the first stage in the task of hermeneutical translation. The two horizons need to be seen with clarity if what was said in the past is to be *understood* in the present. The text must be understood in its own terms before it can be translated into the terms of the present. Yet the exegete can only begin with his present understanding. Such is the complexity of the hermeneutical circle.

Barth also said that 'Paul knows of God what most of us do not know; and his Epistles enable us to know what he knew' (*Romans*, p. 11). Bultmann was in substantial agreement with this point of view (*Th.N.T.*, II, p. 251; *JCM*, p. 53). But Barth's understanding implies a revelation of teaching which was not acceptable to Bultmann. It is this that enabled Barth to stress the permanent nature of the revelation, in form as well as content. Thus the walls which separate the present from the first century can become transparent because man's situation before the eternal God remains exactly the same. From Bultmann's point of view the problem does not concern man's situation before God *per se*, but the way this is conceptualized and understood. The kerygma might remain constant in some sense, but the expression of it is always in some particular form and influenced by a specific cultural context (*Th.N.T.*, II, pp. 239f.).

The separation of the two horizons cannot be abolished. There is no simple transport back into the world of the first century. Nor can the language of the first century simply be repeated as meaningful communication in the present. For example, the changes brought about by the revolutions in industry, science and technology involve us in radically different perceptions from those of the first century (*Th.N.T.*, II, p. 238). We live in another world. The hermeneutical circle, in which the interpreter is involved, does not permit him to begin anywhere but in his own time with its conceptuality, possibilities and problems. While our age is pluralist, the interpreter has his own position and conceptuality.

When the believer asks about the meaning of the New Testament, the question implies no mere antiquarian interest. It concerns the meaning that the text continues to have for him today, with his own problems and possibilities. Concentration on the same subject will not be an adequate means to make transparent the walls which separate the present from the first century, so that when Paul speaks, the man of today hears in his own terms. This result can only be achieved through the complex task of historical reconstruction and hermeneutical translation.

Reference to the hermeneutical circle draws attention to the relation of the interpreter to the text to be interpreted. It is this relationship which constitutes the hermeneutical circle. The relationship constitutes both the posibility of understanding and of misunderstanding. The interpreter cannot but approach the text with his existing understanding and conceptuality. It was for this reason that Bultmann persistently called on Barth to clarify his conceptuality (*Letters*, nos. 2, 23, 29, 31, 45, 46, 47, 48). The interpreter's present understanding and conceptuality is a consequence of human life in the world and the specific history through which tradition is formed. Historical knowledge, in the form of tradition, can be passed on but, as such, it should be regarded as preunderstanding which is subject to the criticism of each new generation in the process of achieving understanding anew (*EF*, pp. 295, 65f.). The situation is falsified only when preunderstanding is taken to be definitive (*EF*, p. 294). Bultmann's intention, through existentialist interpretation, was to make existential understanding a new possibility again today ('Reply', in Kegley, pp. 286f.). Through existentialist interpretation the challenge of the text addresses the interpreter afresh, offering him the possibility of new understanding, a new self-understanding.

Recognition that no understanding of a text is possible without some preunderstanding of the meaning of the text is one aspect of the hermeneutical circle. The interpreter's objective is set by his understanding of the purpose of the text. Understanding of any part of the text depends on understanding the whole text and yet the whole text can be understood only in terms of the sum of all its parts (*EPT*, p. 236). The complexity of this aspect needs to be seen in terms of both small and large scale consequences. The word only has meaning in terms of the sentence but the sentence is the sum of its words; similarly, the sentence in the paragraph, the paragraph in the book, and so on. The book also is an expression of a life moment in the life of the author and is best understood from the vantage of the context of all such expressions. One letter by Paul is better understood from the perspective of all his letters, yet that perspective is built up from the sum of his letters. His letters are better understood from the perspective of other historical data from the period, while at the same time supplying data for the understanding of that perspective (*EPT*, p. 247).

Understanding the parts of the text in terms of the whole naturally means that the understanding of the whole should always be treated as provisional in order that the text might be able to speak authentically in its own voice. This will not happen if the parts are treated in a piecemeal fashion (*EF*, p. 289). The parts need to be understood as bearers of the understanding expressed by the author. From this point of view Bultmann commends the work of C.H. Dodd on the Fourth Gospel.[40]

> The work of C.H. Dodd represents in a masterful way an understanding of the Gospel of John ... which understands the Gospel from the perspective of its own theological centre, and from there illuminates all its details.[41]

However Bultmann was critical of Dodd's failure to deal with the *complexities* involved in placing the Gospel in the history of primitive Christianity. It is this difference which separates Bultmann's treatment of John from that of Dodd. Bultmann himself has attempted to interpret the details of the Gospel in the light of the centre. The hermeneutical role of his reconstruction of the history of primitive Christianity is also clear though not always recognized as it is by D.M. Smith (p. 214).

4. **The Problem of History in the New Testament**

When Bultmann's commentary on the Fourth Gospel appeared in English translation Christopher Evans wrote a review article (*SJT* 26/3[1973], pp. 341-49) in which he gave praise, not only to the commentary but also to the work of the English translators. The translation was in itself a mammoth task involving the linguistic problems bound up with turning the German original into readable English. But the carefully nuanced Bultmann text also posed complex theological problems for which the translators were not adequately prepared. Possibly their own theological positions contributed to this failure though for the most part it seems to have been the consequence of not taking account of the way Bultmann used specific terms. Consequently the English translation must be regarded as an unsatisfactory guide to the *detailed* aspects of Bultmann's thought. Professor Evans says of the commentary (*ibid.*, pp. 345f.): 'The whole work is one of immense weight and profundity.' He does, however, have his criticisms.

> Bultmann nowhere gathers together the scattered insights in the commentary about the author, his readers, their milieu, the occasion of writing etc., or makes a sustained attempt to envisage the *Sitz im Leben* of the Gospel as a whole and to place it in the contours of primitive Christianity.

While these remarks are related to 'the absence of any Introduction', they are clearly meant to indicate that these tasks have been left undone as is clear from the following.

> It may be replied that we know so little about primitive Christianity as to make this a waste of effort. Yet is it not incumbent on a commentator to make the attempt, and are not some of his individual insights and judgments likely to be put to the test when it is asked whether, however plausible in isolation, they stand up in relation to one another? . . . For all the erudition and profundity of Bultmann's treatment his Fourth Gospel still floats in the air.

Professor Evans contrasts the work of Ernst Käsemann with this supposedly contextless approach of Bultmann. While Käsemann acknowledges

> All of us are more or less groping in darkness when we are asked to give information about the historical background of this Gospel, information which would determine our understanding of the whole book and not merely of individual details

he goes on to unfold the complex of theological problems which point to the context of the Gospel within primitive Christian history. This, it is asserted, Bultmann failed to do.

Bultmann does not do this in any introduction to the commentary but all of these questions are treated very fully in the commentary and elsewhere. In the commentary on the Prologue alone Bultmann presents much of his argument concerning the evangelist, his place in the history of religions and of primitive Christianity and his purpose in writing the Gospel. In addition to articles on specific subjects there is also Bultmann's summary treatment in *Die Religion in Geschichte und Gegenwart* and his *Theology of the New Testament*. The way Bultmann approaches these questions is clearly stated in these works.

> The different questions which are found in John's Gospel - questions about the authorship, its relationship to the Synoptics, to the Jesus of history, its place in the history of primitive Christianity and in the history of religions - if they can be answered at all they have to be answered after the recognition of the *literary character* of the Gospel (*RGG*3, III, p. 840).

No less than Käsemann does Bultmann seek to derive answers to his questions from the data of the Gospel initially using formal characteristics (literary) before using the theological emphases to indicate John's place in primitive Christianity. On this basis he discusses the evangelist's relation (A) to Jesus and the primitive Church (B) to Paul and (C) to Gnosis (*RGG*3, III, pp. 845ff.).

There can be no doubt that in Bultmann's mind, as for Käsemann, the location of the Gospel in the development of primitive Christianity has far-reaching implications for the interpretation of the Gospel. It was for this reason that his own critique of Dodd's attempt to locate the Gospel in the history of primitive Christianity specifically asserts that the history of early Christianity is more complex than Dodd has allowed, noting in particular the work of Walter Bauer, *Orthodoxy and Heresy in Earliest Christianity*, which Dodd had ignored.

From what has been said it is clear that both Dodd and Bultmann attempted to place the Gospel in the context of developing early Christianity but each understood its place differently. The reason for this is not only because the Gospel itself gives so little specific data about this question but also because the course of the development of early Christianity is itself hidden. Because of the gaps in the evidence which has survived, and the over-simplification or distortion of what actually happened in the traditional accounts of early Christianity, the task of historical reconstruction is complex. It is here that Dodd and Bultmann part company as much as on the basis of the way they read the Fourth Gospel itself. Dodd, more than Bultmann, accepts the development of early Christianity as described in Acts and Eusebius's *Ecclesiastical History*. However, he also questions this picture at certain points, for example in relation to the authorship of the Fourth Gospel. But Bultmann regards the picture to be almost wholly misleading. For him it was not possible to understand Christianity in terms of an original orthodoxy which, at some later stage, had to overcome heresy. Rather, from the beginning Christianity was diverse and orthodoxy was a later development through which the diversity came to be understood as heresy. This approach is fundamentally that which was put forward by Walter Bauer. However, Bultmann argued that within the diversity of original Christianity we find both 'authentic' and 'inauthentic' manifestations. It is in Paul and John that the 'authentic' understanding of faith finds clearest expression. Hence Bultmann recognized an 'orthodoxy' or 'authentic' understanding but this differs from the traditional 'orthodoxy' which is labelled 'early Catholicism'[42] today, characterized by an institutional view of church, ministry, sacraments and dogma. From Bultmann's point of view this 'orthodoxy' was in many ways, a betrayal of 'authentic' Christian understanding.

Not only did later orthodoxy 'rewrite' its own history as the history of the church, it 'rewrote' the history of Jesus as the founder of orthodoxy, establishing the church with authoritative apostles, sacraments and dogmas. What actually happened was somewhat different. Jesus, like the Baptist, appeared as a prophetic figure within Judaism, standing in the tradition of the great prophets. His message can be distinguished from theirs only by degrees, in his proclamation of the coming Kingdom of God. However he did assert that entry to the Kingdom of God was dependent on response to him.

But he was mistaken about the imminent coming of the Kingdom and instead suffered execution at the hands of the Romans by crucifixion.

In spite of his execution, faith in Jesus emerged in a new way. The one who had proclaimed the Kingdom was himself proclaimed as God's saving act. It has been asked why Bultmann chose Jesus rather than the Baptist as the basis for the kerygma.[43] In one sense this is a pertinent question but not in the way that it is put. The choice was not made by Bultmann. Faith arose in Jesus in spite of his crucifixion. Why? Why this man and not someone else? For Bultmann this is the scandal which faith must overcome (*Th.N.T.*, II, p. 85), but it was not a choice made by Bultmann. It is a fact of history going back to the first believers and from them down through history.

Enough has been said to make clear that there is no self-evident narrative history of Jesus and Christianity in the New Testament period. Just what Bultmann makes of this is the subject of a later section in this chapter. Before turning to this we will examine the significance of 'the (so called) historical-critical method' for Bultmann's reconstruction.

5. **History and the Historical Method**

Talk of '*the* historical method' is a convention. There is no single method which can lay claim to this status.[44] There is in fact 'a multiplicity of methods which are appropriate to the subject matter' of history. However, there is an underlying attitude, or point of view, which is the basis of modern critical history and to which the various methods conform. It is not sufficient to speak of this criterion in terms of the omnipotence of the analogy of the present-day experience of reality unless the nature of the present day experience of reality is spelt out in some detail. It is not as if the experience of reality is an uninterpreted fact in any age. What *interpretation* of reality (*Letters*, pp. 91, 96), is implied by reference to *the present day experience?*

Historical reconstruction of the past is done from the vantage point of the present. In some ways, it can be the case that the modern interpreter is in a better position to understand than the author of an ancient text. There can also be disadvantages due to the separation of the two horizons of past and present. If the past is to be understood at all it must first be understood in its own terms by way of the task of preclude arbitrary interpretations and to gain access to the meaning intended by the author. Such access is obstructed by the individuality of the author, his location in the distant past and the gaps in our knowledge of that past and the author's place in it. Bultmann pays attention to these problems and does not allow them to prevent his attempt to reconstruct, for to fail to do this would be to fail to understand. It is his view that any understanding of a text implies some reconstruction of the past even if this is not made explicit. It is Bultmann's strength that his own reconstruction has been made explicit in considerable detail. Naturally it is the detail that has made his reconstruction a target for criticism.

The language of the text needs to be understood in its broader context. In the case of the New Testament this involves both the lineal connection (with the past) with the Old Testament *mediated through first-century Judaism*; and the lateral contemporary relation to the Hellenistic world. Bultmann's own work emphasized the significance of the Hellenistic influence for Christianity both directly and mediated through Judaism. Awareness of this broad historical context is made explicit in his *Primitive Christianity in its Contemporary Setting* and brilliantly demonstrated in his commentary on the Fourth Gospel. The results of this approach are set out in his *Theology of the New Testament* which is a critical history of the development of Christian thought in the first century. As a critical history it seeks to lay bare the origin and reasons for development in the context of the world of the first century. In doing this the primary concern is to *understand* the thought of first-century Christianity. But as *critical* historical writing some attempt is made to come to terms with the validity or truth in the various writings. The critical approach is undertaken from the perspective of 'present-day experience' or understanding of reality.

Bultmann argues that today the world is understood as a closed continuum of cause and effect and that history is also understood in terms of the causal nexus. Recognition of the causal nexus is, in principle, given in human existence in the awareness of order in the world. So pervasive is this awareness that it came to be applied to what he calls the sense of 'wonder', turning the mysterious into a 'miracle' and attributing such events to God, the 'higher causality'. Such events came to be understood as contrary to nature, contrary to man's understanding of the world, contrary to the modern scientific *Weltbild*. Today what is contrary to our understanding of the world is reconstructing the past ('SOTCF', p. 13 n. 2; *EF*, p. 292). This is done by means of the critical use of evidence. The understanding of the past is primarily transmitted in literary remains so that the interpretation of texts is central to the task while not disregarding artefacts and other data. Of the interpretation of texts Bultmann says:

> It belongs to the historical method, of course, that a text is interpreted in accordance with the rules of grammar and of the meaning of words. And closely connected with this, historical exegesis also has to inquire about the individual style of the text... Paying attention to the meaning of words, to grammar, and to style soon leads to the observation that every text speaks in the language of its time and of its historical setting. This the exegete must know; therefore he must know the historical conditions of the language of the period out of which the text which he is to interpret has arisen (*EF*, p. 291; cf. *JCM*, pp. 51f.).

This statement makes explicit certain procedures. It also involves certain hidden assumptions. Firstly, it is assumed or expected that texts from the past and from far-off places are in principle intelligible to us, even if written in languages other than our own. It is in principle possible to learn those languages and to read and understand the texts provided an appropriate approach to the texts is followed. This assumption implies an understanding of human existence in the world which, in spite of differences of time, place and individuality allows us to enter into the understanding of another. The approach as outlined aims to ensure that it is the understanding of the author into which the exegete enters. While the exegete can only enter the process of understanding where he is at the time it is essential that he allow the text to call his own understanding and expectations into question. To do this he must understand the language of the text, its words, grammar, and style, both as an expression of a cultural context, that is, as an expression of its own time and place, and as a peculiar expression of its author.

Here we encounter the complexity of the hermeneutical circle in its detailed actuality as it affects language, history and thought. Understanding each of these (language, history and thought) is a circular process and each contributes to the understanding of the others. No truly historical work can proceed without the appropriate language skills which enable the interpreter to begin his historical work of reconstruction using methods which are intended to held to be impossible (*FU*, pp. 247ff.; and see Roberts, p. 98). From this perspective Bultmann wrote about the scientific approach to history as the way we view history from this vantage point.

> The historical method includes the presupposition that history is a unity in the sense of closed continuum of effects in which individual events are connected by the succession of cause and effect.[45]

This statement (see *EF*, pp. 291-92) of which the quotation forms only a part, is a model of clarity and lucidity. That is not to say that it is straightforward and uncontroversial. In it is concealed a preunderstanding of the nature of history which is not straightforwardly visible in history. It excludes the possibility of miracles and not only says that dead men have not risen to life, it asserts that they do not and prescribes in advance what can or cannot happen. It does this on the basis of *an interpretation* of present day experience which is analogically applied as a criterion to any understanding of what can or cannot happen. As far as critical history is concerned there is a strong case for the application of this principle. Without it there would be difficulty distinguishing fact from fancy, although there is perhaps some need for qualification. The qualification in view is the role of evidence.

Discussion of the role of evidence in critical historical work can be carried on fruitfully in relation to the problem of the resurrection of Jesus. Granted that in contemporary experience dead men do not rise from the grave,[46] can any evidence put in question the obvious conclusion to be drawn from the analogy of present day experience? According to Bultmann the first Christians believed that Jesus had so risen and Paul even tried to demonstrate this by appealing to eyewitnesses whom he listed in order to demonstrate his case (1 Corinthians 15). But the men of New Testament times were not in the same position as a person in the twentieth century. For them miracles were possible and did not demand an act of double thinking or, what Bultmann calls, a '*sacrificium intellectus*', because their lives were not determined by the modern scientific *Weltbild* and mythological thinking was still acceptable (*K&M*, I, p. 5 n. 1).

The characterization of the naivety of the first century is one-sided. The evidence suggests that the proclamation of the resurrection of Jesus was not generally accepted, hence Paul found it necessary to amass the evidence of witnesses. It is true that apocalyptic thinking provided a ready-made context in which the resurrection could be proclaimed and understood. Such a proclamation would carry with it the implication that the end of the age had dawned, the resurrection being an event of the last days. The historical explanation of the proclamation of the resurrection might assert that, believing that the last days had come, the early Christians proclaimed the resurrection of Jesus, interpreting the proclamation of the physical resurrection as a mythological expression of the Easter faith. To some extent this form of explanation is a consequence of the rejection of miracles, the denial of the possibility of any event such as the one apparently reported. If the event did not occur as reported, some account nonetheless needs to be given of what gave rise to the report. This is *explanation* in the sense already discussed, but with this difference. It is not used in order to set aside the tradition, but as the first step along the way of understanding it.

If the physical resurrection of Jesus were to be allowed as a possibility, the question would arise as to the role of evidence. The New Testament writers proclaim the resurrection and make it the basis for the Easter faith and the belief that the end of the age had dawned rather than the reversed process. The reversal is made on the basis of the assumption that the event so proclaimed did not happen, but is itself a manifestation of faith. At this point there is a need to introduce, in a preliminary fashion, a discussion of faith. Bultmann asserts that faith is not a phenomenon of this world (*EF*, p. 288). Nor can it be based on this worldly phenomena (*FU*, p. 31). Were it to be so, it would no longer be faith. Elsewhere he insists that it is necessary to maintain the paradox that the historical event is the eschatological event (Kegley, pp. 244f.). Only faith perceives the eschatological event *in* the historical event. Bultmann appeals to the cross as the historical event and asserts that the cross had become the eschatological event. But might it not be that the resurrection should be seen, paradoxically as the historical, and at the same time, the eschatological event? What implications would this position have for an understanding of faith?

Historical research can only lead to the recognition of probabilities, even if some have such a high degree of probability that they can scarcely be doubted. Bultmann thought it to be intolerable that faith should be based on such a probability. For him faith is a paradoxical affirmation in the face of the crucifixion. It is faith in spite of the evidence.[47] But is it valid to use a particular understanding of faith to determine what did or did not happen?

The main objection to the evidence for the resurrection is the *Weltbild* from the point of view of which such an event is impossible. How determinative this *Weltbild* should be depends on whether one believes in God and if so, how one thinks of God. It is therefore to be seen as a metaphysical presupposition. Bultmann's view of the world and his understanding of God are closely related. It is this rather than his view of faith that leads to his rejection of the physical resurrection. Such an event would not prove anything beyond that dead men do sometimes come back to life or that we need a more sophisticated definition of death. It does not demonstrate that death has been destroyed, not even that Jesus lives on, for where is he now? Nor can it prove that Jesus is the revelation of God. Thus it is surprising that Bultmann rejects an objective resurrection of Jesus, not only on the basis of his *Weltbild* but also on the basis of his view of faith.

> So it is because he did not objectively rise from the dead that Jesus really . . . rose from the dead (Malet, pp. 157ff.).

That Bultmann's view of faith is compatible with no physical resurrection is clear. It hardly follows that his view of faith excludes such an event. Because of the ambiguity of the event (what is actually proved by it?), it could function only as an historical symbol which communicates the kerygma. Such is 'the new history of the efficacy of the Spirit and the proclamation of the word' (*GJ*, p. 616). The one significant difference from Bultmann's position would be that the event would be seen as the ground of the Easter faith and the basis of the kerygma even if the kerygma cannot be seen as the proclamation of the bare event but faith's interpretation of it.

Why should the faith of the first believers not have been in response to the risen Jesus? Obviously this would allow for the interpretation of the cross as a temporary setback while the resurrection revealed the 'real' act of God. In fact there is evidence of such an interpretation in the book of Acts (e.g. 2.22ff.). According to Bultmann this distorts the meaning of the cross as God's saving act. Bultmann's view of faith goes further. He insists that there is no continuity between evidence and belief. Belief is in spite of the evidence. This goes beyond saying that there is no *necessary* relation between faith and the evidence and appears to make faith anti-rational, a position not consistently maintained but which does appear to be in view here. Such a view of faith is antithetical to a physical resurrection.

The application of the analogy of present experience in determining what can or cannot happen is problematical if the possibility of a unique event is recognized. Here the question concerns the role of evidence in the development of a *Weltbild* and in evaluating claims concerning a unique event (see Malet, p. 126). In assessing the evidence for the resurrection of Jesus it is necessary to recognize that this event is proclaimed as a unique event. However, it is set in a context which raises certain problems. The Bible as a whole contains accounts of miraculous events of which the resurrection of Jesus is one example, even if a special case. How are such miracles to be viewed? This question is easily answered if the modern scientific *Weltbild* is called on to adjudicate what can or cannot occur. But if we set this aside and attempt to assess evidence where do we stand? A number of assessments are worthy of consideration.

First, it might be argued that the Bible contains the history of God's saving acts so that accounts of miracles are to be found there even if evidence of miraculous events is absent from our contemporary world.

Second, a closer look shows that evidence of miraculous events is not to be found uniformly throughout the Bible. There is a manifestation of miracles in the time of Moses, another with the emergence of the prophets, then with Jesus and the beginning of the movement which he began. It has been argued that miracles are special acts of God as signs to validate new directions in his saving work with Moses, the Prophets, Jesus, the early Church, and that after the foundation period the need for signs disappeared.

Third, there are those who believe that miraculous acts of God are always possible and that only apostasy and lack of faith inhibits God's acts. Where there is faith, it is claimed, God still acts today.

This latter view runs into the problem of the evidence of today. If God is so acting where is the evidence? The other views all escape this test by affirming that such acts of God only occurred in the past and we must not expect them today because the special purposes they served belong to the past. In some ways this is a 'lame' response. It is 'unfalsifiable' except in terms of testing the evidence for such events in the past. On the other hand, it is hardly reasonable to expect the crucifixion and resurrection of Jesus to recur down through history. From the point of view of those who are convinced only by the standard of their own experiences of the world this is an unsatisfactory position. For such it is perhaps necessary to become aware that there may be more to the world than our own knowledge of it.

While we have discussed the nature of miracles and argued that Bultmann's *a priori* rejection is unjustified, it has not been our intention to open the gate to a wholesale acceptance of miracles. Rather the point has been to argue that the actuality of events should be established on the basis of evidence. It is also reasonable that evidence for unusual events should be tested more rigorously than evidence concerning everyday events. When this has been said it is important to note that Bultmann allows for 'miracle' in another sense. For him it is possible for faith to perceive an act of God *in an historical event* which is otherwise, on the basis of historical science, intelligible in terms of its own imminent historical causes (*EF*, p. 292). It seems that here we have an example of two forms of history, historical fact, world history, and the new history perceived by faith and perceived *in* the events of world history. To perceive an act of God in the crucifixion of Jesus exemplifies this distinction. A problem only arises when we turn this discussion to the resurrection of Jesus, which, for Bultmann, is no event of world history at all, but only an event of the new history. The new history is to be found in the arising of the Easter faith, the arising of the kerygma, which is an event of world history. In the Easter faith, which is expressed in the kerygma, Jesus is risen. To talk of the resurrection of Jesus is to draw attention to the eschatological nature of the historical event of the cross. That Jesus is risen is perceived only by faith because it is not an event of world history.

6. **The Problem of Two Histories**

The discussion of Bultmann's understanding of history is complicated by a complexity of language that is veiled in English translations. The terms *Historie*, *historisch*, *Geschichte*, *geschichtlich* and *Geschichtlichkeit* are distinguishable in German but in translation appear as 'history', 'historical' and 'historicity'. In popular German use *Historie* and *Geschichte* are synonyms. But since Martin Kähler's essay of 1892, in which he distinguished the historical (*historisch*) Jesus from the historic (*geschichtlich*) biblical Christ, a German theological use of language has developed. In this tradition of use *Geschichte* means the mutual encounter of persons while *Historie* indicates the causal nexus in the affairs of men. The latter is the subject matter of historical science while *Geschichte* 'demands resolve and decision'.[48] Hence it is argued that the distinction between *Historie* and *Geschichte* manifests a dualism between fact and meaning.

R. Batey and J.H. Gill[49] have argued that philosophical empiricists and theological conservatives and liberals have emphasized factual meaning (*Historie*) while existentialists, including the Bultmannians, have stressed the valuational or existential meaning (*Geschichte*). They conclude that this common dichotomy of fact and value is a consequence of a deficient view of language in the two fields of philosophy and theology. This criticism has been taken up by A.C. Thiselton and specifically applied to Bultmann (Thiselton, pp. 39, 80f., 84, 217, 245ff., 440f.). Following R.A. Johnson (Thiselton, pp. 210, 212f.) and Wolfhart Pannenberg (Thiselton, pp. 80f.) he locates the origin of this 'dualism' in Marburg Neo-Kantianism. Against such a 'dualism' it is argued that there is an essential connexion between our most factual utterances and our valuational commitments (Batey and Gill, pp. 14f.). Is this critique of Bultmann's position adequate?

Two aspects of Bultmann's work need to be examined: his understanding of history is general and his understanding of the historical Jesus in particular. The critique of his position is based on the assumption that the problems related to the historical Jesus are examples of the problems concerning the understanding of history generally. In fact this is not the case. First we will show that there is no dualism of fact and meaning in Bultmann's understanding of history before turning our attention to the way his discussion of the historical Jesus complicates the issue.

Bultmann argued that his existentialist interpretation of history did not ignore the factual history ('Reply', in Kegley, pp. 274f.), that 'a historical event or action as historical includes its meaning or importance' (*HE*, p. 117) and that the event evokes interpretation ('Reply', in Kegley, p. 265). Nor would he have disagreed that 'Facts are always experienced in a context in which they have significance' (Thiselton, p. 80). It was for this reason that he argued that a text from the past would be misunderstood if the work of historical reconstruction and hermeneutical translation were overlooked ('SOTCF', p. 13 n. 2). But the criticism of Bultmann along these lines seems to imply that events understood in a particular cultural context are true in the sense understood. There is a movement from the recognition of what makes understanding possible to the affirmation of a 'truth claim'. Traditional understandings appear to be self evident to those who are within that tradition (*EF*, pp. 65f.). Such is a false impression.

An example of this problem can be given in relation to the death of Jesus. That he was 'crucified under Pontius Pilate' is a statement to which few would object. It is a statement which has meaning and implications for an understanding of the event. But the statement that 'he died for our sins' is a statement of a different order. To understand what the statement means we need to be aware of the tradition of which it is an expression. But knowing the tradition and understanding what the words mean does not prove that the statement is true. This example suggests that the criticism of Bultmann arises from a different attitude to tradition. While neither Thiselton nor Pannenberg would advocate that traditions should be accepted at their face value, they argue that not all values are culturally conditioned and that some are theologically absolute (Thiselton, p. 52). But would not theologically absolute values be *expressed* in culturally conditioned forms? The problem is to recognize the theological truth in its culturally conditioned expression.

Discerning the meaning of events is a complex problem. Some events pose few problems of understanding, though the full meaning of any event can only be seen from the perspective of its ultimate consequences. The meaning of other events is dependent on complex and sometimes controversial presuppositions. In such cases it is not possible to show the *necessary* connexion between the event and the understanding. The understanding is possible, given certain presuppositions. But are the presuppositions valid, can their truth be verified? This is a problem for historical interpretation generally.

On the basis of the work of historical reconstruction of past understanding Bultmann attempts what he calls the work of genuinely historical (*echt-geschichtlich*) interpretation ('SOTCF', p. 13 n. 2). Such interpretation concerns the understanding of existence which finds expression in the text which is a challenge to new self-understanding for the interpreter. Such an understanding finds expression in the text and is relevant to the interpreter because of the historicity (*Geschichtlichkeit*) of man. It is the historicity of man which makes Bultmann's existentialist interpretation of history both possible and relevant. Does this not suggest that his use of *Geschichte* will reflect his existentialist perspective as Schniewind and others have argued?

Against this view the following arguments and evidence are relevant. It is possible to have an existentialist interpretation of history without that being reflected in the distinction between *Historie* and *Geschichte* though it is reflected in Bultmann's distinction between history and nature. While man can be viewed as a part of nature, as an object, his significance is not adequately grasped until his 'historicity' is recognized. But the most important evidence of Bultmann's view is his use of *Historie*, *historisch*, *Geschichte* and *geschichtlich*.

Bultmann's use of this language is well illustrated in four of his writings; in his original essay on demythologizing (*K&M*, I, pp. 36ff.), in his essay 'Is Exegesis Without Presuppositions Possible?' (*EF*, pp. 289ff.), in his critique of Barth's view of the resurrection in 'The Problem of Hermeneutics' (*EPT*, pp. 259ff.), and in his commentary on *The Gospel of John*. From these writings it becomes clear that *historisch* describes the mode of knowledge, with its conclusions, appropriate to scientific historical methodology. As distinct from this *geschichtlich* denotes the actual happening of events without reference to the way our knowledge of such events is established.

In *K&M*, I, p. 37, Bultmann says that the cross of Christ is 'no mere mythical event, but a historic (*geschichtlich*) fact originating in the historical (*historisch*) event which is the crucifixion of Jesus' and that 'mythological language is only a medium for conveying the significance of the historical (*historisch*) event'. Given Schniewind's definition we would expect Bultmann to have written 'the significance of the historic (*geschichtlich*) event', but he wrote *historisch*. Rather his language fits the distinction common in scholarly circles where *historisch* refers to the study of actual (*geschichtlich*) events. Hence *historisch* qualifies the mode of knowledge appropriate to the study of history. In *K&M*, I, p. 37, Bultmann says that the cross is an actual event and knowledge of this event can be established by historical methods working on the basis of available evidence. This event, so established has a significance which is not self-evident in the event as perceived by historical methods and this can be conveyed by the use of mythological language. The use of and acceptance of this language are an expression of faith rather than historical methods. But the actuality of the cross as an event of history removes this language from the sphere of myth. One other matter calls for attention here. Bultmann wrote that the cross was 'a historic (*geschichtlich*) fact originating in the historical (*historisch*) event', the crucifixion. What is the point of 'originating'? We shall see that here we have an indication of his view of the paradox that an historical (*historisch*) event is the eschatological event. Before looking at this distinction we will examine his discussion of historical methodology in *EF*, pp. 289ff.

In his essay 'Is Exegesis Without Presuppositions Possible?' Bultmann discussed both the nature of history (*Geschichte*) and historical methodology. There he referred to the historian (*Historiker*), historical science (*historische Wissenschaft*), the science of history (*Geschichtswissenschaft*) and the historical method (*historische Methode*) (*EF*, pp. 291f.). The historian studies history (*Geschichte*) and historical science and the historical method are the appropriate mode of understanding history (cf. also *EPT*, p. 245 line 23 and 'PCKHJ', p. 26 n. 6). From this perspective history (*Geschichte*) and an historical event (*geschichtliches Ereignis*) are viewed in terms of their imminent historical causes. Here *Geschichte* is said to be 'the subject of historical science' though Schniewind said this of *Historie*. Clearly *historisch* defines the approach and mode of understanding appropriate to the study of *Geschichte*.

In this essay Bultmann also deals with the theme of existential encounter with history (*Geschichte*) which grows out of man's historicity (*EF*, p. 294; cf. pp. 92-110 and Young, p. 13). The existential approach to history presupposes the work of historical reconstruction taking account of the forces which connect individual events such as economic needs, social exigencies, the political struggle for power, human passions, ideas and ideals (*EF*, p. 292). Various perspectives can be adopted by the historian. The Reformation can be studied from the perspective of church history, economic history, political history, the history of philosophy, etc. To treat the Reformation exclusively as political history would be a falsification. Bultmann's critics have asked whether his existentialist interpretation is not also such a falsification.[50]

Three responses can be made to this criticism. 1. The existentialist approach is not a sectional interest in the life of man such as economics. It concerns man's whole existence as such. 2. The existentialist approach presupposes an historical understanding of the text in its own terms, whether economic, political or philosophical (*Th.N.T.*, II, p. 251; 'SOTCF', p. 13 n. 2). 3. In the case of the New Testament Bultmann argued that the authors intended to deal with the question of the meaning of human existence for which existentialist interpretation was appropriate. However, he recognized that historical phenomena are many-sided. Because of this the subject of history (*Geschichte*) can be studied from many perspectives such as church history, political history etc. Such histories are not distinguished by different methods but by different subjects.

Bultmann's commentary on *The Gospel of John* (*GJ*) is rich in its use of the language of history. The terms *historisch* and *geschichtlich* are used, in one form or another, about three hundred times. Unfortunately the English translation does not make it possible to recognize the underlying terminology. Here there is no discussion of the science of history and its methodology such as appeared in (*EF*, pp. 291ff.). The following conclusions are clear.

a. *Geschichte* is used frequently in *GJ*. It is used over sixty times to denote the *events* of human history. In this sense it is said that the light has appeared in *Geschichte*.[51]

b. *Geschichte* is also used over one hundred times to refer to a literary unit, a 'story', without reference to the historical actuality or accuracy of the story. For example

> If in this story (*Geschichte*) there is preserved old tradition about the conversion of the first two disciples of the Baptist to Jesus . . . [52]

Given the ambiguity between 'event' and 'story' such phrases as *die Geschichte Jesu*[53] could mean 'the history of Jesus' or 'the story of Jesus'. There are three references to *die Geschichte Jesu* (*GJ*, p. 361) and *Jesu Geschichte* (*GJ*, p. 419). The first should probably be translated 'the story of Jesus'—not 'Jesus' history' as in *GJ*. It is 'a crucial moment' in the story, not the history of Jesus, to which Bultmann refers. No comment on the historicity of the tradition is implied. But the second should be translated 'the history of Jesus', *not* 'the story of Jesus' as in *GJ*. It is the history of Jesus, not the story, which the evangelist sees as the judgment of the world. In the same sense Jesus' history (*Geschichte*) is said to be an event of revelation (*GJ*, p. 234).

c. The adjective *historisch* is used about fifty times.[54] Its use in *GJ* confirms the view that it relates to the establishment of knowledge on the basis of evidence so that events are known in their causal relations. Twice Bultmann refers to an 'historical sense' (*Sinn*) rejecting the view that this was the evangelists' intent (*GJ*, pp. 69, 197). The additional qualifications to 'sense' help to clarify the meaning of *historisch*. 'Johannine "seeing" is not concerned with eyewitnessing in an historical or a legal sense.' That is, there is no attempt to establish facts on the basis of evidence. Again it is said, 'the conversation has no historical significance' (*nicht historisch-aktuellen Sinn*). It has no actual historical meaning, the meaning is symbolic.

There are other references where *historisch* is used in a context which indicates reference to evidence of what happened. Such evidence would be supplied by an 'historical note' (*GJ*, p. 86); an 'historical narrative' (*GJ*, p. 94); an 'historical account' or 'report' (both of which translate *Bericht*) (*GJ*, pp. 108, 554, 626). Thus reference to envoys from the Jerusalem Jews is not an 'historical note'; it stresses the official nature of the witness. Another scene abandons 'the realm of historical narrative' (*den Boden chronistisch-historischer Anschaulichkeit*). Here the translation misses the reference to chronology which is also clear in the context. Reference to the 'historical account' confirms that what is in view is the chronological unity of history determined by its own internal causality.

Historical fact (*historisches Faktum* [*GJ*, pp. 94, 563] or *weltgeschichtliches Faktum* [*GJ*, p. 475]) is the substance of an historical account with its attention to details, dates and facts. Such facts can be established by historical science. As far as Bultmann is concerned the significance of Jesus is not to be found in such facts.

Of John 4.31-38 Bultmann writes that 'no historical interest attaches to the scene' (*kein historisch-novellistisches Interesse*). Reference to 'historical scenery' is said to be a disguise for the real event (*GJ*, p. 297). Nor does the evangelist have any interest in depicting an 'historical farewell scene' but uses the scene symbolically to depict the situation to be overcome by the believer through the revelation (*GJ*, p. 566). Thus the point is not that the farewell is a *unique* historical *occasion* (*GJ*, pp. 558f.). The real event, the eschatological event is contrasted with historical reminiscence (*historische Erinnerung*) (*GJ*, p. 308), and the cultural and intellectual effects of the historical person of Jesus (*der historischen Person Jesu*). The same contrast between the eschatological event (*Ereignis*) and 'historical recollection' of the historical event (*Ereignis*) of Jesus' life as something in the past occurs elsewhere (*GJ*, pp. 493f., 558f.).

What is at stake is not historical contemporaneity with Jesus but a relation with the exalted Lord (*GJ*, p. 424). In these instances *historisch* refers to an event established by evidence and located in the past in relation to its inner-historical causes and consequences. Again and again it has been Bultmann's aim *to deny* that the evengelist's intention has been to portray Jesus in this way.

Other references deny that the beloved disciple can be identified with any of the 'historical disciples' (*GJ*, p. 485). Nor is the newness of the love command an 'historical' characteristic dependent on its appearance at some point in history. As an eschatological phenomenon it is continually new (*GJ*, p. 527). The believing community has its foundation in the eschatological revelation event which is not the historical achievement of a great man in world history (*GJ*, p. 589). The revelation event cannot be comprehended in terms of the inner causality of the unity of history. Nor is the work of the Paraclete conceived as 'historical reconstruction' or 'historical report'; rather it is the community's own witness to Jesus (*GJ*, pp. 626f.). 'Historically' means here as elsewhere the chronological relation of events in terms of cause and effect (*GJ*, pp. 199, 522, 637). In contrast to this the eschatological event, having entered history, it not bound by the chain of inner world causality. As the eschatological event it is realized ever anew in history. Thus the character of the eschatological event is brought out by contrasting it with the event viewed as an event of the past, a *historisch* event.

d. The adjective *geschichtlich* is used over fifty times.[55] The meaning of *geschichtlich* often comes out in a contrast, as does the meaning of *historisch*. Thus the mythological Gnostic redeemer is said to be no specific historical figure (*kein konkreter geschichtlicher Mensch*) (*GJ*, p. 65; cf. *K&M*, I, p. 37). Evidence or causal relations are not in view. What is clear is that the Gnostic redeemer is no actual person. In contrast it is said that the 'I' of eternity is to be heard in an historical person (*in einem geschichtlichen Menschen*) (*GJ*, p. 328). Nothing is implied about evidence and proof though the assertion is that the one spoken of actually lived. In the same sense there is reference to one historical bearer of the revelation (*GJ*, p. 567).

Bultmann uses *geschichtlich* to qualify *Existenz*, *existieren* and *Sein*. Using *Existenz* and *existieren* reference is to actual historical existence (*GJ*, pp. 473, 520, 606, 607, 620f.). Such references are to specific actual events whereas reference to 'all historical existence' (*alles geschichtlichen Seins*) (*GJ*, 501; cf. p. 628), should be translated 'all historical being' which is a general, ontological statement not a reference to actual concrete existence. *Dasein* is historical *Sein*. Thus *geschichtlich* is used to qualify human existence with its freedom and responsibility for the future (cf. *EF*, pp. 92ff.).

The 'historical decision' of faith is not for any inner-historical possibility (*innergeschichtliche Möglichkeit*) but for the eschatological event (*GJ*, p. 501). The inner historical possibilities are outlined in terms of ethical, political or cultural action and values. The eschatological event has happened in the total historical appearance of a man (*in der ganzen geschichtlichen Erscheinung eines Menschen*) (*GJ*, p. 252). The paradox is that the eschatological event is an historical event and that faith and unbelief share in this paradox as the manifestation of eschatological judgment in concrete historical division.[56]

Reference to 'historical reality' (*GJ*, p. 229); 'historical ministry' (*GJ*, p. 254); 'actions they performed' (*seine geschichtlichen Werke*) (*GJ*, p. 501); all draw attention to real actions in history. Such actions are distinguished from the eschatological event which is not to be understood in terms of consequences or 'historical (*historisch*) reminiscences' of the life of Jesus and consequences of the historical (*historisch*) person of Jesus (*GJ*, p. 308; see also *GJ*, p. 562). The eschatological character is perceptible only to those who believe though the events occur in history, and this is the point of *geschichtlich*. That to which this word applies occurred in history (*GJ*, p. 375).[57]

Certain conclusions are clear from this analysis. Bultmann used *historisch* to describe the mode of knowledge appropriate to the science of history, recognizing its inner-historical causality. Such knowledge is based on evidence, making use of criticism and interpretation appropriate to the inner-causality of history. Commitment to this point of view, however justifiable, does involve the adoption of a principle of criticism not self-evident in history itself. As distinct from this *geschichtlich* emphasizes the happening of an event without reference to evidence or inner-historical causality. *Geschichte* refers both to the events in the lives of men and to accounts of such events. No emphasis is placed on evidence, chronology or even the historical accuracy of what is reported when *Geschichte* is used of a story. In such formulations as *Weltgeschichte*, *heilsgeschichtlich*, *geistergeschichtlich*, *dogmensgeschichtlich*,[58]

Bultmann's use is conventional. However, the stress falls on the content rather than the methodology. It is *world* history. Even so, it is assumed that the presuppositions for the study of history are applicable.

Bultmann's understanding of history is complicated by his interpretation of the history (*Geschichte*) of Jesus.

> And faith has its basis in the appearance of Jesus, which broke through the circle of intra-mundane events in order to create a new history (*Geschichte*) - a history of the efficacy of the Spirit, of the proclamation of the word . . . Jesus' life and work have come to an end as an event in world history (*weltgeschichtlich*); the revelation - which he brought will never come to an end. But in accordance with its origin, this new history will not have the character of world history.

World history' is described as 'the circle of intra-mundane events' and here this description is intended to cover all history except the history of the revelation (*Offenbarungsgeschichte*), the new history. The historian recognizes that man stands *within the stream* of historical events. Determinism is suggested by the phrase 'the circle of intra-mundane events'. Man's existential awareness of freedom is taken into account because 'the circle' includes human causality. However, according to Bultmann, man without faith is determined by his own past, which shapes all of his decisions. Only through the coming of the revelation does a new possibility actually enter human history. Only in the faith which is a response to the revelation can man's historicity be realized in freedom. Because of this Bultmann spoke of the coming of Jesus inaugurating a new history. Talk of the *new* history (*Geschichte*) implies that 'the circle of intra-mundane events' is the *old* history (*Geschichte*).

The problems related to the study of the New Testament are only partially recognized in terms of history in general. Peculiar to this study is the problem of the beginning of the new history. The origin of that new history in the history of Jesus distinguishes it from all other history. The ensuing history of the revelation takes its character from the history in which it originated. The peculiar problems for this study relate to the history of the revelation. However, these peculiar problems are paradoxically bound up with the problems of history generally. This peculiar relation comes out in Bultmann's debate with Barth about the nature of the resurrection of Jesus.

In this discussion[59] Bultmann called on Barth to clarify his concepts concerning history. Barth acknowledged that the resurrection of Jesus was not an 'historical fact' (*historisches Faktum*) to be established by historical science (*historische Wissenschaft*). Yet it really did happen in time and space more certainly than any event that the historian can establish. Because the historian cannot establish the event working on the basis of his presuppositions and methods Barth referred to it as '*Saga*' or '*Legende*', not as 'historical fact' (see *Letters*, pp. 143ff.). But it really did happen in time and space even if such history (*Geschichte*) is not called an historical fact.

Obviously there are events which have taken place without leaving any historical trace, of which we *know* nothing. But Barth claims to know about this event though it cannot be established by historical science. How then is it possible to *know* that it did happen? If the reason that the historian cannot establish the reality of the event is the problematical nature of the evidence Barth would not be justified in claiming that the event did happen, more certainly than events the historian can establish. The problem probably arises from the presuppositions and methods of historical science which are incapable of coping with the unique resurrection event. Barth was satisfied that knowledge of a real event could be communicated in a way that failed to satisfy the canons of historical criticism. Bultmann perceived this as a 'blind acceptance of Scripture involving a *sacrificium intellectus*' because the notion of a physical resurrection contradicts the *Weltbild* which he considered to be self-evident.

Evidently Barth conceded the terminology of 'historical fact' to the historians. But there is no doubt that the history (*Geschichte*) of the resurrection did happen, according to him. Hence his terminology is the same as Bultmann's. What separates them is Barth's acceptance that the physical resurrection of Jesus really did happen. At this point he is not impressed by the problematical nature of the evidence in the New Testament or by the analogy of present experience which casts doubt on the reports of the resurrection.

In Bultmann's terms Jesus' life and work are part of world history and as such these events have come to an end. But the revelation he brought will never come to an end. This way of expressing the matter is not to be resolved simply by distinguishing the event from its consequences. Rather the same event can be seen from two perspectives, the perspective of the historian and the perspective of faith. Faith perceives the history of Jesus and the consequent history of the revelation to be different from all other history. As an historical event viewed by the historian Jesus is seen as a Jew whose proclamation is to be understood in the tradition of the great prophets. Perceived by faith the history of Jesus is the eschatological event which never comes to an end. The coming of the revelation brought the possibility of a genuinely new life to those who believed. How this new possibility came about can be set out as follows with reference to *GJ*.

1. The historical (*historisch*) Jesus is the origin of this new possibility (p. 195). Before him the possibility of eschatological existence had not been realized. However, it is not argued that this eschatological existence was realized in Jesus' earthly life nor that it came about through the inner historical consequences of his life. Paradoxically it is asserted that only when Jesus had departed did the possibility actually occur (pp. 475, 493, 500f., 558f., 610f.). Faith in Jesus as the risen one is a miraculous paradox in the face of the crucifixion; it is an expression of the new existence which has come about through his total life viewed from the perspective of his withdrawal from the world. The crucifixion provides no causal historical explanation for the faith in the risen one which, Bultmann argues, is an expression of the new life. But the new life is itself recognized only in faith (p. 475).

2. While historical science can, as far as the sources allow, reconstruct the life and teaching of the Jesus of history, such an approach cannot demonstrate his absolute and exclusive character as the eschatological event, as the revelation of God. Here the discussion touches on one of the most difficult issues facing contemporary Christianity. Is the significance of Jesus exclusive and absolute? What is his place in relation to other religions? From an historical (*historisch*) point of view Bultmann recognized the relative significance of Jesus in the context of his place in first-century Judaism. Historically his message and his actions are part of the continuum of the first-century Judaism.

3. Through his completed life and work something new occurred in human history. Its relative newness is apparent even to historical science but its genuinely absolute newness can be seen only by the faith which emerged through his completed work. This faith is paradoxically in spite of the event of crucifixion rather than a positive consequence of it. Yet the event of Jesus' life, with its ending,

is in a real way the 'cause' of the Easter faith—not in a deterministic fashion but paradoxically, miraculously (pp. 500f., 558f., 589). For this sense of the miraculous see *EF*, p. 292.

4. The coming of the Easter faith is itself an historical (*historisch*) event which can be known by means of historical science. But the validity of such faith can only be known by faith. While the Easter faith arose from the historical (*historisch*) event, faith is not a thing of the past, possible only for those who were there with Jesus. Nor is it bound to a causal chain of consequences which can be traced down through the course of history. To view the matter this way is to overlook the way Jesus, as the eschatological event, can be present in the proclamation. The proclamation is a tradition and, as such, part of a causal chain stretching back to Jesus. But this should not be taken to mean that the preaching simply maintains some sort of link with the past figure of Jesus. On the contrary, Bultmann asserts that Jesus is present in the preaching, that the believer encounters him in his present situation, not simply as a recollection or a reconstructed figure from the past (pp. 195, 308, 475, 562, 589, 610f., 626).

5. The encounter with Jesus as the eschatological event has its beginning in and through the historical (*historisch*) Jesus but historical science cannot demonstrate the necessary connection between the historical and the eschatological. Only faith can perceive this (pp. 195, 475).

6. The exclusively absolute status (his revelation not only excludes others, it is complete) of Jesus for faith has its basis in the awareness that faith arises genuinely only in response to him, that the new life is genuinely a new and miraculous possibility brought about by him. Faith perceives this though it is not possible for it to be demonstrated by historical science. Certainly there can be no doubt about the faith which came into being through the completed life of Jesus and the claim that through this faith new life, eternal life, had entered human life. So much faith professes and historical science can discover what it is that is professed though whether it is true or not is beyond the scope and competency of historical science to ascertain. Each person confronted with this history must decide whether or not it is true.

7. This understanding of history in which no event as historical (*historisch*) can be absolute because it is part of the overall inner-historical causality and is culturally relative, has implications for

Bultmann's reconstruction of the history of 'Primitive Christianity'. Thus it is necessary to distinguish that history, with its historically conditioned understanding of the eschatological event, from the eschatological event itself, though that event is always expressed in culturally conditioned terms. For this event and this event alone, as a continuing present event, makes faith and the new life of faith possible. The appearance of this faith can be discovered by historical science but historical science cannot show such faith to be valid nor demonstrate that it is both the means of and expression of authentic human existence, eschatological existence. Thus some response to the christological problem determines the starting point for any contemporary critical reconstruction which must take account of the problem of relativism and at the same time acknowledge the absolute claim which faith makes for the historical Jesus. This problem is not of Bultmann's making, nor is it exclusive to those of 'existentialist' persuasion. It is a problem for all who treat history critically and do not set the New Testament apart as if special privileges were necessary here.[60]

7. **History and Historical Reconstruction**

Bultmann's understanding of Christianity is a consequence of his reconstruction of the history of 'Primitive' Christianity. This reconstruction has two separate but closely related aspects. First, historical research must establish the relationship of the historical Jesus to 'Primitive' Christianity. Second, it is necessary to reconstruct the 'development' of Christianity in the New Testament period. Naturally the reconstruction of this development is somewhat dependent on what is understood to be the 'origin' of Christianity. It is not surprising that here, as elsewhere, we do not escape the problem of the hermeneutical circle. However, while his understanding of the nature of the origin of Christianity is more or less distinctively his own, his reconstruction of the development of 'Primitive' Christianity is dependent on Wilhelm Bousset's *Kyrios Christos*,[61] as can be seen from Bultmann's Preface to the fifth edition of 1964.

In that Preface Bultmann indicates that the book remains indispensable, introducing the critical questions for New Testament research and bringing together the conclusions of the history of religions school. The significance of eschatology was adequately recognized by this school. Bousset developed this further by arguing that the 'Son of Man' of primitive Palestinian Christianity was replaced by the cultically revered 'Kyrios Christos' in Hellenistic Christianity and that Hellenistic Christianity was the presupposition of both Paul and John. This reconstruction has become the common property of the historical study of the New Testament.

Other themes of importance dealt with by Bousset include the relation of Jesus and Paul, the historical Jesus and the kerygmatic Christ, sacrament and church, and the relation of Hellenistic Christianity to the mystery religions and Gnosticism. By taking his study of Christian origins 'down to Irenaeus', Bousset also drew attention to the artificial character of the canon, from an historical point of view, in the study of Christian beginnings.

The one qualification Bultmann had about the work was the intention to deal with religion, which was the common intention of the history of religions school, rather than theology. He asked whether this intention can do justice to the New Testament or whether it is not necessary to return to the question of the theology of the New Testament. His own answer is given in his classical treatment of *The Theology of the New Testament*. However, even here his critique of Bousset is qualified. He argued that Bousset and the history of religions school generally were reacting to the dominant view of theology of the New Testament as study of 'the so called doctrinal concepts'. From this perspective the move to the study of religion, understood as piety, where 'Christology is interpreted as Christ-oriented piety' is regarded to be a decided advance. Bultmann's existentialist interpretation has its starting point here though it is modified both by existentialism as a perspective and by the theological intention of his interpretation (*Th.N.T.*, II, p. 238). However, the significance of Bousset for Bultmann's historical work on the New Testament has yet to be adequately recognized. His recognition of the distinction between primitive Palestinian Christianity and Hellenistic Christianity paved the way for the recognition of diversity in earliest Christianity.

a. **The Diversity of 'Primitive' Christianity**

Walter Bauer's critique of the distinction between 'orthodoxy' and 'heresy' in early Christianity (second century) was a landmark. The diversity to which he drew attention in the second century is demonstrated in the New Testament period by Bultmann. In his critique of C.H. Dodd's *Interpretation of the Fourth Gospel*[62] he argued that Dodd had failed to take account of the complexity of

Christianity which Bauer had demonstrated. But if 'orthodoxy' was merely the victorious group in the struggle from an original diversity, how can any criteria be discovered that will serve to demonstrate what is or is not permissible to Christian faith? Recognition of diversity has sometimes been used as an argument against Bultmann's practice of 'content-criticism' (*Sachkritik*) (thus Thiselton, p. 290). Does not original diversity imply the validity of diversity? To this question Bultmann answers 'Yes' and 'No'. 'Yes', since faith is always a specific response in an actual situation there can be no definitive once-for-all *expression* of faith. On the other hand, some expressions of faith are more adequate than others. Pre-faith understandings of God, world and man can hinder believing comprehension. Because of this, content-criticism even of the New Testament writings, such as was exercised by Luther, is necessary (*Th.N.T.*, II, p. 238).

Bultmann relates his *content-criticism* to the critique made by Luther in the 'September Testament' of 1522.[63] There Luther showed his preference for the Gospel and first epistle of John and epistles of Paul because they 'show Christ to you' and 'teach you everything you need to know for your salvation'. He goes on to say, 'In comparison with these, the epistle of St James is an epistle full of straw, because it contains nothing evangelical'. In his preface to that epistle he goes on to elaborate this view. 1. James, by ascribing justification to works is in opposition to Paul and the rest of the Bible. 2. James is therefore refused a place in 'the true canon of my Bible'. 3. The primary criterion for this canon is 'whether it emphasizes the prominence of Christ or not'.

Two further points arise from this discussion of Luther. 1. Luther recognized a 'true canon' or a 'canon within the canon'. He indicated that the Gospel of John and the first epistle, the epistles of Paul to the Romans, Galatians and Ephesians, and 1 Peter formed that 'true canon'. The other Gospels and other epistles of Paul also 'show Christ' but not as clearly as the canon within the canon. But James is excluded from the canon altogether because it 'teaches nothing about him'. 2. Luther set James in opposition to Paul's teaching on justification through faith. In this opposition James is said to be out of step with Paul and the rest of the Bible. Thus, justification tends to become a criterion by means of which Luther recognized his 'canon', from which James was excluded. Luther also gave a special place to his 'canon within the canon' made up of works by John, Paul and Peter.

Bultmann added other criteria in his development of 'content criticism'. Firstly, he appealed to the 'intention of the New Testament itself' ('SOTCF', p. 11; cf. *FU*, p. 280). That intention is recognized most clearly in the Christ-kerygma of Paul and John. It is confused by the way this is expressed in the framework of a mythological *Weltbild*, whether Jewish apocalyptic or Gnostic. The problem of such *Weltbilder* is exposed by both the intention of the New Testament and the modern scientific *Weltbild*. A conflict within the New Testament concerning freedom and determinism is also dealt with by the dual criteria of the intention of the New Testament and contemporary knowledge based on the existential awareness of freedom. The kerygma presupposes man's freedom and man is aware of freedom in his existential decisions (see *K&M*, I, p. 11; Johnson, p. 248).

When the kerygma is expressed in the terms of apocalyptic myth it can only be understood by coming to terms with apocalyptic conceptuality. But apocalyptic conceptuality is not the product of the kerygma. Because of this it is possible that it may imperfectly express the kerygma or even distort it. Thus the tasks of understanding and criticism must be distinguished. For understanding the conceptual framework in which the kerygma is expressed is presupposed but on the basis of that understanding the conceptuality is criticized in the light of the contemporary principles of criticism set out above.

There are problems for such an approach. The kerygma is always expressed in culturally conditioned language, whether that be Jewish apocalyptic or Gnostic mythology. Where is the pure kerygma to be found which is to be used as a criterion? Is it not possible to view these differences simply as diverse expressions of the one gospel? This question implies a unity in spite of apparent diversity and does not do justice to contradictions and disagreements in the New Testament, even in individual books.

Bultmann's approach to the canon within the canon is taken up, with modifications, by a number of scholars. David Tracy prefers a 'working canon' appropriate to the full range of expressions in the New Testament (*TAI*, pp. 308f., 333 n. 3). Pluralism is treated as a virtue (*TAI*, pp. 248ff., 264) and his aim is to find 'criteria of relative adequacy' (pp. 246 n. 25, 274, 306-309, 312, 315, 318-22). Relative adequacy indicates that not all expressions are equally adequate. Thus Tracy is closer to the canon within the canon than he acknowledges. His use of 'the major internal corrective' (243 n. 13) allows for other correctives and thus for the diversity of the tradition but by making it the *major* internal corrective it has priority and tends to operate as a criterion even in relation to the other criteria.

Tracy identifies the Jesus-kerygma as the major internal corrective. Here he both agrees and disagrees with Schubert Ogden for whom the Jesus-kerygma is the canon within the canon rather than the Christ-kerygma as used by Bultmann (*Point*, pp. 51-54, 62, 84, 111-14; *TAI*, p. 243 n. 13). The Jesus-kerygma is reconstructed by means of a form critical approach to Q and the early Markan narratives while Bultmann appeals to the Christ-kerygma of Paul and John (*TAI*, pp. 243 n. 11; 246 n. 25; 270f., 289 nn. 21, 27; 300 n. 97).[64] However the Jesus-kerygma is not to be identified with the historical Jesus. Thus Tracy and Ogden stand with Kähler and Bultmann in rejecting the attempt of the 'new quest' to ground faith in the historical Jesus. Rather, the Jesus-kerygma is the earliest recoverable form of the kerygma in which Jesus was proclaimed. The assumption *seems to be* that the earliest is truest. Truest to . . . ? Perhaps truest to the historical Jesus and the faith he evoked.

Bultmann, Ogden and Tracy all recognize the christological diversity of the New Testament and the relative adequacy of the expressions of the kerygma. The various traditions express the conviction that the event proclaimed is to be understood as divine, as the saving revelation event for the believer (*Point*, pp. 76ff.).

Tracy's rejection of the canon within the canon makes it difficult to see how he relates his various criteria unless his 'major internal corrective' is given the weight of the canon within the canon so that the other criteria are understood in terms of the primary criterion. It would be possible to do this while allowing more positive value for the diversity than is granted by either Bultmann or Ogden. If this is not done it is difficult to see how conflicts in the tradition could be overcome.

The difference between the Jesus-kerygma and the Christ-kerygma is significant. Bultmann's position rests on the perception that faith is more adequately expressed in the latter, that the eschatological significance *of Jesus* is not adequately perceived in the former which has not shaken free from the apocalyptic framework and hence does not recognize the eschatological character of the life of faith in the present. Whether the Jesus-kerygma or the Christ-kerygma is more adequate can only be discerned in an examination of the origin and early development of Christianity.

b. **The Roots of 'Primitive' Christianity**

Recognition of the pre-eminence of Paul and especially John, for Bultmann, is one thing. Discovering why this should be so and how it is to be justified is another. Christianity is recognized as a syncretistic phenomenon (*PC*, pp. 11f., 209). However it would be a mistake to understand his approach to Christianity in terms of its religious antecedents as 'reductionism' such as Barth attributed to Jülicher (*Romans*, pp. 7f.). According to Barth the intention of Jülicher was to explain away aspects of Pauline thought by attributing them to Judaism or Hellenism. Bultmann's intention is quite different from this (*Letters*, pp. 4f.). Having briefly set out the syncretistic nature of Christianity in terms of its borrowing from both Judaism and Hellenism he goes on to say that the uniqueness of Christianity is thrown into sharp relief against this background (*PC*, p. 11).

Recognition of syncretistic phenomena does not prejudice the possibility of recognizing a unique or distinctive understanding. The whole context, into which particular motifs are inserted, is the key to a proper understanding of the parts. While various motifs might have been derived from Judaism or some form of Hellenism, the emergence of Christian faith was something new and distinctive in the history of the religions of the world. Perhaps if Bultmann were writing today he would describe his approach as 'holism', because he was looking for the overall pattern of Christian faith in as much as it expressed an understanding of human existence, which perhaps could be described as a new philosophy of life (*PC*, p. 12).[65] What then is the 'pattern' of the Christian faith? The pattern is a functional structure which enables us to grasp the specific meaning. In Christianity that structure becomes visible in its soteriology, in the way to enter into and maintain what the tradition holds out as 'true life'. This might not be clearly articulated in the text but unless the text can be located in relation to this framework it is not likely that it will be understood with any precision. This is a problem, for example, with such a book as James. Is it anti-Pauline or simply non-Pauline? What understanding of 'salvation' and the 'way of salvation' is to be found there?

The comparative study of motifs led Richard Reitzenstein to the indiscretion of calling Paul 'the greatest gnostic of them all'. Bultmann's recognition that the context of Christian faith differs radically from the context of the Gnostic myth led him to reject this view because, although Paul borrowed Gnostic themes and motifs, these were transformed by the framework of their new context. The motifs mean one thing in the Gnostic 'pattern' of religion and another in the Christian 'pattern'. Hence, the most obvious need is for the recognition of 'types' or 'patterns' of religions (the 'holistic' approach) in the study of the relationship between different religions such as Judaism and Christianity. But neither Judaism nor Christianity is, or was in the first century, a simple monochrome unity. Each religion manifests a number of patterns. Because of this it is necessary to reconstruct both the developing patterns which 'evolve' historically with the passage of time—religions change in the course of history—and set out the spectrum of the variety of positions within the religion at a given time. The problem of 'mixed types' is evident where religions have interacted, as was the case with 'Primitive' Christianity in relation to Judaism and Hellenistic Paganism. Obviously Christianity owes much to Judaism. There is also evidence which suggests that Judaism was not left unaffected by the birth and growth of Christianity.

Bultmann's reconstruction is a clarification and elaboration of Bousset's programmematic approach. The outlines of his work are set out in his *Primitive Christianity* and in more detail in *The Theology of the New Testament*. His aim in *Primitive Christianity* 'is not an original piece of historical research' but 'rather that of *interpretation*' (*PC*, p. 12). That he succeeded quite brilliantly with this aim there is little doubt. The interpretation aims to go beyond description and summary to discover the understanding of existence, the philosophy of life, which finds expression in the texts under discussion. But if the aim is 'interpretation', the method is genuinely historical. The method shows 'Primitive' Christianity in relation to Judaism and Hellenism and in the process illuminates the distinctive nature of Christian faith.

c. **Judaism in the Hellenistic Age**

The opening of this reconstruction in *Primitive Christianity* treats 'The Old Testament Heritage'. This title indicates that the Old Testament was not the immediate context of Jesus. That immediate context was Judaism, whose heritage was the Old Testament. The themes treated in this section should not be considered as a comprehensive survey of the themes of the Old Testament. Rather they are the heritage presupposed by Judaism in the period. From the

Old Testament these themes were of living and vital significance for Judaism. Even so the Old Testament is not treated uniformly. Account is taken of historical development in the treatment of the various themes. This suggests that there were various 'types' of Old Testament religion all of which need to be distinguished from Judaism in the first century. The fundamental themes of 'the Old Testament *heritage*' are presupposed at a stage of development appropriate to the time. Further, in dealing with first-century Judaism he notes that it was not a completely unified entity, that there were distinctions between Pharisees and Sadducees, between the teaching of the Law and apocalyptic. There were even opposing viewpoints ('Reply', in Kegley, p. 282). Consequently, when dealing with the setting of 'Primitive' Christianity in Judaism he does so in terms of Jewish Legalism, National and Cosmic Eschatology, and Hellenistic Judaism. His intention was to depict Judaism in its own terms and to illuminate its structure and dynamics. This is done on a broad canvas, together with his reconstruction of Hellenistic life and thought, as the context for his reconstruction of 'Primitive' Christianity. That this perspective has influenced his interpretation should not be denied, though it was Bultmann's aim to see how Judaism, as distinct from Christianity, perceived man, his plight and his salvation and hence also how God was perceived. It remains to be seen whether his view of Judaism is only a Christian perception, and hence a distortion.

Bultmann's discussion of Judaism could have been more detailed and in some respects needs to be modified. For example, having defined Hellenistic Judaism as 'the Judaism of the Graeco-Roman world' the ensuing discussion concerns the Jews of the Diaspora and Philo in particular (*PC*, pp. 111ff.). This understanding has serious implications for Bultmann's reconstruction of the history of 'Primitive' Christianity for which the earliest Church is the Palestinian Church, while the Hellenistic Church is the Church outside Palestine. But if the Jews of the Graeco-Roman world constitute Hellenistic Judaism, does this not include Palestine? Obviously Bultmann considered hellenization to have been more complete in the Diaspora (*PC*, p. 111). While it can hardly be doubted that, as a generalization, this view is valid, it tends to obliterate the recognition that Palestinian Judaism was also Hellenistic and that no hard and fast distinction between Palestinian Judaism and the Judaism of the Diaspora is possible in terms of hellenization. The same criticism needs to be made concerning the distinction between earliest (Palestinian) Christianity and Hellenistic Christianity.[66] Certainly Bultmann gives the impression that we have here a geographical distinction though this contradicts his earlier definition of Hellenistic Judaism. Were we to take the distinction in terms of degrees of hellenization in Judaism and 'Primitive' Christianity—without geographical reference —we would be on safer ground. However, there is a need to recognize Jerusalem and Palestine as forces which retarded the influence of some aspects of hellenization.

While the Qumran sect might not have escaped hellenization, it is difficult to imagine such a community existing outside of Palestine. The Zealot movement was also native to Palestine. Thus it would seem that the tendency to see a Judaism more or less uniformly hellenized, regardless of its location, is an over-statement. The distinction between Palestinian and diaspora Judaism remains valid though the differences might not be as clear-cut as Bultmann supposed. The same conclusion is probably valid in relation to Christianity. On this issue see now G. Vermes, *Jesus and the World of Judaism*, p. 26 and passim.

Bultmann's picture of Judaism was not monolithic, nor did he accept any view of a 'normative' Judaism in the time of Jesus. Such he regarded to be the picture of a later time, after the fall of Jerusalem (*PC*, pp. 74f.). He also agrees with Samuel Sandmel that it is 'one-sided - even false - to characterize Jewish piety simply as legalism' ('Reply', in Kegley, p. 282). But Bultmann asserts that legalism was to be found in first-century Judaism and in Rabbinic Judaism. Because of his critique of Jewish legalism it is sometimes asserted that he has a distorted picture of Judaism in the first century.

It has become common for some Old Testament scholars and experts on Judaism to criticize the interpretation of Judaism to be found in the writings of New Testament scholars. An example of this criticism is to be found in the important book by E.P. Sanders, *Paul and Palestinian Judaism*.[67] Sanders' work is important because of his thesis that a succession of scholars going back to F. Weber is largely responsible for this distortion (p. 44). The succession is F. Weber, E. Schürer, P. Billerbeck, Wm Bousset, R. Bultmann. It is argued that Bousset broadened the scope of Weber's interpretation of Rabbinic Judaism to cover all of Judaism and that these views were more widely disseminated by Bultmann (p. 47). Sanders 1. identifies the nature of the distortion; 2. locates its origin; 3. traces its development; 4. shows how it became popular; and 5. indicates why it has seemed convincing to New Testament scholars.

The distorted view of Judaism is said to be a construct based on Paul's criticisms, assuming that he was criticizing empirical Judaism when he criticized Jewish legalism. The 'succession' then read this picture of Judaism into the sources (p. 4). Here we are concerned with Sanders' contention that Bultmann was dependent on the 'succession' and disseminated this distorted picture of Judaism.

Sanders argued that Bultmann had no independent access to the sources of 'late Judaism' but was dependent on 'the succession' naming as his 'principal authority for the history, literature and *religion* of Judaism the work of Schürer . . . ' (Sanders, p. 43). From a patchwork of quotations he then attempted to demonstrate the distorted view of Judaism in Bultmann's *PC* (Sanders, pp. 44f.). He also argued that Bultmann mistook Paul's criticism of Judaism from the perspective of Christian faith for a phenomenological critique.

Sanders can be answered briefly. Schürer was not cited as 'the principal authority for . . . but as 'the basic work on . . . ' in a bibliography which was by no means exhaustive. The footnotes of *PC* also show that Bultmann did have independent access to the Jewish sources and this is confirmed by his other writings on Judaism. Sanders also ignored, in his critique, the section in *PC* on the Old Testament heritage in which Bultmann treated many of the themes said to have been ignored by the succession. Nor did he take account of Bultmann's insistence that Judaism in the time of Jesus was not uniform, and that there were even opposing points of view (*PC*, pp. 74f.; cf. Kegley, p. 282). His patchwork of quotations from *PC* also presents a distorted picture of Bultmann's position which is little more than a caricature. The reason for this is that Sanders did not recognize that Bultmann presented two views of Judaism: one that of the Jew and the other that of the believer from the perspective of the kerygma. From the point of view of the former the law is not a burden as it is from the perspective of the latter.

In his 1940 essay Bultmann clearly repudiated the '*false picture of Jewish legalism as an oppressive burden*' (*EPT*, pp. 36ff.; see also his 'Reply' to Samuel Sandmel, in Kegley, p. 282). But Sanders argued that Bultmann's true opinion of Jewish legalism was that it made life intolerable because he based Paul's soteriology and his view of the law on his view of man's plight (Sanders, p. 474 n. 1; cf. pp. 435,

442f., 454 n. 25, 475, 481f., 548). Sanders recognized that this was contrary to what Bultmann said in his article on Romans 7. We have noted that it is contrary to the article in *EPT*, pp. 36ff., and to the 'Reply' to Sandmel. Sanders' case is based on his view of Bultmann's relation to 'the succession' and to the fact that in *Th.N.T.* Bultmann's treatment of the theology of Paul deals first with 'Man Prior to the Revelation of Faith' before moving to 'Man under Faith'. He concluded that the latter must be based on the former. This is contrary to Bultmann's statement on Romans 7.15ff. Here he affirms that the struggle with the law becomes apparent only from the standpoint of faith and is not perceived as such by the Jew (*EPT*, p. 40). The point is made emphatically in *Th.N.T.*, I, p. 191, 'that man prior to the revelation of faith is so depicted by Paul as he is retrospectively seen from the standpoint of faith'.

Bultmann has two views of Jewish legalism: one from the point of view of the Jew who keeps the law and the other that of Paul in the light of faith and the kerygma. The same point is made in referring to Paul's conversion (*Th.N.T.*, I, p. 187).[68]

Sanders also failed to perceive Bultmann's distinction between 'unconditional obedience' and 'radical obedience' (Sanders, p. 45; cf. pp. 112f., 120 n. 84). This distinction is crucial for Bultmann's presentation of Jesus in the context of Judaism. Reference to 'the unconditional obedience of the religious man' to the Law comes from Bultmann's book on *Jesus*.[69] Bultmann explains that by *unconditional obedience* he understands obedience that is dependent on a formal authority. The commandment is to be obeyed simply because it is commanded, not because of *what* is commanded. Therefore all commandments are equally binding. Because this involves 'obedience to a *purely formal authority*', moral and ritual laws are not distinguished. The consequence is the emphasis on ritual and ceremonial which was denounced by Jesus (*Jesus*, pp. 54f.; and *PC*, p. 80, where the same point is made).

Bultmann nuanced his position somewhat by recognizing that the Judaism of Jesus' time attempted to formulate a priority of principles and that some of the rabbis developed a criticism of legalism. But even in these developments, he argued, the will of God remains identified with the formal authority of Scripture. Thus he presents Judaism as a religion of obedience arising out of reverence before the majesty of God (*Jesus*, pp. 56f.; *PC*, pp. 78f.).

Radical obedience is understood quite differently from this. The first mark of the difference is to be seen in the way the Scriptures are evaluated on the basis of their content. 'Jesus sets one passage against another...' Clearly it is not the formal authority that is binding because man has the insight to recognize what is demanded by God. The content of the command determines whether the word of Scripture is God's command or not. In this Jesus is not only opposed to specific laws, the laws of purification are annulled, but also to the Old Testament as a formal authority. On the basis of the recognition that God's commands are intrinsically intelligible, the idea of obedience is first *radically* conceived. Because the commands are intelligible, man can assent to what is required of him with his whole being in the choice between good and evil (*Jesus*, pp. 59-60; *PC*, pp. 80f.; Kegley, p. 283).

Bultmann argues that radical obedience liberates man from the burden of formal authority where it is necessary to know all the detailed commands in order to act rightly (*Jesus*, pp. 64f.). But it involves the burden of decision between good and evil, God's will or man's. Radical obedience then assumes the intelligibility of the demand of God. In so doing ritual laws are dismissed as unintelligible but the principle by which they are dismissed is more radical than the critique of ritual laws might suggest. The principle also applies to moral laws such as those concerning divorce. Further, because God's will is not identified with the numerous laws it is possible to recognize that God's will demands the response of the whole person, complete obedience. What God demands can never be satisfied because he demands all, not simply the fulfilment of this command or that. Hence the term *radical* obedience seems justified. Whether Bultmann's expectation that what God demands will be known in the decision of the moment is over-optimistic is another question. Naturally obedience is possible only in terms of the *known* will of God and this does not rule out the possibility that men of goodwill can be misled. But errors of judgment do not necessarily indicate that God's will is unintelligible. Perhaps such errors indicate only false conceptions, expectations and a failure to take account of situations and consequences, all of which are important, according to Bultmann, if man is to respond responsibly to the will of God.

Granted then that for Bultmann, as much as for Sanders, Paul's critique of the Law, Judaism and 'the religious man', is retrospectively from the stand-point of faith, what light does this shed on the critique of Jewish legalism? First, Sanders draws attention to the view that

> Paul, according to Moore, was not addressing himself to Jews to refute them on their own terms but to Gentile converts, to prevent their being persuaded by Jewish propagandists that observance of the law was necessary along with allegiance to Christ (Sanders, p. 6; cf. p. 442).

This observation appears to be eminently probable; cf. Acts 15.1, 5 and Galatians, though perhaps we should say that the 'propagandists were Pharisaic Jewish Christians'. But what are the implications of this demand? Surely if in addition to faith it is necessary to be circumcised and keep the Law of Moses this is a demand for works of the Law, and it does justify the charge of legalism. Further, if Paul's critique of the Law in terms of works and legalism arose out of the situation where there were those who sought to impose the Law of Moses on Gentile converts, this still leaves unexplained Jesus' critique of the Law according to the Gospels. Bultmann argued that this critique was central to the message of the historical Jesus. How then is this to be understood? It is Bultmann's point that there was a movement to apply the ritual laws more widely (*PC*, p. 77). Jesus' response is to be seen as a critique of the Pharisaic demand of obedience to the formal authority of the Old Testament and, in particular, of their own application of this authority. Such a demand constituted legalism according to the critique of Jesus. Because Sanders's book was on Paul he ignored the problem of the critique of legalism in the Gospels. He also ignored the fact that, for Bultmann, the critique of legalism is not merely a critique of Judaism but a critique of 'the religious man' as such.

d. **Jesus the Jew**

Those who criticize Bultmann's understanding of Judaism seldom note that Jesus is treated as a Jew in the context of the diversity of Judaism. This is made clear in his book *Jesus*, *PC*, and *Th.N.T.*, I. Historical analysis of Jesus' proclamation locates him firmly within the Jewish framework. Despite this Bultmann is charged with disregarding the factual history of Jesus,[70] of asserting that nothing can be said about the historical Jesus and that he has no relevance for faith.[71] Yet Bultmann has written *HST*, *Jesus* and summarized the message of Jesus in *PC* and *Th.N.T.*, I. Perhaps his statement in *Jesus*, p. 14, has something to do with this misunderstanding.

> We can know almost nothing concerning the life and personality of Jesus since the early Christian sources show no interest in either, and other sources about Jesus do not exist.

Here Bultmann appears to surrender to his critics. But it is the 'life and personality of Jesus' about which little can be said. He could also say

> Hence, with a bit of caution we can say the following concerning Jesus' activity: Characteristic for him are exorcisms, the breech of the Sabbath commandment, the abandonment of ritual purifications, polemic against Jewish legalism, fellowship with outcasts such as publicans and harlots, sympathy for women and children; it can also be seen that Jesus was not an ascetic like John the Baptist, but gladly ate and drank a glass of wine. Perhaps we may add that he called disciples and asssembled about himself a small company of followers—men and women ('PCKHJ', pp. 22f.).

More can be said of the teaching of Jesus: 'we know enough of his *message* to make for ourselves a consistent picture' (*Jesus*, pp. 16f.; 'PCKHJ', p. 23). Further, Bultmann argues that for one like Jesus, who worked by means of word 'his purpose can be comprehended only as teaching' (*Jesus*, p. 15). That teaching places Jesus firmly in the context of Judaism and distinguishes him from Christianity.

Bultmann's distinction between the two histories is important here. From the perspective of the 'old history' Jesus is a Jew and his message is to be comprehended in terms of Judaism. However, viewed as the beginning of the 'new history', the eschatological event, the history of Jesus takes on a new significance. That significance is not *self-evident* in the history of Jesus but is perceptible only through the faith which the event itself evoked, paradoxical as that might seem. Because of this Bultmann was not disturbed by the fires of historical criticism. All that they burned was the fanciful portraits of 'the life-of Jesus' theology (*FU*, p. 132). Further, the state of the sources, making it impossible to reconstruct the life of Jesus, did not bother him either because 'the historical Jesus is a phenomenon among other phenomena, not an absolute entity' (*FU*, p. 31), not the ground and object of faith.

Bultmann's rejection of the attempt to establish the *life of Jesus* as the basis of faith implies that the ground of faith must be 'absolute', not a relative phenomenon. Does the teaching of Jesus constitute such an absolute? Is this the reason for Bultmann's concentration in this area? The answer to this question must be an emphatic 'No'. The treatment of the proclamation of Jesus as a phenomenon of Judaism and as a presupposition for the theology of the New Testament rather than as an aspect of it makes this clear. Jesus was a Jew whose message is to be understood in terms of the Old Testament prophets. At this level Jesus can be understood in terms of immanent historical causes (*EF*, p. 292). Individual motifs of Jesus' proclamation can be found in the writings of Judaism, including attempts to set up moral principles as fundamentally important and criticisms of formal legalism (cf. e.g. *Jesus*, p. 56). Further, Jesus shares with Judaism its fundamental concern of obedience to the will of God. Bultmann claims, however, that Jesus went 'beyond anything known to us in contemporary rabbinic criticism' (*Jesus*, p. 59). In rejecting the 'formal legal authority' of the Old Testament Jesus 'first radically conceived' the idea of obedience by asserting that God's commands are intrinsically intelligible (*Jesus*, p. 61). Does this element of the teaching of Jesus constitute the absolute basis of faith?

The answer to this question is not easy to give. Perhaps the best answer is 'Yes' and 'No'. 'Yes' because the absolute demand of God is intelligible; but 'No' because not even this aspect of Jesus' proclamation constitutes the basis of faith as such (*Th.N.T.*, I, pp. 34f.).

Here while Bultmann stresses continuity with Judaism in his treatment of the proclamation of Jesus, he recognizes the radical direction of various aspects and asserts that what happened through him was unique. He makes a distinction between the content of Jesus' proclamation, which is an expression of prophetic/apocalyptic Judaism, and the sheer fact of Jesus, which is unique. The event of Jesus gave rise to the Easter faith. In this regard it is not so much what he proclaimed but the fact that *he proclaimed* it. The newness is not in what Jesus proclaimed as such, though there is a relative newness in its radical form. What is new is that *he proclaimed* it and in so doing became the one who was proclaimed, the eschatological event. Bultmann crystallizes what can hardly be disputed at a factual level into a brilliant theological formula which at once raises historical problems and at the same time demonstrates the absolute uniqueness of Jesus as the ground of faith. 'The proclaimer became the proclaimed' (*Th.N.T.*, I, p. 33). Faith perceives the revelation of God *in* an historical event which is completely intelligible in the natural or historical connection of events (*JCM*, p. 55; cf. *EF*, p. 292 and Kegley, pp. 274f.).

The historical problems involved in the formula concern the *legitimacy* of making the proclaimer the essential message. Should this not be seen as a distortion of his historical significance? On the other hand there can be no doubt that this is what happened. The one who had previously proclaimed the message of the Kingdom of God was now himself proclaimed in the message. It was not John the Baptist or Peter or Paul who came to be proclaimed, but Jesus. It was his life which gave rise to the Easter faith and the new life of faith, which Bultmann interprets as being uniquely possible through the faith which arises from the proclamation of Jesus as the eschatological revelation of God. Hence, according to Bultmann, there is no point in asking why the revelation should be tied to this man alone and not others as well. The historical reality is that it was Jesus' life, not the Baptist's, which gave rise to the Easter faith.

e. **The Earliest Church**

An historical picture of the Earliest Church can only be achieved 'by route of reconstruction' making use of sources which do not, in the form known to us, come from the Earliest Church. The paucity of sources leaves vast gaps in our knowledge. Such sources as do exist do not give us a straightforward picture of that history. Because of this complexity there are diverse interpretations. But Acts, the letters of Paul and the Synoptic Gospels all make use of material which was shaped by the Earliest Church. Hence critical historiography attempts to reconstruct a picture of the Earliest Church on the basis of the detection of this material.

The message of Jesus was passed on in the preaching of the Earliest Church, where he was depicted as teacher and prophet. But he was also proclaimed as the coming Messiah, the Son of Man. His earthly ministry was not yet seen in messianic terms. The proclamation of Jesus as the coming Messiah or Son of Man fits the frame of Jewish apocalyptic and eschatological expectation. Whereas Jesus had proclaimed the coming Son of Man, the Earliest Church identified the crucified Jesus with this eschatological salvation-bringer. The proclaimer had become the proclaimed. Yet this was not yet radically understood because he was proclaimed as the coming one who would bring history to an end. As yet the fact that the one who was to come had already appeared was not sufficiently taken into account. For this reason the Earliest Church had not broken the frame of Jewish eschatology and was in danger of remaining a Jewish sect. Yet, in one respect it anticipated the development that was to come to clarity in the writings of Paul and John. It already conceived of itself as the eschatological congregation (*Th.N.T.*, I, p. 37). If this was already the case then surely the eschatological event had already occurred. But this understanding was not consciously developed by the Earliest Church.

The Earliest Church was separated from Judaism by its identification of Jesus with the coming Messiah and its nascent awareness of itself as the eschatological community. This, however, was maintained in a fundamentally apocalyptic mode of thought and, in view of this, the Earliest Church might have retained a place as a sect within Judaism. This was a possibility because its *explicit* kerygma failed to take account of its *implicit* self-understanding as the eschatological community, and rendered its kerygma inadequate as an authentic expression of Christian faith.

f. **The Hellenistic Church**

Bultmann considered Paul to be an example of Hellenistic Christianity. But he was in no way a typical example. For this reason he attempted to reconstruct 'pre-Pauline Hellenistic Christianity' from sources all of which come from a later time than Paul, but which embody relevant evidence. Here Bultmann lists traditions in Acts, in the letters of Paul and evidence from later non-Pauline Hellenistic Christianity in the Gospels and other sources (*Th.N.T.*, I, p. 64).

It is immediately obvious that pre-Pauline Hellenistic Christianity was not a unity but was formed under the impact of varying dominant influences such as the Synagogue or Gentile religions, especially Gnosticism (*Th.N.T.*, I, p. 63). Hence it makes good sense to distinguish Hellenistic Jewish Christianity from Hellenistic Gentile Christianity. Bultmann does not do this *explicitly*, though it is implied by his treatment and made explicit by some of his pupils. Walter Schmithals[72] argues that Paul encountered Gnosticism first mediated through Hellenistic Jewish Christianity, where the language had already been 'demythologized', but he came into conflict with the Gnostic meaning of the language in Hellenistic Gentile Christianity at Corinth. The distinction is implicit in Bultmann's recognition of the diversity of pre-Pauline Hellenistic Christianity. In addition he says

> Paul originated in Hellenistic Judaism . . . he was won to the Christian faith by the kerygma of the Hellenistic Church (*Th.N.T.*, I, p. 187).

Bultmann's reconstruction of Hellenistic Christianity presupposes this diversity and from time to time it is made quite explicit. It seems, however, that certain characteristics were commonly found in the kerygma of the Hellenistic Church. Because this mission first made its impact amongst those for whom polytheism and idolatry were a living force it followed the precedent of the Jewish mission in preaching monotheism. But the Old Testament/Jewish concept of God is frequently modified by the concept of God from Greek philosophical tradition with its 'natural theology'. God is proclaimed as Creator and Judge and because of this the heathen world is called to repentance. In the proclamation of judgment Jesus Christ appears as the eschatological saviour and judge of the world and, as such, corresponds to the Son of Man of Jewish apocalyptic, a 'title' which drops out of use in Hellenistic Christianity apart from John. But the eschatological saviour and judge who was proclaimed was the crucified Jesus whom God had raised from the dead. The themes of resurrection and judgment were combined in the proclamation of the general resurrection of the dead.

The preaching of the evangel or kerygma called for faith in the one God and his saving act in Christ, and this involved conversion to a new religion and thus was bound up with a Church-consciousness in which individual congregations were formed into one Congregation—the Church. This Church consciousness was expressed in the idea of the 'new covenant' which linked the Church with Israel's history. Identification with this history separated the Church from the world, excluding Christians from all non-Christian cults and moral uncleanness. Because of this Hellenistic ascetic influences also find expression, heightened by reference to the imminent end of the world. Hence Church-consciousness and eschatological separation from the world could be called an eschatological *dualism* with cosmological motifs. Both stoicism and Gnostic dualism find a point of contact in opposition to the *flesh* and *desires*. Gnosticism also produced a consciousness of a world-renouncing community. These developments all produced tensions for the relation of Hellenistic Christianity to Judaism, including Jewish Christianity and the Old Testament, tensions which were resolved in various ways.

The title '*Kyrios*' was conferred on Christ by the Hellenistic Church. Confessed as such he was believed to be present in the worshipping community. In this confession he was recognized as 'Son of God', a divine figure who paradoxically appears as man and suffers as a man. This aspect (the crucifixion) of the proclamation was a stumbling block in the Hellenistic context. Clearly the conception of Christ as Son of God constituted no problem, though there was no uniform understanding of it. For example, 'Son of God' is understood in terms of divine power which descended on Jesus at his baptism and was revealed in his power to work miracles. Second, the Son of God was understood as a pre-existent figure who became man. Third, probably under the influence of Gnosticism, the cosmological significance of the Son of God was stressed alongside his soteriological significance.

In the worship of the congregation the *Kyrios* is present and the individual entered the congregation through baptism which was regarded as a sacrament, a natural means to which supernatural powers were bound. Those powers were believed to purify, to mark out the baptized as the property of the *Kyrios*, to bestow the Spirit and, on the analogy of initiation in the mystery religions, to enable the believer to share in the death and resurrection of Christ which could also be spoken of as re-birth and illumination. But the decisive contribution of the mystery interpretation was to link baptism with Jesus' death and resurrection as God's saving act.

In Hellenistic Christianity the Lord's Supper was also understood as a sacrament in the sense of the mystery religions. But the basic idea of communion was probably not derived from that source. This should be understood in terms of the transformation of a meal which was an expression of fellowship into a sacramental celebration in Hellenistic Christianity. The *Spirit* also seems to have been interpreted in various ways in which two trends are discernible. First, the Spirit is the power conferred in baptism. Second, the Spirit is given to Christians on specific occasions.

While the Hellenistic world must be recognized as a complex diversity, the most important single influence on Hellenistic Christianity was Gnosticism. Bultmann sets out the specifically Gnostic motifs which find expression there. While the development of the *Kyrios-cult* drew Hellenistic Christianity into the syncretistic process, the influence of the Gnostic doctrine of redemption took this process further. But Hellenistic Christianity retained its drive towards its own understanding of God, world and man. This drive had to be expressed theologically and it was here that Gnosticism provided possibilities and dangers because, as a rival mission, its mythology expressed a new understanding of the utter difference of human existence from all worldly existence which was recognized first in Gnosticism and Christianity. The shape of the Gnostic myth is well known. With many variations it tells the story of the fate of the soul, its origin in the world of light, its fall and imprisonment in this world of darkness and ultimate redemption through the coming of a heavenly figure of light who brings knowledge, who awakens the sparks of light, the souls from the world of light, so that they are 'reborn', teaching them the way back to the world of light.

The Gnostic movement found expression in baptizing sects around the Jordan through which it influenced Judaism. As early as 1925 Bultmann was looking to sectarian Judaism as the medium through which Gnosticism was mediated to Hellenistic, specifically Johannine Christianity.

> If we could get a clear picture of the Essenes, we would perhaps make progress. In any case the Jewish and Jewish-Christian baptismal sects, thorough investigation of which is urgently needed, show what possibilities there were.[73]

This was a view which Bultmann was to confirm by stages.

> At first, Gnosticism probably penetrated into the Christian congregations mostly through the medium of a Hellenistic Judaism that was itself in the grip of syncretism (*Th.N.T.*, I, p. 171).

The earlier quotation shows that Bultmann also allowed for Gnostic influence in some forms of Palestinian Judaism. The clearer picture of groups like the Essenes became possible with the discovery of the Qumran texts which, in Bultmann's view, confirmed his argument, originally based on little evidence (*Th.N.T.*, II, p. 13). The Gnostic movement was also widespread throughout the Near East, having an influence on the mystery cults as well as various Hellenistic religious philosophies, including the philosophy of Philo of Alexandria.

The conflict with Gnosticism was first expressed in terms of eschatology and christology, both of which manifest an underlying contrast in anthropology. The Gnostics taught that the 'spiritual ones' were saved by nature and already had entered into this reality through the sacraments. They also denied the real humanity of Jesus. Against this, Christianity taught the resurrection of the dead and the last judgment and defended the true humanity of Christ. Only at a later stage does the doctrine of creation emerge as the main point of conflict (*GJ*, pp. 28ff.; *Th.N.T.*, I, p. 170; II, p. 13).

Bultmann makes an important statement about the relation of Hellenistic Christianity to Gnosticism.

> It is clear: Hellenistic Christianity is in the maelstrom of the syncretistic process; the genuinely Christian element is wrestling

> with other elements; 'orthodoxy' does not exist at this early period but is still to develop (*Th.N.T.*, I, p. 71).

Here we see that although Bultmann accepted Walter Bauer's assessment of the development of 'orthodoxy', nevertheless he maintained a view which enabled him to distinguish 'the genuinely Christian element' from 'other elements'. This is a problem to which we shall return. For the moment our attention is turned to those elements of Gnostic myth, thought and terminology, which influenced Christian theology and contributed to the development of Christian theological language.

1. Eschatological dualism was developed beyond the bounds of 'salvation-history' through the influence of Gnostic cosmological thinking. Naturally this influence made use of those elements within the tradition which were open to interpretation in this direction. Mythological figures such as Satan and the terminology in which dualism is expressed show the influence of Gnosticism.

2. These figures and the dualism presuppose and give expression to the idea of the fall of creation so that man's situation in the world is depicted as under the dominion of demonic powers and destined to destruction. The *terminology of parenesis*, using light/darkness dualism and calling on men to awaken, to become sober, is drawn mainly from Gnosticism.

3. The most important contribution was the use of Gnostic concepts to clarify the *history of salvation*. The Redeemer is presented as a cosmic figure, the pre-existent divine Son of the Father who descends to bring knowledge and re-ascends to lead the way back to the heavenly world of light. In so doing he triumphs over the powers of this world and sets the captives free.

4. The cosmic triumph of Christ means emancipation from the demonic world-rulers for the believers. In Gnosticism this emancipation depends on the kinship between the Redeemer and the redeemed and traces of this teaching remain in the New Testament. This involved (in Gnosticism) the notion of pre-existent human selves (souls?).

5. Gnosticism assumes that all 'the Spiritual' form a unity quite distinct from the world. This is expressed in terms of the notion of 'the body' of the original figure of light and use is made of this in the development of the idea of the Church. But in this there is a potential conflict with the idea that the Church is open to all who believe.

6. To come to faith from polytheism was to come to knowledge of the truth, which was emancipating knowledge. The hidden conflict lies in that from which and for which 'the believer' was emancipated.

7. The Gnostic myth provided terminology which could be used to interpret the eschatological event in a way that showed that the consummation had already begun in the history of Jesus. Naturally this possibility also involved dangers.

The distinction of the Hellenistic Church from the Earliest Church can best be summed up in terms of the change from the framework of the apocalyptic-eschatological myth to the framework of the Gnostic myth. This change enabled the Hellenistic Church to take account of the fact that, not only was Jesus expected, he had already appeared. His appearance in history had changed the whole course of history for those who believed. However, if this can be seen as pure gain, the myth also carried the suggestion of the divine origin of the Redeemer and his cosmic role, which threatened his real humanity. It also suggested that only 'the Spiritual' could follow the Redeemer and that this following was fully possible in this life and involved an ascetic repudiation of the world, though this sometimes appears to have been expressed in terms of libertinism. Such tendencies surrendered the idea of creation and abandoned history by rejecting the world in 'dehistoricizing' ecstasy instead of affirming love (*Agape*) as the fulfilment of the believer's life in history. It is against the background of this confusion that Bultmann interprets the work of Paul and John as exponents of the kerygma of the Hellenistic Church.

Bultmann treats Paul as a representative of Hellenistic Christianity, but not as an average representative. He must be regarded as one of the creative influences. He was a Hellenistic Jew of Tarsus who was won to the Christian faith by the kerygma of the Hellenistic Church. Consequently he took over the kerygma of the Hellenistic Church. In so doing he subjected it to his own considerable theological powers of reflection. This theological understanding has its origin in faith and speaks of man from this perspective, man prior to faith and man in faith. The mythological tendencies of Hellenistic Christianity were thus held in check while at the same time use was made of Gnostic language and concepts to portray the significance of Christ for the believer. Paul taught that Christ paradoxically freed the believer from the dominion of the world by enabling him to live in true freedom for the world. Hence, for Paul, the idea of creation was not lost, though he was able to recognize the believer's alienation in the world. The paradoxical nature of faith was also maintained in the affirmation that, while redemption was a present reality, its fulfilment awaited the future. At this point Paul had not radically demythologized Jewish apocalyptic eschatology; this task was only carried through consistently by John.

Johannine Christianity is also seen as representative of Hellenistic Christianity in a form distinct from the Synoptic Gospels and Paul. Johannine Christianity has its origin in a form of Judaism saturated by Gnosticism (*Th.N.T.*, II, pp. 6, 13). The Gospel also appears to have been shaped in the conflict with the Jews (though this aspect is not adequately recognized by Bultmann), perhaps indicating a phase in the history of Hellenistic Jewish Christianity. But in its final form it is an expression of Hellenistic Christianity (*RGG*, p. 845). John, like Paul, made use of the Gnostic myth with its conceptions and terminology. By writing a Gospel the myth was more obviously *historicized*, being embedded in the life of Jesus.

John, like Paul, reinterprets the Gnostic understanding of the unworldly character (*Unweltlichkeit*) of human life and like Paul directs this life back into the world. Here John's distinctive contribution is to affirm that all that the world searches for is in fact truly to be found only in the Revealer, in Jesus. Hence Gnostic cosmological dualism becomes a decision dualism in John. In this way John too safeguards the understanding of creation while affirming the 'unworldly' character of true life which, paradoxically, is to be lived in the world in love, not found in escape from the world in ecstasy.

This more extended treatment of Hellenistic Christianity is given in recognition that Bultmann considered the relation to Hellenism to be decisive for the emergence of Christianity. Even Judaism was mediated to Christianity in its Hellenistic form. But more important, it was Hellenism, especially Gnosticism, which provided the concepts in which the kerygma could be expressed adequately.

g. Development Towards the Ancient Church (Early Catholicism?)

Again and again throughout his treatment of the Earliest Church and the Hellenistic Church Bultmann raised questions on various issues asking whether a genuine understanding of the kerygma and faith would be maintained or whether this would be lost in tendencies which were already emerging. From the Earliest Church certain tendencies call for comment. Would the awareness of being the eschatological community find theological expression? Would the tendency to remain a sect in Judaism be overcome? Would the apocalyptic-eschatological framework be modified to take account of the fact that the Messiah had already appeared? How would the community maintain itself through history? Already there were tendencies towards the recognition of an authoritative tradition, 'apostolic' leadership and the authority of the 'elders'. Thus the question had already been posed concerning the living authority of the kerygma *or* a formal institutional authority. These questions were not settled by Hellenistic Christianity. The prolongation of the two possibilities probably was increased with the development of cultic, sacramental Christianity. On the other hand both Paul and John saw their way through these problems to affirm the authority of the kerygma and the freedom of faith.

The answers of Paul and John were not easily reconciled with the emerging 'orthodoxy' of the Ancient Church which, in the fight against Gnosticism, developed dogmas, an authoritative scripture, an institution with its priests and sacraments. In this Church the apocalyptic-eschatology of the Earliest Church also survived. It is against this background that Bultmann argues that the ecclesiastical redactor modified the Fourth Gospel in order to make it acceptable to the Ancient Church. The modifications took the form of introducing apocalyptic eschatology, a sacramental interpretation of baptism and the Lord's Supper and an authoritative witness guaranteed by the Beloved disciple. Much the same could be said about the treatment of Paul in Acts and in the Pastoral Epistles.[74]

h. The Purpose of Historical Reconstruction

The purpose of historical reconstruction is understanding. If texts are to be understood they must be understood in their own context. Much of this has already been said in relation to the 'historical method'. Consequently it is important to understand the historical development of Christianity in order that the various texts should be accurately placed.

Bultmann's own reconstruction confirms Walter Bauer's view of the diversity of Primitive Christianity out of which an orthodoxy developed towards the end of the first century. A naive view might suggest that what we have here is a single straight line of development from Jesus to orthodoxy. In fact the diversity of 'Primitive' Christianity allows no such straightforward view. Even this would entail placing the various texts at some point on the line of development. However, apart from being able to distinguish the Earliest Church from the Hellenistic Church and the tendencies towards the development of the 'Ancient Church', Bultmann stresses diversity in the Earliest Church which continued and passed into the life of the Hellenistic churches under the varying influences of their time and context such as the synagogue, mystery cults, Gnosticism and Hellenistic philosophy. An understanding of the course of development enabled Bultmann to uncover the sources employed by the Fourth evangelist and to detect the process of redaction by means of which that Gospel was made acceptable to the Great Church. Likewise the reconstruction throws light on the sources used by Paul and helps to distinguish his genuine letters from others that were later circulated in his name. Naturally there is room for different opinions in this reconstruction.

While Bultmann admits that a *synchronic diversity* must be recognized in 'Primitive' Christianity he also argues that there is a *diachronic unity*. Put more simply, from the first and at any given time Christianity has never been uniform. In the beginning there was no orthodoxy. That diversity does not, however, mean that there were no historical developments, only a perpetuation of diversity. Rather it is the case that underlying tendencies in the beginning became dominant characteristics by the end of the century and altogether new understandings of beliefs and practices also emerged in the course of time. All of this raises the question of whether any belief and practice can be called Christian in the light of the recognition that 'orthodoxy' was a 'late' development. Bultmann's reconstruction is a response to the problems raised by this question.

From earliest Christianity onward Bultmann asserts that there emerged a new understanding of existence, existence in faith or eschatological existence. Even the earliest community was aware of being the eschatological community though it had not adequately taken account of this in the apocalyptic form of its proclamation. The awareness of this underlying unity, which could be expressed in various forms, such as that of Jewish apocalyptic or Gnostic myth, suggests a line of response to the problems created by the recognition that 'orthodoxy' does not belong to the beginning of Christianity. It is the task of historical reconstruction, which creates the problems by putting the existence of an original orthodoxy in question, that also provides an answer by revealing the underlying unity in the diversity of Primitive Christianity.

Finally, historical reconstruction can serve the purpose of allowing an 'encounter' with history to occur (*Jesus*, p. 13). Such an encounter, when it is with the history in which the *kerygma* is embedded, allows for the possibility that the one so encountered by the text will enter into the eschatological life proclaimed by the text. But, as Bultmann notes, all he can do is indicate that this was so for himself. Whether it will be so for another only that person can say (*Jesus*, pp. 13f.). Thus we have returned to the important recognition that what Bultmann identifies as essential to Christianity is the new life of faith which is claimed as an expression of the 'new life' which emerged in history. That history, with which it is inseparably associated, is bound up with the *kerygma* which proclaims the historical event of Jesus to be God's saving eschatological event.

Bultmann's historical work was addressed to two questions. First, what was the early Christian proclamation according to the New Testament? Second, how did the New Testament writers come to know what they proclaimed and what does it mean? The second question reminds us of Bultmann's epistemological concern. An analysis of the teaching of the New Testament only begins the task. What this does is to reveal the diverse ways in which Jesus was proclaimed from the beginning of Christianity. Some account needs to be given of that diversity. Bultmann's account appeals to the various traditions, with their characteristic conceptions, by means of which the early Christians expressed their proclamation. It has been the purpose of the presentation of his reconstruction of the history of Christianity in the first century to indicate how he understood this process. What the early Christians proclaimed, in their varying fashions, was that Jesus was the bringer of salvation.

The second question asks how Jesus was known to be the bringer of salvation. Bultmann's answer asserts that he was recognized as such by those who came to believe in him, who came to know his salvation (his benefits). The varying ways in which the bringer of salvation was confessed are due to the variety of cultural contexts. What they say of Jesus, in various ways, is that salvation is known and received through faith in him.

Obviously this position depends on Bultmann's reconstruction of the development of early Christianity, which began with the Easter faith, was expressed in terms of Jewish apocalyptic, then in terms of Gnosticism, and in the Ancient Church the expressions of both of these forms were interpreted dogmatically. This dogmatic interpretation provided the basis for 'orthodoxy'.

Not all historians will agree with Bultmann's reconstruction. Indeed his position is sometimes criticized in a way that suggests that the critic occupies some independent position of objectivity. Is such a position possible? perhaps by taking the New Testament simply as it is? But the New Testament is a *collection* of writings which are not self-evidently uniform. The fact that the collection exists is the result of a struggle in the early Church. The collection had its defenders, for instance Irenaeus. But it was also attacked from early times by Marcion, for example, and particular books now included were contested by such pillars of orthodoxy as Eusebius (Revelation) and Luther (James, Revelation). The *canon* was a consequence of a struggle in the Church. By bringing these books together the church declared that they belonged together. But to exist together as a unity they had to be read in terms of the dogmas of the Church.

Bultmann's challenge concerns the question of the canon. How are unity and diversity in the New Testament to be handled? Historically or dogmatically? For those who are not content to follow the line of a developing tradition of interpretation the only way would seem to be to follow Bultmann, either in accepting his reconstruction, or working out a more satisfactory understanding than was possible for him. It is not enough to criticize his view at this point or that if a more convincing reconstruction is not offered.

i. **History and Theology**

Bultmann's reconstruction of the history of Primitive Christianity has a considerable bearing on his theology. It provides him with the paradigm for his understanding of the intention of the New Testament authors in terms of the new life of faith brought by the Christ event. That paradigm is also basic to his understanding of the way the kerygma is translated from one conceptual framework to another and must continue to be translated if it is to be understood. Such understanding is the task of hermeneutical theology. It opens up conceptual understanding, which provides the opportunity for existential understanding, when the word about God becomes the Word of God, the Word from God.

We need now to stress the importance of Bultmann's theology for his understanding of history. The process is an illustration of the hermeneutical circle. Naturally, Bultmann the historian does not renounce Bultmann the theologian. Nor does Bultmann the theologian think without the influence of the study of the historical tradition which began with Jesus, who himself stood within the Jewish tradition, which is also seen as an historical tradition intertwined with other traditions in the ancient world. The historian - theologian, in Bultmann's case - was committed to critical historical methodology. In general terms that methodology is the common heritage of critical historians in the twentieth century. Not all such historians are Christians. According to Bultmann, however, this should not influence the use of methods. It could influence views concerning what is or is not possible. Indeed, Bultmann's understanding of God and the world should be seen in this way. God and world stand in a relation in which the understanding of the one implies a particular understanding of the other. It is a moot point whether Bultmann's understanding of the world has influenced his understanding of God's transcendence with consequences for his understanding of God's act.

Chapter Three

Signals of Transcendence

Synopsis

Bultmann's understanding of transcendence is the basis for his recognition of the difficulty of speaking of God. How can anything of meaning be said of him? Why then does man speak of God? What gives rise to the question of God, and how are the various answers to this question to be understood from the perspective of Christian faith? Bultmann understands these answers as myths. But myth is itself a notorious problem in the writings of Bultmann. The problem involves both definition and evaluation. An understanding of Bultmann's position is not possible without this distinction. In his understanding of myth Bultmann is not far from Eliade, Jung and Tillich, though his definition is more restrictive than theirs. But it is in his evaluation of myth that the distinctive nature of his position becomes clear. His evaluation is based on his understanding of the kerygma which is intimately related to his own ontological position and has three aspects: the transcendence of God and his revelation; the order of the world and its inner-causality; the freedom of man and his openness to the future. In Bultmann's mature position his existentialist interpretation of the kerygma is made the basis for his critique of myth. From this perspective myths are recognized as responses to 'signals' of transcendence. But the signal has become obscured in 'this-worldly' objectification common to all myths. Even so, the kerygma, which is the expression of the transcendent Word of revelation, can be expressed in mythological terms. It is this that makes demythologizing both complex and controversial.

Evocative Epigram

> God's existence is questioned today. But our problem is not simply to cope with this question. There remains the struggle of a different kind with the insecurity of human existence, which has existed from time immemorial. And since the emergence of modern, rational man, there has been an almost desperate struggle with the problem of human certainty. Where, we wonder, is there a rocklike, unshakable certainty on which all human certainty could be built?
>
> HANS KÜNG, *Does God Exist?*, p. 1.

Chapter Three

SIGNALS OF TRANSCENDENCE

1. **Defining 'Religion'**

Defining what we mean by 'religion' is a notorious problem (see Tracy, pp. 156ff.). Empirical studies tend to shatter theories concerning a common 'essence' and even a Wittgensteinian approach to family traits is hardly satisfactory as there is no single trait which is common to all so-called religions (see Edwards, *R&R*, pp. 15ff.). In spite of this problem it seems to be necessary, or at least expedient, to speak of 'religion', because there is something which makes the category 'religion' meaningful as a description of this diverse set of phenomena. This brings us back to the basic question as to what this something is. Attempts to discover a common 'experience' have met with as little success as the attempted definition of a common essence.

In his *Speeches on Religion* and *The Christian Faith*[75] Friedrich Schleiermacher attempted to define religion in terms of 'the feeling of absolute dependence', a description which has been widely misunderstood. The words 'feeling' and 'dependence' have been troublesome, especially where 'absolute' has been ignored in its qualification of 'dependence'. Hegel suggested that, given this definition, a dog would be the most religious animal. This caricature not only ignores the '*absolute* dependence', it does violence to Schleiermacher's understanding of 'feeling'. Clearly, he was referring to what we might call 'existential awareness'.[76] In so doing he developed what could be seen as an existentialist interpretation of Anselm's ontological argument. Such an approach hardly demonstrates the existence of God in any way. It simply shows how and why the question of God arises. Schleiermacher himself did not make this distinction but it becomes crucial for Bultmann. For Schleiermacher the essence of religion is positively identified with the feeling of absolute dependence. His interpretation prepares the way for Schubert Ogden's interpretation of 'original revelation' which is developed differently by Bultmann.[77]

The identification of the essence of religion with what can be described broadly as experience is also important for the work of Rudolf Otto.[78] He taught that religions have developed as a consequence of the rationalizing of man's experience of the *numinous*, for which some men have a greater faculty or sensitivity. All speaking of this experience is regarded as the rationalizing of what is essentially non-rational. At Marburg Otto was one of Bultmann's colleagues and the controversy between them was extremely lively ('AR', in Kegley, p. xxii). Bultmann rejects both the notion of a special religious faculty and the idea of specific religious experience (*EPT*, pp. 135, 137).

Paul Tillich's definition[79] in terms of *ultimate concern* is also in the Schleiermacher tradition. From the existential point of view, religion is that which concerns us ultimately, our top priority. For many people, what concerns them ultimately (e.g. money, football) is not an *ultimate* concern. To treat as ultimate that which is not is idolatry, false religion. Only the ultimate should concern us ultimately. Had Tillich at this point developed his distinction of question and answer, the existential raising of the question (questions about the meaning of the mystery of life in the world) and the ontological answer given in the revelation, he would have been moving in the same direction as Bultmann.

For Bultmann there is no suggestion of a common essence in all religions or a common experience underlying all. His approach does full justice to diversities and differences. What then can religions have in common? What they have in common is not what they are, rather it is what *constitutes* them, that is, what, in some sense, causes them. They are constituted by what Bultmann calls man's quest or search for life, authentic life, which man glimpses somehow and is aware of without possessing. This awareness, without possession, constitutes the quest or search for something more.

2. **Man's Search - for God?**

Bultmann saw a precedent for his position in some words from Augustine to which he appealed on a number of occasions.

> O God, you have made us for yourself, and the heart of man is restless till it finds its rest in you (*JCM*, p. 52; *EPT*, pp. 257f.; *K&M*, I, p. 192; Kegley, p. 275).

He assumed that this implied that the search for life and the search for God are identical, or, perhaps more precisely, that those who search for life are in reality, whether they know it or not, searching for God (*JCM*, p. 53). Of course this is a Christian understanding of the search, an understanding which is influenced by the supposed answer to the search, namely, God (*EPT*, pp. 90-98, 257f.; *JCM*, pp. 52f.; *FU*, pp. 53-65, 318ff.).

To exist is to search for an answer to the question of what it means to exist. But this quest or search can be answered in different ways as the multiplicity of religions forcefully demonstrates. The universality of the search is, for this discussion, more significant than the diversity of answers. That universality can be spoken of in the context of the understanding of man as *possibility*. What man is is not self-evident, and it is important for man to have some understanding of himself. But what man is is not fixed, determined. Man is aware of possibilities. In which of these will he find or lose himself? This is the double basis for the search, that man is driven to understand himself, but what he is is not fixed, it is something to be discovered in the possibilities of human existence.

If man is depicted as one who seeks, this is only part of the picture. In his search man is driven to find some answer to his question about 'happiness', 'the meaning of the world and of history'. The existence of the great variety of religions attests not only to the fact that man is a 'seeker'. It indicates that the seeker must find some answer to his question. What unites religions is that they are all responses to the inquiry about the nature of human life. That inquiry is frequently carried out in terms of those elements which are fundamental to sheer physical life—bread, water and light, which are universal religious symbols. In the great historic religions of the world the question about life goes beyond the concern to sustain sheer physical life. Those fundamental elements of the physical world remain central, but in a way that enables them to point beyond themselves. The reason for this is the inadequacy of sheer physical life. That it comes to an end is problem enough, without taking account of the question of the quality of life, which becomes central in the religious quest for the 'authentic life'. How this is conceived varies in the different traditions, often using similar symbols. However it is conceived, the search for it is the common constituitive element in the various religions.

While there is no great problem in understanding how and why the search for authentic life is alive in human existence generally, the diversity of responses poses a more complex problem. Various solutions are possible. If man is to be understood as 'possibility', might not authentic existence be anything that man *chooses for himself*? After all, man has no fixed being. Why should it not be (as for some existentialists) that authenticity should be defined simply in terms of what man chooses for himself? Such a position would be possible apart from belief in God.

If the various religions give such different responses to the question about the meaning of life what follows? All responses might be wrong; there might be no such meaning. All responses might be partially right and partially wrong. Some responses might be more adequate than others. Only one response might be true. The situation has been stated hypothetically. It is not possible to do more than this because there is no *known* objective standard outside the situation of conflicting beliefs and opinions. Because of this a relativism of values pervades the thought of the western world. We should also recognize that there are also non-religious answers to the question raised by human life. But there would be no religious answers without the existential question.

From the perspective of faith in response to the revelation Bultmann asserts that the search for life and happiness is the search for God. Further it is his view that: 'outside the revelation man is always a seeker' (*GJ*, p. 378), because pseudo-answers do not satisfy man's longing. From this perspective Bultmann explores Christian faith in relation to both the search and the answer. This approach does not provide a methodology for the study of religions. It is rather to be seen as a Christian interpretation of other religions on the basis of the recognition of the absoluteness and finality of the revelation in Christ.

> *The Christian belief therefore criticises* on the basis of its knowledge not the *non-Christian inquiry about God—it can only penetrate into it and illuminate it—but first of all the answers which the non-Christian enquiry constructs* . . . It asserts that *all answers* apart from the Christian answer are *illusions* (*EPT*, p. 98; cf. *FU*, pp. 264, 319f.; *GJ*, p. 530).

The ancient hopes, dreams, and myths appear to have a seductive and tenacious power over the minds of men. Bultmann's stress on the role of the modern scientific world view might suggest that, as far as he was concerned, such hopes, dreams, myths could be of no significance. This is not the case. They should not have any power over the minds of men. Even today, however, not every person, perhaps not even the majority of people, is guided by the knowledge based on modern science. There are many surviving varieties of superstition (*K&M*, I, p. 5 n. 1). Bultmann was well aware of this. Had he not been so from the beginning, the violence of the demythologizing debate would soon have made him aware. His debate with Karl Jaspers had, as one of its major issues, the question of whether myth was or was not indispensable. Hence it is naive to suggest that Bultmann was unaware of the continuing power of myth. Bultmann's so called 'modern man' is what we call an *ideal type* rather than the average twentieth-century man. As an *ideal type* he is man guided by the knowledge based on modern science. The fact that myths and dreams are sustained in the face of such knowledge is an indication of their power over the minds of men.

Bultmann asserts that '*all answers* apart from the Christian answer are illusions'. From one point of view such illusions can be said to be a consequence of the fact that man 'twists his negative knowledge into a positive knowledge ...' (*EPT*, p. 115), that is, he turns his question into an answer, his not knowing into knowledge. Why does man do this? In agreement with Ludwig Feuerbach Bultmann says that myths are a form of 'wish fulfilment'. This association with Feuerbach is explicit in response to the question of what it means when other religions speak of God or to God (*FU*, pp. 318f.). What they speak of or to is an '*illusion*'. However, unmasking the illusion is only part of the task. Bultmann also asks, 'what is meant by the illusion?' To this question all sorts of answers are possible and are hidden in the speaking of God. Such speech can be seen as an expression of man's flight from himself, from the responsibilities of existence, from his own being disclosed in anxiety (*Angst*) (*AET*, p. 65). Bultmann expresses this view concisely in *FU*, pp. 318-22 (see also *GJ*, pp. 61f.). In addition to the stress on the role of anxiety in this passage a number of other points are made, the importance of which can be brought out in the following statements. While the search does not establish the reality of the God of the revelation, without the search the revelation of God would be unintelligible. However, in as much as the search becomes a finding, the revelation is in opposition to it. This contradiction is to be seen as the point of contact which the revelation creates.

Unbelieving existence *always* turns the question into an answer

(*FU*, p. 323; *EPT*, p. 115), it treats not knowing as knowing, preunderstanding as understanding. Such understanding is an illusion, a fantasy. This radical, pessimistic anthropology is traced by Bultmann through Paul to Jesus. The problem lies with *man* who 'twists his negative knowledge into a positive knowledge'. To be human is to search. What is more, there is revelation in creation which would give man knowledge of God *if* he continued to search and did not twist his question into an answer. But because man is a sinner this possibility remains unfulfilled, apart from the judging and gracious Word of revelation (*EPT*, pp. 114f.; *GJ*, pp. 61f.).

The fact that *man* always twists his negative knowledge into positive knowledge is an indication of man's sin which is the point of *contact* with the contradicting Word of grace, the revelation. The revelation contradicts man in his whole existence (*EPT*, p. 137) because his life is built on a lie, a false understanding of himself (*GJ*, p. 317). For this reason 'the revelation consists in a calling into question of the natural man' (*GJ*, p. 317); it is a word of contradiction, of judgment. Paradoxically it is also a word of grace and life. The necessity of this paradox is nowhere more clearly stated than in Bultmann's work on the Fourth Gospel, where he expounds the way the revelation takes the form of judgment. In the 'I am ...' statements, as understood by Bultmann, Jesus presents himself as the one for whom all men are searching (*GJ*, p. 225). This is both an affirmation of the validity of all searches and a rejection of all answers which are not found in him. Man who is driven in his search, implicit or explicit, is confronted by the word of the Revealer, 'I am he, for whom you seek' (*GJ*, p. 364, and p. 107 n. 2; see also *TDNT*, I, pp. 871f.). The revelation resonates in the lives of those who respond to the contradiction and hear the new word that it speaks as a new possibility for human life.

Because the revelation is absolute and intolerant in its demands on man, there is no room for the believer to adjust the demands it makes on him. Because all men are seekers, all he can ask of others is that they seek honestly, and attempt to understand their seeking, and that they in turn should recognize his search and what he understands, and the way he understands himself. This position is forcefully set out in *GJ*, pp. 378ff. Whether the security of faith, to which Bultmann refers as a security which the believer has in believing, is well based or not each one will decide for himself. For Bultmann, as a Christian, such faith has its basis in the reality outside the believer, that is, in God.

Because man is aware that he is not what he wills to be, an inner necessity drives him to speak of God, the transcendent ground to which the order and reality of the world also point. There is some relation between the life which man seeks and the transcendent source of life to which the world somehow points (*GJ*, p. 182). Upon this relation is based the analogy between the life which man has (with the means by which it is sustained) and the authentic life for which he searches. That which sustains earthly life is used to point beyond itself to the transcendent source of authentic life. The world is a *storehouse* of symbols because man *perceives* the world as pointing beyond itself to whatever is conceived as the source of authentic life. While the symbols are universal, the understanding of the symbols varies according to whatever is conceived as 'salvation' or authentic life. This varies from tradition to tradition. The universality of the symbols corresponds to the universality of the search, while the variety of interpretations or meanings expresses the different answers given by the various religious traditions.[80] But only in the revelation do the symbols actually communicate knowledge of the *transcendent creator* of all things.

For Bultmann, God's act, the revelation event, is to be found exclusively in the Christ event into which the kerygma is caught up. Not all contemporary Christian approaches are in agreement with this position. The 'process theology' of Schubert Ogden, based on the writings of Charles Hartshorne, could be seen as a significant alternative. The development by Ogden was worked out with the intention of overcoming problems in Bultmann's theology. Three such problems are the claims concerning: 1. the exclusive nature of revelation in the Christ event; 2. the illusory nature of the answers given in the religions of the world apart from Christian faith; and 3. the identification of authentic existence with Christian faith.

Ogden's understanding is derived from his understanding of God. He argues that God's relation to the world should be understood on the basis of the analogy of the relation of mind and body. Everything that happens is an act of God. But this is not necessarily recognized. In this regard the Christ event is of *decisive* significance. It is decisive because it persistently reveals God's action and is the criterion for recognizing God's action everywhere. In most ways this view is hardly distinguishable from Bultmann's (see *JCM*, pp. 71, 78f.). There are differences. The revelation is decisively but not exclusively effective in the Christ event. Positive, real knowledge of God is to be found outside Christian faith. Such a view provides possibilities for dialogue in the encounter of world religions. But is it true to Christian faith? Bultmann would argue that it is not true to the intention of the New Testament authors. However, Ogden argues that Bultmann's view is inconsistent with the New Testament understanding of the universality of God.[81]

John Robinson's *The Human Face of God* presents a position quite similar to Ogden's in many ways. The interpretation of the New Testament evidence gives this book an importance of its own, especially the treatment of the Johannine witness to the incarnation of the *Logos*. Robinson's interpretation can be seen in relation to Ogden's position and should be understood as a 'process christology'. The *Logos*, which is everywhere present, was decisively present in Jesus who can be thought of as a decisive mutation, in the realm of the Spirit, in the process of world becoming. In his interpretation of the incarnation as a decisive 'mutation' Robinson's interpretation goes beyond Ogden's in the direction of Bultmann. The analogy from the field of biology is powerful but deceptive. How it is to be understood needs careful elaboration. But this is not given. The appearance of Jesus, according to Robinson, opens up the possibility revealed in his life, to those who follow him. How does this new 'mutation' transmit itself? Is it a mutation in the world of ideas? The details of Robinson's position call for further clarification. However, his book is a constructive attempt to say how christology remains decisive and definitive while taking Jesus' humanity seriously and recognizing truth and value in human life in the world in the variety of forms that it takes. For Robinson, the difference between Jesus and other people is one of degree. The *Logos* was more fully expressed in his life than others and his life is somehow instrumental in its fulfilment in the lives of those who followed him. Because of this Jesus plays a permanent and decisive role in the birth of the new humanity.

For Bultmann, God's act in Christ was both decisive and definitive as for Ogden and Robinson. But for him, in a way quite different from either of them, the Christ event is *the* 'act of God' *to save* humanity, to save the world. Because of this, for him, apart from faith the world is in the darkness of death. It does not know God. In the Christ event the believer comes to know God.

3. **To Speak of God**

Bultmann's understanding of God is the key to the understanding of his hermeneutical theology. In the light of this his view of the two histories becomes clear and the importance of this view for his reconstruction of the origin and history of 'Primitive Christianity' becomes apparent. The *transcendence* of God is the key to his theology (Ogden, in *EF*, p. 14). God is the 'Wholly Other' (*TBDT*, p. 234; *FU*, pp. 55ff., 60ff.; Johnson, p. 64). However, transcendence is a complex concept. It involves the invisibility of God, his visible absence from the world. It excludes the possibility of God's interventions in the natural and historical order of the world and this view is confirmed by Bultmann's understanding of the modern scientific *Weltbild*, the *Weltbild* that seems self-evident to us today (*K&M*, I, p. 33) though it is open to revision (*JCM*, pp. 37f.; *FU*, p. 59; *K&M*, I, p. 3; II, pp. 118, 181). But even more important is 'the infinite qualitative distinction' between time and eternity. This can be characterized as the distinction between man the sinner, the sinful world and the holy God (*EPT*, p. 153; 'AR', in Kegley, p. xxiv; *Th.N.T.*, II, p. 239).

Because of the transcendence of God knowledge of God would seem to be impossible. Pre-understanding as some kind of awareness of the absence of God is understandable but there seems to be no room for knowledge of God. It is for this reason that the revelation event *as revelation* is 'new history' in which the 'otherness' of the revelation can be preserved while at the same time affirming actual revelation. Bultmann's understanding of the transcendence of God is qualified by the belief that actual revelation occurs in Jesus Christ, and that an actual relation is created between God and the believer through the revelation.

Paradoxically the revelation, which preserves the otherness of God, encounters man in the world. But this point of contact (*Anknüpfung*) can only be the contradiction (*Widerspruch*) in which man as a sinner finds himself in relation to the revelation (*JCM*, p. 40; *GV*, II, p. 120; *EPT*, pp. 133-150). It is because man is a sinner that God encounters him as 'Wholly Other'.

Paradoxically, to speak of God, the 'Wholly Other', man speaks of himself. But this is not to be understood as a projection or as 'wish fulfilment' in terms of religion as criticized by Feuerbach, though this is Barth's criticism of Bultmann (*KD*, III, 2 [1948], pp. 534f.), a criticism repeated in different terms by Roberts (p. 257). Bultmann rejected the association of his thought with Feuerbach (*JCM*, pp. 70ff.; *EPT*, p. 260). Ironically, Bultmann's criticism of the answers of religions apart from the Christian answer was that they are 'illusions' (*EPT*, p. 98). Bultmann himself claimed to speak of God, not just of man (*FU*, p. 29; *EPT*, p. 98). But he could only speak of God in relation to man, he could only speak of God on the basis of the revelation.

Bultmann distinguished speaking about God from speaking of or from God (*FU*, pp. 53-65). Speaking about God is possible on the basis of pre-understanding, on the basis of the search for God. Because of the question about God the concept of God is meaningful. But to know the concept is not the same as knowing God. The distinction is important for Bultmann though his own use of language is not completely consistent with it (*JCM*, pp. 52f.). Only on the basis of the revelation is it possible to speak of God, from God. The revelation is the revelation of God *to man*. For this reason to speak of God man must speak of himself in *relation* to God. It is an illusion when knowledge about God is treated as knowledge of God. Such knowledge is used to reinforce man's self-understanding. Consequently the revelation must overthrow man's understanding of himself, the world and God (*FU*, pp. 29, 46, 55, 61; *EPT*, pp. 96ff.; Roberts, pp. 247f.).

The distinction between speaking about God and speaking of or from God is set out in an essay in *FU* (pp. 53-65). The essay itself is ambiguous on a number of points but can be clarified by reference to other essays. Briefly, speech about God is possible because we understand the concept. But it is inappropriate because if God is not, it is meaningless; if he is, it is sin because it is a way of speaking which stands outside of faith. Speech of and from God is only possible if God reveals himself and in the response of faith the believer speaks from God. Such speech is beyond human control. Only if God reveals himself is such speech possible. But how does man 'encounter' God, the 'Wholly Other'?

Bultmann's understanding of revelation also presupposes God as 'Wholly Other'. Only that which is 'other' can make man other. In theory the encounter with the neighbour in history provides man with a basis to become other than he is. Because of this the understanding of history opens up the possibilities of existence. But such encounters do not in fact make man other because the 'Wholly Other' is not encountered in history generally. Nevertheless, faith grows out of such encounters in which the claim of the neighbour is heard, because it is in this way that the Word of God addresses man

(*JCM*, pp. 71f.). But God's Word is beyond the believer's control (*JCM*, p. 71).

Because God is 'Wholly Other' there is no continuity between the world and God, man and God, history and God. His presence cannot be demonstrated from any of these. It is because man is a sinner that no continuity can be seen. Consequently the revelation must overthrow man's understanding of himself, the world and God. The word of the cross both preserves the paradox of the revelation (an historical event is the eschatological event) because in the cross life is revealed, and negates man's self-understanding and seems to negate reason. In this word/event the otherness of God is preserved. In this event man is called on to decide whether he will give up his claim on himself, the world, and God because the revelation of God, the 'Wholly Other, can make man other, can give him authentic existence (*K&M*, II, p. 201; Malet, pp. 19f.).

Because God is 'Wholly Other' there is no continuity between God and this world. The cross is a negation of this world. Faith is a miracle because 'We can believe in God only in spite of experience' (*JCM*, p. 84). This miracle in response to the Word of revelation moves the world of sin off its axis so that it becomes again God's world, the creation.

The 'encounter' with the revelation is contrasted with 'experience' by Bultmann. The reason for this is the suspicion of the word 'experience' which might be totally subjective. Bultmann stresses the reality of the encounter with the revelation, or perhaps better, with the Revealer. His use of the language of 'encounter' falls between what Frederick Ferre (*Language Logic and God*) has called 'the logic of obedience' and 'the logic of encounter'. The 'encounter' is a matter of faith, not experience. In the 'encounter' the believer responds in obedience to the demand which is laid on him in the situation which is expressed in love to the neighbour and responsibility for the world.

What is 'experienced' is the new life which is a consequence of faith in the Revealer who is believed to have been encountered in the proclamation. The charge that Bultmann has reduced everything to self-understanding is *almost* correct. But Bultmann affirms that the self-understanding of faith is a consequence of the encounter with the Revealer. Outside the community of faith this conviction is called an illusion. Is such faith based on an illusion? We can only answer in faith or unbelief. Outside faith the decision of faith appears to be based on an improbability but faith is convinced 'in spite of experience'. Whatever evidence there is lies hidden except for faith (*JCM*, pp. 61f., 64, 71). The believer is convinced that it is God who has given him new life.

The language of encounter/obedience used by Bultmann is based on the analogy of personal encounter. It needs further clarification. Schubert Ogden has developed lines of interpretation which clarify the meaning of analogy by relating God's action in relation to the world to the analogy of the relation of mind to body. Bultmann's intention was to maintain the analogy of personal relations and this involves taking seriously the understanding that Jesus really is risen and encounters the believer in the kerygma bringing him new life. What is experienced is the new life. What is believed is that Jesus is risen and through him the believer has new life. Yet the resurrection of Jesus was not a physical event in history as the crucifixion was. Through and in that history God acted to bring new life to the believer who believes in Jesus risen. But faith cannot *demonstrate* that Jesus is risen or that he has brought new life.

The understanding of the transcendence of God is the key for the separation of the kerygma from myth. That view of transcendence is reinforced by 'the modern scientific *Weltbild*'. On the basis of this understanding Bultmann has developed three criteria (which constitute his ontology), for his criticism of mythology. They are the transcendence of God, the order of the world, and the freedom and responsibility of man (*K&M*, I, p. 11; *JCM*, pp. 83f.; *Th.N.T.*, II, p. 238). These criteria are used in the criticism of the biblical language. It is important that the three criteria be recognized because the recognition of the order of the world in the modern scientific *Weltbild* has destroyed the awareness of transcendence and puts the awareness of freedom in question (*K&M*, I, pp. 10f.). The question might well be asked whether this *Weltbild* has influenced Bultmann's understanding of transcendence. Does transcendence exclude the idea of God's intervention in the world? Is the idea of such intervention myth?

How are we to understand myth and mythology?[82] How adequate is Bultmann's treatment of this subject? It is frequently asserted that his attitude to myth is wholly negative. This is hardly surprising in the light of his demythologizing programme which has attracted so much attention. Concentration on this controversial aspect of his work has tended to obscure his description of the function of myth which is expressed in so much of his work. In fact, the negative evaluation should be seen to apply to one limited point of view. How does authentic Christian faith evaluate myth? From this perspective alone does Bultmann call for demythologizing, because myth obscures authentic Christian faith. Even from this point of view some myths offer more valuable insights than others. Gnostic myth shows much more affinity to Christian faith than most other forms of mythology. This complexity is frequently overlooked in discussions of this subject. However, the critics are generally right in the assertion that Bultmann offers no systematic treatment of mythology as a basis for his programme. In this context he limits himself to a few scattered descriptive statements which are often taken to be inconsistent (Dunn, *NTI*, pp. 292, 297; Johnson, pp. 7ff.). Whether the statements are inconsistent or not will need to be discussed and attention will be drawn to his more positive description of myth in contexts not dealing with demythologizing. Further, Malet's claim (p. 46 n. 9) that Bultmann's talk of *demythologizing* should not be confused with demythicizing will need to be assessed.

In concentrating on the demythologizing programme the debate has tended to set Bultmann squarely against a growing positive evaluation of myth. At first sight, his approach appears to be out of step with those who find myth to be an essential facet of religion, for example Karl Jaspers,[83] C.G. Jung,[84] M. Heidegger,[85] M. Eliade,[86] P. Tillich,[87] etc. (thus Thiselton, p. 256). This is a false impression. What distinguishes Bultmann from the others named is *not so much* his understanding of myth and its functions as his *evaluation* of myth and the distinction he makes between Christian faith and the religions of the world. That is not to say that there are no differences of understanding, but to note that the differences are not as great as generally thought on account of the confusion of evaluation with understanding. Bultmann's evaluation of myth is a consequence of his understanding of Christian faith, rather than his understanding of myth.

4. **Myth and Religion**

While Bultmann does not write about the significance of myth as such, it is possible to reconstruct his views from clues which appear from time to time. These are even more fragmentary than the scattered statements which provide such definition of the nature of myth as he finds necessary to give. His definitions are used to identify those elements in need of demythologizing. Bultmann's understanding of the significance of myth must be discovered elsewhere. His understanding of man is relevant to this problem.

Man exists in the world in which his meaning and significance are not self-evident. In fact, meaning and purpose can only be asserted over against the threat of chaos and meaninglessness. The threat of chaos and meaninglessness find expression in fundamental human anxiety (*Angst*). Awareness of the source of this *Angst*, and the human response attempting to cope with it, are two aspects of the significance of myth. We could say that myth is man's response to 'the chaos of experience', his attempt to perceive order in the chaos (Frankfort, p. 11). The awareness of the chaos evokes the anxiety which man seeks to silence by one means or another (Zuurdeeg, p. 162).

Bultmann's discussion with Karl Jaspers throws considerable light on his understanding of myth (see *K&M*, II, pp. 185f. = *M&C*, pp. 61f.). First, myths are 'ciphers' of transcendence, 'signals' of man's awareness of 'the ground and limits of his being', that he stands before the threat of chaos and meaninglessness. Such awareness of this is evident in all myths.

Second, mythological traditions are diverse (Indian, Greek, Biblical) and that diversity is not a matter of indifference. The common awareness of transcendence is the shared pre-understanding while the diversity of actual mythologies is a consequence of the actual understanding constructed on the basis of the question of transcendence. In Bultmann's terms the signal of transcendence is in man's experience of finitude, his encounter with the threat of meaninglessness, the enigma of existence. In man's anxiety (*Angst*) there is a signal of transcendence if man will listen to it. This is one side of myth, that which gives rise to myth. Without this *Angst* there would be no motivation for myth and because nothing has been discovered in our modern world to allay man's anxiety myths still have the power to grip and obsess the minds of men. Myths are not only signals of transcendence, they are man's constructions as a kind of fortress to safeguard him against the threat to his being. Hence they can be seen as a flight from *Angst* (*EPT*, pp. 318-22; *AET*, p. 65).

This flight from *Angst* has taken many different forms. For example, whereas the world had been 'home' in ancient mythologies, for the first time in Gnosticism and Christianity it became a foreign place, in Gnosticism, a prison (*Th.N.T.*, I, p. 165; cf. *PC*, pp. 193ff.).

The myths of ancient man answered his insecurity by assuring him of his place in the world as his home. Even here there are variations which are not without consequence. The views expressed in the Old Testament are distinguished from those of 'classic Greece'.

Third, the existential awareness of transcendence is mistaken for a 'guaranteed and guaranteeing presence'. This is another way of saying that the genuine existential question that is alive in myths is turned into an answer with consequent confusion. Man 'hypostasizes his dream wishes' (*EPT*, pp. 318ff.). From this perspective the construction of myth is seen as an expression of man's flight from himself, from the responsibilities of his existence, from his own being disclosed in his anxiety.

> And is not the flight from before God into cosmology, into a world-view, the knowledge of the creator hidden from itself (*EPT*, pp. 318ff.).

The interpreter of myth then has two tasks. First, it is necessary to clarify the signal of transcendence. Second, because myths present various responses, it is necessary to discover what understanding of existence is expressed in the myths. In the answers to the threat of transcendence myths present a variety of understandings. From the perspective of Christian faith none of these is authentic. Further, the interpreter is faced with the task of bringing out the existential meaning in the context of the myth which has confused this with empirical reality. Thus it is not the empirical reality as such which is important. But, in the myth, because it is confused with empirical reality, it is claimed to be self-evident and therefore authoritatively unquestionable (*K&M*, I, p. 10 n. 2; II, p. 185 n. 1 = *M&C*, p. 61 n. 1). On the basis of such evidence the order of man's life in the world is guaranteed. Hence, man's life is secured in the face of *Angst*, or better, his anxiety is suppressed.

On the basis of this understanding of myth, many would regard myths to be of great importance. By means of myth man secures his existence in the world, he knows his place and finds his meaning. But Bultmann wrote of myth from the point of view of his understanding of Christian faith. From this point of view myth is man's flight from himself, from his responsibility and from God. In this flight man secured himself and set up barriers against God. From the point of view of Christian faith the answers of the non-Christian religions are to be seen as myths, man's wishes and dreams. But what of the

Christian answer, how is it related to myth? According to Bultmann the Christian answer is the negation of myth and at the same time the true answer to man's longing and searching. However, the Christian answer can also be expressed in mythological language and even confused with a mythological understanding. Such is the seductive power of myth.

5. Understanding Myth

Myth is an expression of man's attempt to secure his existence in the world. This alone does not clarify the nature of myth because man attempts to secure his existence in the world by all the means at his disposal. The religious man of the first century sought to secure his existence before God by means of the Law, while today, 'modern man' seeks to secure his existence in the world by means of science.

> By means of science men try to take possession of the world, but in fact the world gets possession of man (*JCM*, p. 40).

It is not science itself that Bultmann criticizes but the existential stance which man adopts in relation to science by means of which he hopes to subdue, not only the earth, but also his own anxiety. While this attitude to science has much in common with what Bultmann calls myth it does not qualify as such. Rather it is what he calls 'ideology' (*K&M*, I, p. 10 n. 2). Bultmann's definition of myth is much more restricted than what is understood as myth by many modern scholars who would include what Bultmann calls 'ideology' in their definition and perhaps even all 'God-talk' (*JCM*, p. 62; Kegley, p. 261). Differing definitions have produced confusion, especially in the demythologizing debate, where wider definitions of myth have led scholars to suspect that Bultmann is attempting to demythologize all God-talk. Bultmann's 'Reply' to Edwin M. Good illustrates this point ('Reply', in Kegley, p. 259).

Clearly Good had not understood that Bultmann's definition of myth involves a *confusion* of God with the world. It is not a matter of using the world to speak of God, who is not the world, but to confuse God with the world or the world with God. Similarly Schubert Ogden's misunderstanding is evidenced by his insistence that demythologizing logically excludes belief in God's action in Jesus Christ as actually the unique possibility of authentic existence (Kegley, pp. 272f.). Bultmann's point is that the act of God is not visible as such nor is it verifiable by objective criteria. Rather it is perceptible to faith in historical events. The genuine paradox of the eschatological event as an historical event distinguishes the act of God from myth. Hence, as Hans Werner Bartsch recognized, what Bultmann meant by myth has been misunderstood (*K&M*, II, p. 211). Bultmann did not provide a systematic treatment of myth because he did not consider this to be important for demythologizing (*K&M*, II, p. 180; Johnson, p. 14).

Nothing like a formal definition of myth has yet emerged in our discussion. Yet it should be clear that, in Bultmann's view, myth is not ephemeral. It takes its rise in the structure of man's being. Myth is not an occasional or accidental occurrence. Rather it seems to have a perennial power over the minds of men (*K&M*, I, p. 5 n. 1). In fact, if we seek to define man from this perspective it would be something like *homo mythopoeticus*, man the mythmaker. From Bultmann's point of view, this is not an ideal definition but an actual definition—man as he actually is. Man is the mythmaker because his relation to the transcendent is always tainted (Malet), man is fallen, the sinner. Because of this, he seeks to manage and control what he has become aware of in its transcendence, because in its otherness it threatens his existence.

Because both myth and science can be used by man in his attempt to secure his existence in the world it might be thought that myth should be understood and defined in terms of science, as primitive science. 'So it is in part ...' (*JCM*, pp. 18f.). Because of this, Bultmann appeals to the role of the modern scientific *Weltbild*, developed on the basis of empirical observation (*JCM*, p. 72) and worked out logically by reason, in a law-like fashion. This is to be contrasted with the mythological *Weltbild* which also takes account of observation but lacks the critical awareness involved in the modern scientific *Weltbild* which, for this reason, displaces it. However, it should not be thought that the modern scientific *Weltbild* is absolute—time and again Bultmann asserts that it is not (*JCM*, pp. 37f.; *K&M*, I, pp. 3, 10, 210; II, p. 118; *FU*, p. 59 and Johnson, p. 158). What makes it superior is its openness to modification and change on the basis of its own critical approach (*JCM*, p. 38). In this presentation of the fundamental conflict between the two *Weltbilder* Bultmann developed an awareness of mythology recognized in the Enlightenment and developed by D.F. Strauss. But Bultmann differs from this point of view in that he asserts that to designate Myth as 'a primitive science' is a partial description—'So it is in part ...'

What more can be said of myth? In myth man expresses his existential relation to the world. It is the instrument by means of which he expresses that relation, a relation that is analogous to his relation to God. Man's life is determined either by God or the 'world'. The 'world' is not simply the created order, it is that order *perceived by man to be at his disposal* rather than that order by means of which God makes his claim on man. As the former it is the 'world', while perceived as the latter it is God's creation. Hence by means of *both* myth and science man can express his 'fallen' relation to the 'world'. In so doing both are used illegitimately because neither by means of myth nor science can man gain from the 'world' that which he seeks. Does this illegitimate use of science constitute it as a form of myth? Not for Bultmann, because the confusion of transcendent reality with the 'world' is missing and because of the *critical* relationship of modern science to empirical observation which means that the modern scientific *Weltbild* is always open to modification on the basis of new data. Its approach to the objective world is, from this perspective, correct in principle. It is misused when it becomes an expression of man's existential relation to the 'world' in his attempt to secure his existence. This existential relation is characteristic of myth.

The role Bultmann gives to the modern scientific *Weltbild* is that of exposing an aspect of what is not valid in mythology. The *Weltbild* of myth is the science of a bygone age. But that does not exhaust the meaning or significance of that *Weltbild*. It was developed expressly to assert man's relation to the world. Here man's use of both myth and science highlight the nature of the human predicament. The problem is man himself whose aim is to gain control of the world rather than simply to understand it. If myth is *in part* 'primitive science' it is also evidence of man's search for life, for authenticity, for God. At least, this is the Christian interpretation of the search which finds expression in myth. But myth also claims to be the solution to man's predicament. Hence the myth proclaims the way of 'salvation', the nature of authentic existence, not necessarily in these terms, but in the concepts and terms appropriate to the framework of the myth according to the religious tradition within which it makes its appearance.

Defining myth is a problem. What is meant by myth needs to be clear before any critique is possible. Perhaps Bultmann comes closest to a definition in a note in his essay 'The New Testament and Mythology',

Myth is here used in the sense popularized by the 'History of Religions' school. Mythology is the use of imagery to express the other worldly in terms of this world and the divine in terms of human life, the other side in terms of this side. For instance, divine transcendence is expressed as spatial difference. It is a mode of expression which makes it easy to understand the cultus as an action in which material means are used to convey immaterial power. Myth is not used in that modern sense, according to which it is practically equivalent to ideology (*K&M*, I, p. 10 n. 2; see the clarification in *K&M*, II, p. 185 n. 1).

Johnson (p. 232) regards this appeal to the 'History of Religions' school as an 'historical anachronism' arguing that Bultmann had long ceased to work with that primarily literary understanding of myth (Johnson, p. 89 n. 2) which he described as 'a soteriological narrative recited in the context of the cult and in the form of a cosmic drama' (Johnson, p. 89; cf. p. 162).

Johnson argued that, in the 1920s, Bultmann's 'History of Religions' understanding of myth involved only the Iranian prototype of the Primal Man and related matters, which he had taken over from Reitzenstein and Bousset (Johnson, pp. 8ff., 93ff.). Here we have a problem. Bultmann appealed to a 'definition' or understanding of myth which he attributes to the 'History of Religions' school. Johnson argues that Bultmann's 1941 definition never appears in his *religionsgeschichtlich* discussions of the 1920s (Johnson, p. 232). If this is true, the 1941 'definition' does not come from the 'History of Religions' school.

Johnson argued that Bultmann's concept of myth is an eclectic construct consisting of three elements logically and historically independent of each other (Johnson, pp. 30, 35, 155).

1. He argues that the *religionsgeschichtlich* formulation was the only one used by Bultmann from 1920-1926, remaining dominant until 1933 but receding into the background after 1934 until reference to it in 1941 is considered historically 'anachronistic' (p. 232) in the loose sense of that term, indicating the assigning of an earlier practice to a later time.

2. The Enlightenment formulation was not used by Bultmann prior to 1930 (Johnson, p. 128), but from this time onward it has an important place in his discussion of myth.

3. The existentialist formulation is said to have two phases.

a. *From 1925 to 1933* Bultmann was developing his theological exegesis using Heidegger's existentialist categories. During this period Bultmann continued to regard myth as the necessary form for the revelation, and thought of theology as myth interpretation (Johnson, pp. 104, 107-13, 203).

b. *From 1934*, under the influence of Hans Jonas, Bultmann began to use the concept of myth as 'objectifying' and to develop systematically the connection between his *religionsgeschichtlich* understanding of myth and his Heideggerian anthropological categories. Myth is now seen, under the impact of the Enlightenment formulation, as an historically conditioned and limited phenomenon which needed to be systematically overcome in theological interpretation (Johnson, pp. 30f., 109ff., 113).

Much of this historical reconstruction throws light on Bultmann's work. However his reconstruction is questionable at several points. (1) The *religionsgeschichtlich* formulation was not the only one until 1926 nor was the appeal to it 'anachronistic' in 1941. (2) The *Enlightenment* view antedates 1930 and finds expression at the beginning of a 1920 essay (*TBDT*, pp. 205ff.). (3) The *existentialist* interpretation antedates Heidegger and is independent of him.[88] (4) The emphasis on the influence of Hans Jonas is misleading (Johnson, pp. 115-23, 169-231). (5) The importance of the then 'new theological movement' is overlooked. (6) At no time did Bultmann consider myth to be the essential form of the revelation. (7) Bultmann, as much as Jonas, recognized the understanding of existence new to its time that had emerged in Christianity. Bultmann had already in 1920 spoken of the unworldliness (*Entweltlichung*) of the religion of Primitive Christianity (*TBDT*, p. 219; cf. 'DJNF', p. 510). (8) Bultmann retained the motif analysis of the *religionsgeschichtliche Schule* in his exegetical works alongside the demythologizing of his hermeneutical works.

Bultmann's understanding of myth was complex from 1920 onwards. That is not to say that there were no developments. His understanding is best seen as it emerges in his writing from 1919. In his review of *Die Formgeschichte des Evangeliums* by Martin Dibelius (*Th.L.Z.* [1919], pp. 173-74) he said that John had transposed the tradition into the sphere of myth. In much the same sense he said in 1921 that 'the Christ myth gives his book (Mark)... a unity based on the myth of the kerygma' (*HST*, p. 371) and in 1920 he argued that the 'kyrios cult' and the 'Christ myth' were essential for Primitive Christianity as a religion (*TBDT*, p. 232). Palestinian Christianity, being without cult or myth was in danger of remaining a sect within Judaism. But myth is not religion nor is it to be mistaken for God or the revelation (*TBDT*, p. 234). In this essay he identified his position with the liberal theology (*TBDT*, p. 230). By 1924 he was to indicate that he had moved away from this position and identified himself with 'the new theological movement' (*FU*, p. 29). In 1920 as a member of the History of Religions School and a representative of the liberal theology he interpreted the religion of Paul and John in terms of mythical and mystical religion (*TBDT*, pp. 221-35). But this was to change, as can be seen in Bultmann's Preface to Bousset's *KC* (p. 9). Bultmann's change of attitude to religion, myth, mysticism and the liberal theology was a consequence of his identification with the new theological movement. From here on his concern was for the theology of the New Testament rather than religion and the subject of theology is God.

Identification with the new theological movement made no difference to Bultmann's motif analysis of myth in relation to the New Testament. The approach used in the articles 'Der religionsgeschichtliche Hintergrund des Prologs zum Johannes-Evangelium' (1923) and 'Die Bedeutung der neuerschlossenen mandäischen und manichäischen Quellen für das Verständnis des Johannes-evangeliums' (1925) is the same as he continued to use in *GJ* and *Th.N.T.* By this means he identified those mythical elements that had been taken over by the authors of the New Testament in order to understand how they were to be interpreted in the New Testament. The same point is made in his 1926 review of Karl Barth's *The Resurrection of the Dead* as well as, in 1927, 'DJNF' (p. 510) and 'SOTCF' (p. 13 n. 2). 'Mythological-historical research' is the preliminary but indispensable step which makes understanding the New Testament in its own historical context possible.

Myth in the sense of the Christ myth and the myth of the kerygma is to be distinguished from the discussion of mythological-historical research. By reference to the Christ myth Bultmann was indicating his relation to the tradition of Bousset. It is also an indication that the kerygma cannot be established by historical research. It is an expression of faith. Once he had focused attention on Hellenistic myth, Bultmann came to distinguish the kerygma from myth and this distinction was to remain characteristic of his work.

Bultmann made use of Reitzenstein's reconstruction of the Iranian myth of the Primal Man. His precis of Reitzenstein's position is given in 'Urchristliche Religion' (Bericht über die Literatur 1919-

1925) also in *Archiv für Religionswissenschaft* 24 (1926), pp. 83-164 on pp. 100f. (see also Johnson, p. 93; and his summary understanding of Gnosticism is set out in *PC*, pp. 194f.). When Reitzenstein's position was attacked[89] Bultmann could appeal to Gnosticism as a decisive influence on Christianity, though he nowhere admits that Reitzenstein's theory had been disproved. Johnson (pp. 164f., 124f.) concluded that as Reitzenstein was unable to prove his theory it was disproved. But unproved is not disproved and Bultmann used the same arguments as Reitzenstein because the full Gnostic myth is also the product of reconstruction from sources some of which are Christian. Johnson (p. 56 n. 4) argued that the pre-Christian origin of the myth had been disproved. Reitzenstein's arguments, which Bultmann had summarized (pp. 101f.), are applicable. The fragments of myth which appear widely spread presuppose the complete myth. Johnson was over confident that the pre-Christian origin of the myth had been disproved.

From 1920 Bultmann recognized the 'unworldliness' (*Entweltlichung*) of the religion of Primitive Christianity (*TBDT*, p. 219). Later this 'unworldliness' is said to be the understanding of existence new to its time which appeared in Gnosticism and Christianity (*Th.N.T.*, I, p. 165). The recognition of this emergence is often attributed to Hans Jonas. But, as we have seen, Bultmann had already made this observation in 1920. The point made is that for the ancient world man was at home in the world but in Gnosticism and Primitive Christianity man stands lost in the world, a stranger ('DJNF', p. 510). But we should not conclude that for Bultmann as for Jonas this was due to the common *Geist* which finds expression in Gnosticism and Christianity (pace Johnson, pp. 121ff.). Rather, Christianity was influenced by Gnosticism and in Christianity the interpretation of 'otherworldly' (*entweltlicht*) was paradoxical, not mythological as in Gnosticism (1 Corinthians 7.29ff.; *Th.N.T.*, I, p. 165; Kegley, p. 270; *PC*, p. 164). While Bultmann saw both Gnosticism and Christianity as syncretistic phenomena (*PC*, p. 193, 209), this description does not exclude the recognition of a distinctive understanding of existence ('DJNF', p. 510). In this 1927 essay Bultmann indicates that John is not mythology but uses myth to express the revelation of God without giving up the understanding of creation as was done in Gnosticism.

The 1927 essay ('DJNF') is important. In it Bultmann asserts that Gnostic myth is an appropriate form to express the revelation. There is no suggestion that myth is necessary to express the revelation and it is quite clear that myth is not the revelation. Gnostic myth is an appropriate form because it knows the transcendence (*Jenseits*) of God, the *idea* of revelation, and of man's lostness in the world. But it should be recognized that Gnostic myth does not know either God or the revelation. It knows the idea of revelation, that is, it has the necessary pre-understanding for which the revelation would be meaningful. However Gnostic myth is not the revelation. It speaks of man's lostness, the revelation speaks of God; the revelation also speaks of the historical figure of Jesus Christ. It was the intention of the New Testament writers to speak of God using myth as the form of communication. Hence the revelation is not myth.

In his 1928 essay on 'The Eschatology of John' (*FU*, p. 179) many of the same points are made. The evangelist used and interpreted mythical language to bring out 'the real question which lies hidden' in such language. Only the term 'demythologize' is missing. If the real question lies hidden in such mythical language this is much the same point that Bultmann was to make by talking about the 'confusion' inherent in the myth (*K&M*, II, p. 185). Bultmann's 1930 article on Paul lays down the lines which are developed in *Th.N.T.*, I. In it much of what was said of John in the 1927 and 1928 articles is said of Paul. It is a case of 'demythologizing' without the term (*EF*, p. 122).

The influence of Hans Jonas on Bultmann is argued at length by Johnson (pp. 115-23, 169-231). The point of view in the summary statement (p. 174) is somewhat more moderate than the overall impression of his treatment. Thiselton (p. 256) follows Johnson in arguing that Bultmann's treatment of myth was dependent on Jonas. Both make reference to the views of J.M. Robinson who stated that Jonas' dissertation 'was written under Heidegger and followed with great interest by Bultmann as it was being written' (*Interpretation* 20, p. 70 n. 17). The point of this statement is to assert Bultmann's dependence on Jonas which is the basis of the claim that Bultmann's approach was radically changed between 1933 and 1934.

Jonas's own accounts of the situation differ dramatically from Robinson's (see Hans Jonas, 'A Retrospective View', in *PICG*, pp. 8, 10f.; and 'Is Faith Still Possible? Memories of Rudolf Bultmann and Reflections on Philosophical Aspects of his Work', in *HTR* 75/1 [1982], pp. 1-23). Jonas followed Heidegger to Marburg and attended the seminars of both Heidegger and Bultmann. It was Bultmann who introduced him to the study of Gnosticism and to the leading scholars on the subject. Jonas became fascinated with the subject and Heidegger agreed that he could write his dissertation on the subject with Bultmann as '*Korreferent*' (*PICG*, pp. 4f.). From this perspective we need to recognize Bultmann's influence on Jonas. (See now also K. Rudolf, *Gnosis*, pp. 2, 33.) In his 1920 essay (*TBDT*, p. 219) Bultmann had recognized the 'unworldliness' (*Entweltlichung*) of Christianity which is later said to be the understanding new to its time discovered by Jonas. The recognition of this understanding is developed in Bultmann's 1927 essay 'DJNF'. However, 'mythological-historical research' involved interpreting the meaning of the mythical language as used in the New Testament. According to Johnson this did not involve demythologizing if demythologizing involved the rejection of a mythical *Weltbild*. Certainly Bultmann did not use the term 'demythologize' in this period. Johnson (pp. 31, 214) argued that Jonas introduced the term 'objectifying' to the discussion of myth and that from this perspective to 'demythologize' is to deobjectify' which was what Bultmann did in his exegetical works including *GJ* and *Th.N.T.* What we note at this point is that Bultmann had already recognized the confusion inherent in mythical language by 1927 though he had not described the confusion as 'objectifying'.

Bultmann's advocacy of Jonas's work must be seen in the context of Germany in the 1930s and 40s. Jonas was Jewish, after 1933 a Jewish émigré. Without Bultmann's support his work on Gnosticism might never have been published and without Bultmann's continued insistence that the work was important it might have vanished without trace. However, Jonas does seem to have contributed the concept 'objectification' to the discussion of myth and to have invented the term we translate 'demythologize'.[90]

Bultmann's concentration on the problem of 'demythologizing' did not appear until his programmatic essay of 1941. His subsequent concentration on the subject was partly a consequence of the controversy caused by his essay. But the essay was intended to be programmatic, laying out the work that remained to be done by the next generation of scholars. Does not the movement from the interpretation of the language of myth to 'demythologizing' suggest that Johnson is right in seeing a transition around 1934 under the influence of Hans Jonas? But 'demythologizing' is a method of interpretation. However, there is a difference.

In his exegetical work Bultmann was interpreting the language of the New Testament in its own historical context. This was a work which did not cease in 1934 but continued in *GJ*, *Th.N.T.*, and the commentary on the *Johannine Epistles*, 1967. 'Demythologizing' is developed in his more hermeneutical writings where his concern was for the meaning of the gospel *for today*. Even so, there is not as much difference between the two hermeneutical practices as Johnson suggests. The difference is a result of the context of interpretation, the one in its own historical context, the other from the perspective of our own time for which the acceptance of myth involves a *sacrificium intellectus* (*JCM*, p. 17). Modern man and the 'modern scientific *Weltbild*' have no relevance for a discussion of the evangelist's use of myth nor do they play any part in Bultmann's commentary on the Fourth Gospel.

Johnson distinguished the mythological *Weltbild* from the objectifying confusion of myth. He argued that when Bultmann uses 'demythologize' of Paul and John it means only to 'deobjectify' because Paul and John, as men of their times, were subject to the *Weltbild* of their times. Johnson refers to a number of passages to prove his point (*EJ*, pp. 104, 189–91, 270, 285, 330, 379, 448 [= *GJ*, pp. 250ff., 145, 355, 374f., 431, 496, 581]; *Th.N.T.*, II, pp. 9–10, 12–13, 17; Johnson, p. 214 n. 1). However, apart from *Th.N.T.*, II, p. 10 the term 'demythologize' was not used by Bultmann. Rather he said that the evangelist freed himself from the mythology while retaining its terminology or that the mythological motifs were 'historicized', etc. Thus Bultmann continued to use *motif analysis* to elucidate the evangelist's intention in his use of the language of Gnostic myth. But in *Th.N.T.*, II, p. 10 the rejection of the Gnostic *Weltbild* is in view. 'Both Paul and John demythologize Gnostic cosmological dualism ... the world continues to be understood as God's creation ...' Further, when Paul and John made use of the motifs of Gnostic myth they did not presuppose the framework of the Gnostic myth. The motif was dislocated from that context and located in the history of Jesus. That is what 'historicized' means. Thus, though the term 'demythologize' is not used, the Gnostic *Weltbild* is removed because it is not presupposed nor is it what the New Testament writers intended to communicate in their use of mythical motifs (see Nethöfel, p. 20 n. 24).

Bultmann's understanding of myth was complex. Two major developments can be identified. The impact of the new theological movement with its stress on the infinite qualitative distinction between time and eternity had direct implications for his understanding of myth. Myth confuses this distinction. From the early 1920s Bultmann was clear about the distinction as a consequence of his involvement in this movement. In spite of this 'demythologizing' did not emerge as a programmatic concern until the epoch-making essay of 1941. What was it that brought this development at that time? Perhaps it was because there were those who persisted with a mythical understanding even where this had been 'jettisoned' by Paul and John. But this was nothing new in 1941. Rather 'demthologizing' was Bultmann's theological response to the mythologically based Nazi gospel of 'Blood and Soil'. While this is an hypothetical explanation, a good case can be made for finding the motivation for programmatic 'demythologizing' in the mythologically based gospel of the German Christians in Nazi Germany.[91]

6. The Problem of Demythologizing

From the very beginning Bultmann's critics have not been clear about what 'demythologizing' entails. Understandably, the suspicion that he intended to eliminate myth persists—what else could 'demythologizing' mean? Barth was right in suggesting that the use of this term was responsible for much of the misunderstanding (*K&M*, II, p. 102). But the word was not the only cause of confusion. Bultmann made a strategic mistake in his original essay, by opening with a discussion of the modern scientific *Weltbild* as a means of demonstrating the problem of the mythological *Weltbild* in the New Testament. This gave the impression that he was absolutizing his notion of the modern scientific *Weltbild* and subjecting the New Testament to an 'alien criterion'. Bultmann considered that the error of earlier research was that it used critical methods 'in dependence on a modern world view' (*FU*, p. 280; cf. pp. 72, 86). He argued that the canon of criticism should be 'the intention of the New Testament' ('SOTCF', p. 11).

What then is the role of the modern scientific *Weltbild*? Modern man can only begin with his own *Weltbild*. In his attempt to understand the New Testament, he must be aware of the chasm which separates him from the text, otherwise he will not understand the text. He must also understand whether or not the New Testament is calling him to give up his *Weltbild* in favour of a *Weltbild* of the first century. There are those who argue that this is not the case, thinking that their position is in conflict with Bultmann's at this point (Dunn, in *NTI*, p. 297). On the other hand there are those who continue to read the New Testament from what Bultmann considers to be a mythical point of view. Bultmann's position does not depend on the naivety of Paul and John but on the naivety of the modern reader who misunderstands the use of mythical language which has been used to express the nature and meaning of the revelation event.

In his hermeneutical essays Bultmann contrasts the mythical *Weltbild* with the modern scientific *Weltbild* to clarify the essential confusion in myth. Mythical *Weltbilder* belong to a past age. In their own time *Weltbilder* are self-evident and this accentuates the problem of the clash of *Weltbilder*, all of which are historically conditioned. The *Weltbild* of our day is the modern scientific *Weltbild* which represents our present state of knowledge of the 'natural world'. It is also historically conditioned and subject to critical revision based on new observations and hence is not final or absolute (*JCM*, pp. 37f.; *K&M*, I, pp. 3, 10, 210; *FU*, p. 59; *K&M*, II, p. 118; Johnson, p. 158). Because the New Testament writers were concerned to communicate the kerygma there is no point in demanding the acceptance of the mythical garb which was appropriate to their time, as a precondition for the acceptance of the kerygma.

Myth is not simply an outmoded *Weltbild*. Essentially myths express an understanding of existence (Kegley, p. 261) which has become confused with the objective *Weltbild*. Such confusion is characteristic of myth (*K&M*, I, p. 10 n. 2, pp. 11, 197; II, p. 185 n. 1) and is clarified by Jonas' term 'objectification'. As an expression of man's understanding of his existence myth falls outside the legitimate area of concern of modern science (*JCM*, pp. 38, 65; *K&M*, I, p. 17). 'Myth expresses man's knowledge of the grounds and limits of his being' (*K&M*, II, p. 185 n. 1).

Once the understanding of existence has found expression in the objective terms of a *Weltbild*, which is self-evident in its own time, that *Weltbild* becomes the guarantee and evidence for the existential understanding. The original existential meaning is hidden in the myth which has become an authoritative guarantee of the understanding. 'This is precisely what makes demythologizing necessary' (*K&M*, II, p. 185 n. 1). It is also necessary because historically conditioned *Weltbilder* become outmoded. As long as the kerygma appears to be tied to a mythical *Weltbild* it is a crisis for the kerygma when that *Weltbild* becomes obsolete. In principle Bultmann's case must be recognized. But a question remains. What is myth and what is kerygma?

The modern scientific *Weltbild* is an important factor in identifying the need to demythologize, but it does not provide the fundamental motivation for the task. 'The invisibility of God excludes every myth which tries to make him or his acts visible' (*K&M*, I, p. 210). The primary criterion for demythologizing is Bultmann's understanding of God and the revelation. The 'invisibility' of God is opposed to 'every conception ... formulated in terms of objective thought'. Invisibility is another way of speaking of the transcendence. God is not objectively present in the world. Transcendence also draws attention to the infinite qualitative distinction between God and man who is a sinner. Paradoxically, the revelation of God occurs in the Christ event proclaimed in the kerygma, which only faith perceives (*K&M*, I, p. 200), and which is misunderstood in terms of myth when viewed as an objective guarantee. This understanding obscures the 'real intention of myth, namely to speak of authentic human reality' (*GV*, IV, pp. 134ff.; cf. Roberts, p. 218).

Because God is not an object in the world, he cannot be observed as an object is observed in the world. Even if the world and man's own life raise the question of God, the question does not provide knowledge of God. From this perspective to 'demythologize' might be thought to exclude all 'God-talk' (Johnson, pp. 15-18).[92] But this is to misunderstand Bultmann's position as Hans Werner Bartsch recognized (*K&M*, II, p. 211).

Though Bultmann asserts that 'demythologizing' as an aspect of his hermeneutics is a method of interpretation (*JCM*, p. 18) the word implies that something must go. Andre Malet (p. 47 n. 4) suggested that it was no accident that Bultmann called his method 'demythologizing', not 'demythicizing'. Hans Jonas had used both *entmythologisiert* and *entmythisiert* (see J.M. Robinson, in *Interpretation* 20 [1966], p. 70). Malet argued that the 'logos' in 'demythologizing' indicated that what was meant was 'derationalizing'. Bultmann's linguistic use does not support this view. He uses the terms 'myth', 'mythical' and 'mythology' without distinction and in *K&M*, II, p. 185 n. 1 he characterized 'mythical thinking' as 'objectifying' which 'makes demythologizing necessary'. It is 'mythical thinking' which needs 'demythologizing'. If 'demythologizing' is 'derationalizing' it is not because of the 'logos' in 'demythologizing'.

Demythologizing is a method of interpretation, but something must go. The mythical *Weltbild*, as an objectifying 'guaranteed and guaranteeing' presence, is rejected because it is a misunderstanding of the 'real intention of myth' which is to give expression to an understanding of existence. To demythologize is to free faith from every *Weltbild* expressed in objective terms, including the modern scientific *Weltbild* which, like all *Weltbilder*, is historically conditioned and relative (*JCM*, pp. 37f.; *FU*, p. 59; *K&M*, I, p. 3; II, p. 181). To express the kerygma in the terms of a *Weltbild* causes no problems as long as the *Weltbild* is current. Problems emerge when the *Weltbild* becomes obsolete. Then the kerygma can be mistaken for the *Weltbild* and the obsolescence of the *Weltbild* mistaken for the obsolescence of the kerygma.

Rather than translate the kerygma from one *Weltbild* to another Bultmann advocated existentialist interpretation free from any *Weltbild* (*GV*, IV, pp. 134ff.). Given Bultmann's narrow view of *Weltbild* ('picture of the natural world') he is right in asserting that Christian faith is not dependent on any particular *Weltbild*, though it could be incompatible with some. However, his existentialist interpretation presupposes an ontological understanding of God as transcendent; of the world as subject to order; and of man as open to the future and free. This approaches what Bultmann describes as a *Weltanschauung* and is not recognized as such only because it seems self-evident to us today. Recognition of pluralism, which is true in every age, does not invalidate this analysis because differences generally only affect details within the common *Weltanschauung* of the day.

Because *Weltbilder* appear to be self evident they do not call man to decision but silence his anxiety by telling him who he is. Myth establishes man's existence by setting him in his place in the Cosmos (Zuurdeeg, pp. 18, 19, 89, 90, 115, 162, 173, 188). The 'convictional' character of the language of myth is obscured by the objective language of the apparently self-evident *Weltbild* (Zuurdeeg, p. 189). Thus myth obscures the character of faith and makes the acceptance of myth the precondition of faith and faith becomes the willingness to accept dogma. To demythologize is to recover the existential meaning which becomes lost in myth.

Bultmann, with others such as Küng and Zuurdeeg, stresses that, in the midst of insecurity and anxiety, man is obsessed with the search for security. Myth is a means by which man seeks to secure his existence. In 'demythologizing' or 'historicizing' the mythical motifs from Gnosticism and apocalypticism Paul and John rejected their mythical understanding of human existence. But because the New Testament writers used mythical language this is not always recognized by modern interpreters, nor were the New Testament writers uniformly successful in their use of mythical language. Because of this a strange contradiction appears in the New Testament. Man is sometimes depicted as a free and independent 'I' while at others we are told that his life is determined by the cosmic forces (*K&M*, I, pp. 11f.; Johnson, pp. 223, 229, 248; Roberts, p. 22).

Recognition of such contradictions in the New Testament has confirmed (for Bultmann) his view that 'content criticism' (*Sachkritik*) is necessary. To resolve the contradiction it is necessary to discern which side of it best accords with the writer's intention; which side conforms best to contemporary knowledge and which side has arisen from the use of mythical motifs. Bultmann considers that the view of man as free and responsible accords with our contemporary understanding of the kerygma while the view that man is determined by cosmic forces has a mythical origin. Of course Bultmann's understanding of the kerygma is related to his theological position (cf. 'AR', in Kegley, p. xxiv).

Demythologizing is not a method of *myth* interpretation. It is the interpretation of the kerygma which has been expressed using mythical motifs by the writers of the New Testament. As an terpreter of myths Bultmann recognized that the mythical traditions of the world expressed different understandings of human existence. Especially important for him was the distinction between the mythologies of the ancient world, for whom man was at home in the world, and Gnosticism, for whom man was an alien, a stranger in the world. But he also distinguished the mythologies of India, Greece and the Bible (*K&M*, II, p. 185). These differences are not without their importance and value. But over against the kerygma they are all mythical, providing man with the means by which he ordered his life in the midst of chaos. The question is, can man proclaim the order for himself or can it only be proclaimed to him as a word from beyond, a word from God?

According to both Karl Jaspers and Bultmann, myths can be spoken of as 'ciphers of transcendence' (*K&M*, II, p. 185). However, it is Bultmann's view that the 'cipher' or 'signal' is the question about transcendence which, in myth, is confused with the presence of transcendent reality so that transcendence is objectified in worldly terms. It is this which makes demythologizing necessary ('Reply', in Kegley, p. 261). Again it must be emphasized that demythologizing is self-consciously developed on the basis of his understanding of the kerygma and from this perspective myth confuses existential reality with objective reality and transcendent reality with this world.

Karl Barth, like most of Bultmann's critics, recognized the legitimacy of existentialist interpretation but objected that the vast variety of myths cannot be comprehended in terms of man's self-understanding (*K&M*, II, pp. 115f.). The criticism is *partly* a consequence of misunderstanding. (1) For Bultmann self-understanding is always relational, involving all the relationships in terms of which man understands himself, whether that be God, neighbour, or world. (2) Bultmann's aim was not to interpret the mythical traditions of the world in their own terms but to understand the mythical motifs in the New Testament as the form in which the kerygma is expressed. Babylonian myths, understood in their own terms, might well have an objectifying intent, as is true of Gnostic myth (*GJ*, pp. 30, 65, 76 n. 1, 138 n. 1, 318). But this was not the meaning intended by the evangelist in his use of motifs from Gnostic myth.

Roberts (p. 128) also objected to Bultmann's 'totalitarian' approach to myth. Bultmann argued that the kerygma could not be saved by subtracting some mythical pieces but that the mythical view of the world must be accepted or rejected (*K&M*, I, p. 9). What Bultmann was asking for was a systematic criticism of myth rather than an arbitrary rejection of some aspects (*EPT*, p. 261; Roberts, p. 129). Roberts mistook this to mean that Bultmann demanded 'a single principle of selection' when what he asked for was a methodical rather than an arbitrary approach. Bultmann had attempted to outline criteria and methodology for his hermeneutical approach, all of which is open to criticism. His criticism of Barth was his lack of criteria and methods. Here, as elsewhere Roberts's work on Bultmann is characterized by lack of that sympathy which makes understanding possible. It is as if, having decided that Bultmann is in error, he has searched for faults.[93]

Roberts's approach exemplifies the arbitrariness criticized by Bultmann. Roberts acknowledged that not all the problems were created by Bultmann and noted the paradoxical strangeness and universality of the New Testament (Roberts, p. 125; cf. *K&M*, I, pp. 11f.). While criticizing 'demythologizing' he inadvertently acknowledges the process. Paul might have held the three-story view of the universe but that is not the point of his writings (Roberts, pp. 133f.). The devil is a picturesque way of speaking of evil in the world (Roberts, p. 131). He also says that most Christians do not believe all that Paul believed but asserts the importance of the belief 'that Jesus is the Son of God who died for our sins' (Roberts, p. 128). But he does not ask what such a belief might mean, nor does he set out any principles for his critical method.

Apparently he sought to restrict demythologizing to a marginal role and gives up only those elements which can no longer be defended such as the mythical *Weltbild* and the devil. But how did he decide that the devil was of only marginal significance? He did not ask whether belief in the devil was common in the first century, or what such language meant then. What if the evangelists thought that the devil was real? Bultmann would not have accepted the reality of the devil on this basis because it was not the intention of the New Testament writers to teach belief in the devil. The devil is part of the fabric used for the presentation of the kerygma.

Roberts concluded his section by arguing that Bultmann's reconstruction of the mythical *Weltbild* was more crude than anything in the New Testament (Roberts, p. 131; cf. Dunn, *NTI*, p. 297). He is right in this but the criticism has little significance as Bultmann argued that the mythical *Weltbild* has no relevance to the message of the kerygma. What is clear is that Roberts handled the problem of myth in an arbitrary and unsystematic fashion and is closer to Bultmann's position on certain issues than he recognized.

Bultmann's aim in highlighting the mythical *Weltbild* was not to prove that it was accepted by the New Testament authors, though it might have been by some. His aim was to show how mythical motifs were used to express the kerygma not to teach any *Weltbild*.

In addition to the mythical *Weltbild*, which Roberts willingly abandoned, he mentioned three other components of Bultmann's understanding of myth. (1) miracle as opposed to causality; (2) possession by good or evil spirits as opposed to human freedom; (3) eschatological cataclysm as opposed to the continuation of the world.

Miracles, in the 'normal' sense, are designated by Bultmann as an aspect of the mythological trappings of an outdated world view. This 'normal' sense is the view of miracle criticized by David Hume and more recently by Anthony Flew, where it is understood as a straight-out violation of a 'law of nature'. Miracle in this sense *appears* to affirm the reality of an occurrence which breaks an inviolable law. If appeal is made to the *descriptive* character of the laws of nature—rather than prescriptive—all this does is to question the reality of the miracle. Perhaps it is only an unusual event regarded as miraculous on account of the limited sampling of uniform experience which constituted the understanding of that particular 'law of nature'. It has been argued that for this violation interpretation of miracle to be accepted the miracle must be an event, the occurrence of which is an empirical certainty, and at the same time a conceptual impossibility. It might well be that theists are as much responsible for this understanding of miracle as Hume who so stringently criticized it.

Bultmann's criticisms of miracle appear to be aimed at the 'violation model'. However, he had introduced a factor not taken into consideration in the above description, though it is also involved in Hume's understanding. Hume wrote:

> A miracle may be accurately defined, a transgression of a law of nature by a particular volition of the Deity, or by the interposition of some invisible agent (*Enquiries*, p. 115).

In the Bible, when a miracle is described, what happens is that another causal factor is introduced. This is clearly the view of miracle which Bultmann criticizes. 'Normal' causality does not produce normal effects because another factor is introduced into the situation, that is, super-natural causality (see e.g. 'On the Problem of Demythologizing', *JR* [April 1962], pp. 96-102). If God is conceived as a secondary cause amongst other causes, this constitutes a mythical confusion, according to Bultmann's definition. However, it would be otherwise if God's action is thought of as indirect, that is, occurring in and through means that are of this world but in a way quite extraordinary. It is a question of whether the divine becomes *visible as divine* in God's act or whether God's act occurs in worldly events. Bultmann affirms the latter but without any appeal to anything extraordinary (*JCM*, pp. 61f., 64, 71). In fact, he makes a point of emphasizing that God's act occurs in ordinary historical events.

In what way would a divine act be visible as divine? How would it be recognized as such? Bultmann rejects the view that there are criteria by means of which the divine could be recognized; there are no criteria for recognizing the revelation. However, if by miracle what is meant is a divine act which occurs in worldly events, there are three main possibilities, all of which should be seen as alternatives to the violation theory criticized by Hume and others.

(1) The divine act occurs within extraordinary worldly events.
(2) The divine act occurs in particular but quite ordinary worldly events.
(3) The divine act is latent within all worldly events though this is not always perceived.

Schubert Ogden supports the third possibility, though he allows that certain events might be decisively important for the recognition of the divine act in all events. This position has much to commend it and Bultmann is in broad agreement with Ogden here. However, Bultmann is of the view, a combination of (2) and (3) above, that the intention of the New Testament is to assert that the Christ event is not only of decisive significance, it is the exclusive way to God and authentic life because God's actions in the world are hidden to all but the believer. Naturally it is possible that Ogden is in advance of the New Testament, which at this point might be mythological and in need of criticism. But this way was rejected by Bultmann. For him only the Christ event opens up authentic understanding of God and existence for man. Here the distinction between *ontological* and *ontic* possibilities becomes necessary. This understanding is ontologically possible for all men and there is potential revelation everywhere in the world. But its ontic realization occurs only in the faith called forth by the kerygma. This is the act of God of which Bultmann speaks as occurring in ordinary historical events. The act of God is perceived and evidenced in the miracle of faith which is brought about through the Christ event and its continuing proclamation. In terms of Bultmann's phenomenology he begins with faith and interprets the understanding of its ground and object (*JCM*, p. 73). The self-understanding that belongs to faith and the understanding of the world and the neighbour arise from the ground and object of faith. Faith occurs; that is the fact which provides Bultmann with his starting-point. But there are *other* faiths. How should their claims be heard? Is it any answer to say that for the Christian believer that question has already been answered? Perhaps that is true, but can nothing be said about the basis for such a decision?

Bultmann's failure to address this problem is not an oversight. He refused to do so. That refusal is a consequence of his view that nothing can be said. Either you believe or you do not believe. This does not mean that understanding cannot aid belief. Without some understanding belief is impossible. But the most adequate understanding does not guarantee faith. It is this that Bultmann makes clear in his distinction between speaking about God and speaking from God. Any one who takes the trouble can learn to speak about God but only God can enable man to speak from God by encountering him in and through the kerygma evoking faith. What alternatives are there to Bultmann's position? Is it possible to provide any evidence to which faith might appeal?

With the first possibility listed the act of God occurs within extraordinary worldly events. In fact what is extraordinary *might* be essential to the way in which the worldly event *becomes perceptible* as an act of God. However there is no suggestion that the divine is visible *as divine* in such an event so that all the criteria for recognizing divinity are manifestly satisfied, whatever they might be. Here our attention is directed to the most significant aspect of the problem concerning God's act or miracles. This problem concerns recognition, knowledge. How is God's act to be recognized and known? When are extraordinary events justifiably spoken of as miracles in this sense? Can they only be seen as such by the eyes of those who already believe in God? If this is the case, what is the relation between such miracles and faith? What is the basis of faith?

Further, if emphasis is simply placed on the extraordinary nature of events it is necessary to recognize that such events produce both good and evil effects. Theists would be reluctant to assert that all such events were to be seen as God's acts, revealing his purpose. Bultmann, recognizing this problem, asserted that 'we can only believe in God in spite of experience'. This statement recognizes the weight of the problem of evil for Christian faith, a problem which is no greater for Bultmann than for any other *Christian* theologian. Indeed, it might be possible to argue that his theology has taken more account of this problem than most. Certainly he argues that the event that is proclaimed as God's act takes account of the crisis of human existence in a world where human evil and suffering are always present. The proclamation of the cross as God's act is the revelation for a fallen world. It is God's act within the evil and suffering of the world which, as an event, has opened the possibility for faith through which the world of sin becomes again God's creation (see also Jüngel, *God as the Mystery of the World*).

The early Christians proclaimed Jesus risen from the dead, *raised by God* from the dead, as the seal of the saving event. Bultmann's response to this, not unexpectedly, is that 'dead men do not rise from the grave'. The Easter stories are an objective form in which to proclaim the coming of faith. Bultmann acknowledges one certain fact. After the crucifixion, against all reasonable expectations, the disciples came to believe in Jesus as the one in whom God had acted to save the world. Does this faith explain the Easter stories? Are the inconsistencies in the various narratives an indication of this process rather than an indication of variety in reporting an historical event? Did the proclamation take objective form because it was an age of 'miracles' and thus such a miracle would provide a good 'medium for the message'? Was it proclaimed as a *proof* of the truth of the message? Many questions emerge at this point.

First, recognition that the *prima facie* case of the New Testament evidence supports the view that Jesus was actually raised from the grave does not solve the problem. Stories of miracles, even the raising of the dead, were not uncommon in the ancient world. Second, the literary accounts of the resurrection are not altogether consistent and it is not easy to see how they could be reconciled. Third, the actual resurrection of a dead man must be considered most unlikely. Fourth, there are alternative hypotheses to explain the evidence, e.g. it was not Jesus who was crucified; the body was stolen; what the disciples saw was a vision, an apparition or hallucination.

Response to this critique is necessary. Not everyone in the first century was gullible, perhaps no more than today. It is not easy to demonstrate that all of the Christians were 'simple' folk. The evidence that they actually *believed* Jesus to be risen is difficult to deny. Bultmann recognized this to be true of Paul in 1 Corinthians 15, but he asserts that Paul was wrong. Paul's list of witnesses is impressive. If he was wrong it would seem that many others were wrong also. Hence, even if, from a literary point of view, the Gospels present conflicting evidence, and that *is* a real problem, the early conviction of the reality of the physical resurrection is difficult to deny. In fact the faith of the first Christians *appears to be bound to this event*. What is more, none of the alternative hypotheses seems to be adequate.

Bultmann interprets the situation differently. He argues that through Jesus' life and death the disciples came to believe and to experience 'new life', and that in the awakening of their faith Jesus was risen. As a consequence they proclaimed this event in terms of the physical resurrection of Jesus. His approach leads naturally to the attempt to reconstruct the development of the resurrection narratives from the basis of the Easter faith to the completed stories replete with angels and empty tomb. The tacit assumption of such an approach is that no such *physical* event occurred and that the development of the stories has to be worked out on the basis of the dawning of the Easter faith.

Obviously there can be no simple answer to this problem. Yet the Bultmannian solution is not fully persuasive. The fact remains that Paul and others appear to have believed in the physical resurrection of Jesus. What is more, it has not been demonstrated—but simply assumed—that the idea of proclaiming the dawn of the Easter faith in terms of the physical resurrection of Jesus would have been intelligible to Paul and the earliest Christians. The fact that it makes sense to a twentieth century theologian is no guarantee of its validity for the first century.

We need also to ask if 'miracles', perhaps understood differently from Bultmann's approach, even the resurrection of Jesus, need be incompatible with his theology. They are incompatible if God is somehow evident in them or if they provide proof or a guarantee which makes faith unnecessary. But there is no way that this can be so, if God's act in these events is a hidden action, remarkable though the events might be. There are alternative hypotheses by means of which they might be explained. Miracles, including the physical resurrection of Jesus, can prove nothing beyond themselves. However, they might become vehicles for the revelation. This appears to be the Johannine understanding of 'signs'. They are real miracles, but the emphasis is not on the miraculous. It is on the revelation which occurs in the event. Likewise John emphasizes that the dawn of authentic faith comes *through* the resurrection of Jesus (see my *JWT*, pp. 132-33). However, Bultmann is right in seeing that faith in Jesus involves the perception of the significance of the revelation *in the cross*. The resurrection should not produce some form of triumphalism. Rather, as Paul was to express the matter, it was to see the power of God in the crucified Messiah. What the resurrection does is to signify that the cross is to be understood as an act of God.

Bultmann recognized that in 1 Corinthians 15 Paul was appealing to the actuality of Jesus' resurrection in physical terms. He argued that in so doing Paul had fallen away from his true position. One reason for adopting this position appears to be that, if there were such a miracle, faith, as he understood it, would not be possible. It would have a ground which guaranteed security. But is this assumption correct? If Jesus were raised from the dead what would be proved thereby? Even if this happened it could be questioned whether he really had been dead. Or perhaps death is not always final. It is only faith which affirms 'God raised him from the dead'. No one saw God do it. Only those who take God into account in their thinking are likely to conclude 'God raised him'. The belief in the resurrection of Jesus must therefore be understood in the stream of history and tradition of which Jesus and his disciples formed a part. That stream reaches back into the Old Testament and on into what now constitutes the New Testament.

The second component of Bultmann's concept of myth, according to Roberts, is '*psychic interference*' which is said to have been rejected by Bultmann because it contradicts his (and modern man's) idea of human freedom (Roberts, p. 127). Roberts has made a number of mistakes here. First, the view of freedom to which Bultmann appeals is presupposed by the kerygma of the New Testament (*K&M*, I, pp. 11f.) and not only by modern man. Second, while Bultmann does presuppose freedom, it is not true that man is free from all determining powers. In fact, Bultmann asserts that though, from an *ontological* point of view, man has the *possibility* of freedom, *actually* he is not free apart from the faith which is a response to the kerygma. But this does not involve possession by good or evil spirits.

Finally, Roberts mentions the *eschatological* component of Bultmann's concept of myth. Bultmann regards the prediction of the cataclysm which would bring this world to an end and bring in the new age as myth. Not *only* because that predicted end has failed to materialize is it considered myth, but also because what is predicted is a future confusion of the other world with a this-worldly reality more or less as with miracle in the mythical sense. Speaking in terms of such a confusion, whether it be past, present or future, is precisely what Bultmann calls myth. Further, there is the epistemological problem of the origin of such knowledge. Knowledge of an eschatological cataclysm presupposes an idea of revelation in terms of the communication of knowledge which could only be given on authority because it is outside the experience of man.

Roberts argues that these three areas ought to be dealt with in a piecemeal fashion. He is content to give up the mythological *Weltbild*, and facets of the other areas, arguing that the New Testament writers were not committed to them. But are the three aspects in question not manifestations of a mythological *Weltbild*? Bultmann also recognized that the New Testament writers could use mythological motifs and language without espousing mythological understandings. All of this is in Bultmann's favour and, if this approach is accepted, modern man ought not to be required to believe those aspects of myth. It is primarily at the level of what the New Testament means to us today that demythologizing comes into focus. Beyond this, however, Roberts needs to give some justification for his particular set of choices when it comes to demythologizing.

Bultmann himself offers a basic set of criteria. The invisibility of God (one aspect of transcendence), which is not only a philosophical presupposition, if it is that at all, is the most prominent criterion. It is primarily a recognition from day-to-day experience. Hence, talk of God, or his acts, as if they were visible and *demonstrably divine*, is myth (*K&M*, I, p. 210). God's action can only be perceived by faith in events which occur in the world. Though God is not an object in the world, nevertheless faith confesses that God acts in the world in a way that calls for faith and is perceptible to faith. From this perspective some response can be given to the following question raised by Barth. In talk of God why must man talk of himself? In his interpretation, why does Bultmann speak of self-understanding? (*K&M*, II, p. 86). Bultmann's reference to self-understanding is not conceived as isolated and subjective, but an understanding in relation to the world and 'others'. The *self*-understanding of faith is a response to the Word of God expressed in the kerygma. Consequently, the *self*-understanding of the believer also provides a basis to speak of that Word of revelation.

7. **Kerygma and Myth**

According to Bultmann, the invisibility of God excludes every myth which tries to make him and his acts visible (*K&M*, I, p. 210). This is not intended to exclude speaking of visible acts *as* acts of God. It excludes the idea that such acts are *visibly acts of God*. Only faith perceives such acts as acts of God because neither God nor his *activity* are visible *as such*. That does not mean that God does not exist apart from the faith (*K&M*, I, p. 200).

From the controversies surrounding Bultmann's work the reader could perhaps be forgiven if he drew the conclusion that God is generally visible, except to the blind. Naturally, this assertion would not be so difficult to defend if blindness were understood as *spiritual blindness*. Such an approach simply ignores the problem of the invisibility of God by treating sight as an analogy for faith. But God is not generally *visible as God*. Consequently, those who speak of such visibility, of necessity, must speak of it either in the past (in myths of creation), or in the future, because the present is characterized by God's absence or invisibility. Knowledge of God's visibility in the past can only be passed down by an authoritative tradition, just as God's action in the future must be accepted on the basis of authority, because neither can have any analogical relation to our experience in the present which is an experience of the visible absence (invisibility) of God. If man does find himself in such a position, how is he to choose between the authoritative traditions which clamour for his allegiance?

Bultmann's ontology provides him with the criteria to distinguish kerygma and myth. There are three interrelated aspects: the transcendence of God and his revelation, the order of the world, and the freedom of man. Yet these do not constitute a speculative *Weltbild* such as is to be found in mythology. Nor do these three aspects, as understood by Bultmann, provide man with a basis for securing his own existence. It is not possible, on the basis of them, to produce an objectifying confusion of transcendence with this world.

These differences between Bultmann's ontology and a mythological *Weltbild* are important because of obvious similarities. Certainly it is not 'speculative' in that each of the three aspects is rooted in existential awareness. The affirmation of the transcendence of God is based on the actual invisibility of God as God in the world or the absence of God from the world. The order of the world with its inner-causality is perceived in day-to-day experience and all men live on the basis of it. Of course, as Hume has shown, the idea of causality is an interpretation of a regular succession of events. It is not a self-evident fact. Yet it is treated as self-evident in daily life. The presupposition of freedom arises from man's existential awareness of freedom and is also presupposed by the kerygma which calls man to decision. But the idea is not based on the kerygma. Rather, the kerygma correlates with man's existential awareness. From the perspective of faith it is claimed that the existential possibility of freedom is realized in response to the kerygma.

Bultmann's appeal to the kerygma, which is bound to the historical person of Jesus, appears to be an appeal to an authoritative tradition. To draw such a conclusion would be to make a mistake. The authority of the kerygma is not that of an authoritative tradition. To be sure, it is not insignificant that the kerygma is passed on by tradition. However, it is not the tradition which gives authority to the kerygma.

> Rather it has grown out of the reflection on human existence. Whether everyone so discovers his nature when he reflects on it must be left to him. All the Christian proclamation can do is point it out to him and ask him if he understands himself in this way, if he is willing to acknowledge that this is true of him (*EF*, pp. 215f.).

It might well be asked, on the basis of this statement, whether God, or the kerygma, can be considered essential for this self-understanding. The question is put succinctly by Dunn (*NTI*, p. 298). Does not the concept of a cosmologically transcendent God demythologize into the concept of self-transcendence? Dunn refers to the work of F. Buri; J. Macquarrie; S.M. Ogden; Van A. Harvey; and A. Kee as those who advocate the criticism manifest in these questions. It is obvious that Dunn himself is sympathetic to this line of criticism of Bultmann's position (*NTI*, p. 299). He argues that Bultmann saves himself from this position only by an unsatisfactory and arbitrary appeal to faith born of the kerygma, which he terms 'fideism'. In note 84 Dunn quotes Bultmann to illustrate what he means by fideism.

> The word of preaching confronts us as the word of God. It is not for us to question its credentials (*K&M*, I, p. 41; cf. his reply to Jaspers, *K&M*, II, p. 190; Schmithals, *Bultmann*, pp. 193f.).

A number of problems raised by Dunn need to be clarified. Has he understood Bultmann correctly with regard to fideism? Is the appeal to the kerygma arbitrary? Is Bultmann's understanding of myth confused? Are 'dekerygmatizing' and 'detheologizing' the logical consequence of his understanding and treatment of myth?

First, while it must be acknowledged that Bultmann's language about myth, is his original essay, is not sufficiently precise, in that it could be interpreted to cover all forms of speech about God, this clearly was not his intention. The clarification, in his subsequent writings, does not represent a change of position. Myth is speech about God in terms of this world in such a way that the differences between the two is not perceived. Myth involves this confusion. Consequently, myth must be distinguished from both symbol and analogy. Specific mention of these distinctions constitutes a clarification, not a change of positions.

Second, Bultmann probably would have agreed that

> the first century concept of a cosmologically transcendent God (does) demythologize existentially into the concept of self transcendence (Dunn, *NTI*, p. 298).

Perhaps this statement reveals the basic confusion which leads to a misunderstanding of Bultmann on this issue. Dunn wrote of 'the first century *concept*', not of the transcendence of God as such, nor of the understanding of transcendence in the kerygma. The *concept* is the *preunderstanding* of transcendence which makes possible the actual understanding of transcendence. It is an expression of the question about and the search for transcendence which is alive in human existence and makes the encounter with transcendence meaningful. But the problem is that the concept is mistaken for reality, the question for the answer, and man who seeks, on this basis, to speak of God, speaks only of himself. Such a way of speaking about God is merely a speaking about self-transcendence. It is on this point that Bultmann criticized the old liberal theology (*FU*, p. 29).

Third, any suggestion that Bultmann's approach leads logically to 'dekerygmatizing' is a consequence of a misunderstanding of his understanding of myth as Hans Werner Bartsch (*K&M*, II, p. 211) recognized. In spite of this clarification Bultmann continues to be misunderstood. Bultmann's definition of myth is expressed in his statement concerning the essential confusion involving the 'guaranteed and guaranteeing physical presence' (*K&M*, II, p. 185 n. 1). The paradoxical character of the kerygma distinguishes it from myth because the eschatological event is present in an ordinary historical event and only faith perceives it as the eschatological event.

Fourth, the call to 'dekerygmatize' mistakes Bultmann's starting-point. It is Bultmann's expressed intention to expound the understanding of the faith which is a response to the kerygma ('AR', in Kegley, p. xxiv). The decision to start with faith is not arbitrary. On the contrary, the whole enterprise is an attempt to expound the understanding that belongs to faith, which exists only as a response to the kerygma, in which faith perceives the Word of the transcendent God. This is not arbitrary. Faith does not decide to hear the kerygma as the Word of God. On the contrary, faith is a consequence of the kerygma being encountered as the Word of God. When Bultmann says that it is not for us to question the credentials of the Word of God he is not giving expression to a taboo. Rather, he is indicating that *there are no criteria* for definitively recognizing the Word of God. But then, does this not suggest that faith is an arbitrary response? Might one not just as easily not believe? Obviously this is true, at least from one dominating point of view, and this problem is not peculiar to Bultmann. In fact, only a minority of those who hear the kerygma hear in it the Word of God.

Finally, while the 'decision to believe' might appear to be arbitrary from outside of faith, it does not appear this way to the believer. Nor is unbelief arbitrary to the unbeliever. Because, for Bultmann, theology has to do with the understanding of the believer, he naturally deals with 'the logic of belief and unbelief' and from the believer's point of view. This is the perspective of the New Testament and Christian theology. From this point of view, man without faith is seen as anxious, because of the fundamental insecurity of existence, and seeking to overcome this by securing his own existence. Faith perceives this fundamental drive, by man, to secure his own existence, as sin. Zuurdeeg draws attention to this phenomenon in terms of the way man speaks. Man speaks aggressively, assertively because of insecurity and anxiety, because his life is at stake. By speaking assertively he seeks to establish his existence by drafting his convictions and wishes into authoritative pronouncements about the structure of the universe. By projecting a *Weltbild* he subdues his anxiety about the chaos and meaninglessness of existence (Zuurdeeg, pp. 89, 90, 162). From Bultmann's point of view this is a characterization of man the sinner. Contrary to this, the kerygma encounters man *in his insecurity*. It calls man to recognize that he is not master of his situation, that his life is not something he can establish, but comes to him as a gift. The essence of the kerygma is nothing other than that:

> God has spoken his forgiving word to sinners in Jesus Christ and that word is valid also for me ... (*EF*, p. 220).

According to Bultmann, through this faith, the world,[94] as man's construct to secure his own existence, is restored so that it is seen once again as God's creation, and this corresponds to reality. The believer then understands himself as God's creature, whose being comes to him as pure gift. To the believer, the Word of God in the kerygma makes the whole world intelligible as God's creation. This theme is impressively treated in Bultmann's commentary on the *Fourth Gospel* (e.g. *GJ*, pp. 44, 46f., 52ff.). For the believer, the Word is authenticated by the quality of the new understanding of existence that it brings.

Here it is important to clarify the way in which the kerygma is different from the words man speaks in his quest to secure his own existence. The kerygma addresses man, is spoken to him by another. It is transcendent in this sense. It is transcendent in the proper sense also, because the Word comes as the Word of God. That Word speaks to man of the gift of his being in the midst of all insecurity. That Word calls man to live in response to that Word, without concern for his own security, but in concern for the world and the neighbour in whose need the claim of the Word of God is heard (*EF*, pp. 216ff.). The faith, which is a response to the kerygma, is quite different from the aggressive speech of man who seeks to establish his own existence. The decision (*Entscheidung*) of faith is submission to the claim of God in the kerygma, submission to the claim of the moment, submission to the claim of the neighbour.

Chapter Four

The Transcendent Word of Grace: The Kerygma

Synopsis

There is no simple statement of the relation of the historical Jesus to the kerygma and faith in Bultmann's theology, nor has the complexity of the relation always been untangled successfully by his critics. Without clarity at this point his understanding of the kerygma cannot be grasped and his theology can only appear as an enigma. According to Bultmann, the history of Jesus raises a question the authentic answer to which is perceived as such only by faith. The kerygma, as the proclamation of this perception, is itself taken up into God's saving act, not only because it has its origin in the history of Jesus, but also because Jesus is really present in the kerygma—'the proclaimer became the proclaimed'. However, his presence is to be understood christologically, that is, as perceived by the Easter faith. The proclamation, which rises from faith and itself evokes faith, is transmitted in the tradition of the church and is accessible nowhere except in the historical tradition. From this perspective, the relation of the historical Jesus to faith and the kerygma is clarified, and the importance of the community of faith, as the matrix for the transmission of the kerygmatic tradition, comes into sharp focus.

Evocative Epigram

> For the message of the cross is foolishness to those who are perishing, but to us who are being saved it is God's dynamic power in action. Scripture says,
>
> > I will destroy the wisdom of the wise and bring to nothing
> > the cleverness of the clever.
>
> Where is the wise man? Where is the scholar? Where is the debater of this age? Has not God made foolish the wisdom of the world? For since by the wisdom of God the world did not know God through wisdom, it pleased God through the foolishness of the kerygma to save those who believe. Since Jews ask for signs and Greeks seek wisdom, but we preach Christ crucified, to Jews a scandal, to Gentiles foolishness, but to those who are called, both Jews and Greeks, Christ, God's power in action and God's wisdom.
>
> PAUL: *1 Corinthians* 1.18-24

Chapter Four

THE TRANSCENDENT WORD OF GRACE: THE KERYGMA

What place does the kerygma play in Bultmann's theology? Is it an 'afterthought', some form of escapism, or a fundamental presupposition? James Dunn, having drawn attention to the criticisms of Buri, Macquarrie, Ogden, and others, concludes that Bultmann's appeal to the kerygma is a form of arbitrary *fideism* (*NTI*, pp. 298f.), an 'afterthought' arbitrarily called in to salvage faith which has no justifiable place in *his* theology. But is such an interpretation plausible? Robert Roberts also concludes that the kerygma has no *essential* place in Bultmann's theology, but that Bultmann derived his understanding of the kerygma from his notion of human authenticity for which this kerygma is a correlate (Roberts, pp. 83f.).

Roberts recognized that, as far as Bultmann is concerned, actual authentic existence is not achieved apart from the kerygma (*ibid*., p. 85). But this did not alert him to the inadequacies of his argument. If the kerygma can be derived from the understanding of authentic existence this is because this understanding is itself a manifestation of the kerygma ('Reply', Kegley, pp. 260, 271). Further, Roberts appears not to have understood the *formal*, as distinct from material, understanding of authentic existence, which is crucial for Bultmann.

The analysis of the possibilities of human existence in terms of authenticity and inauthenticity at a formal level makes no attempt to specify exactly what constitutes authenticity or inauthenticity. The precise character of authenticity and inauthenticity is a question of a material nature, not merely *formal*. For example, to specify that authenticity involves decision, at the formal level, makes no attempt to specify what is involved in the decision, or which decision to make. Bultmann's understanding of authentic existence is *not* merely formal. Its precise character can be understood only in relation to the kerygma. What he learned from Heidegger was 'not what to say, but *how* to say it' in order to be understood today ('Reply', in Kegley, p. 276). Hence 'authenticity' involves decision, but not any decision. It involves the decision of faith in response to the kerygma.

1. Faith and the 'Rise' of the Kerygma

The kerygma and authentic existence belong together, according to Bultmann, so that you cannot find authentic existence without the kerygma. The kerygma is the criterion of authentic existence and is accessible only in the faith of the believing community ('AR', in Kegley, p. xxiv). Bultmann aims at a 'phenomenology' of existence in faith, which faith declares to be the existence which is a response to the Word of the transcendent God.

Is believing existence truly authentic, and is the word that gives rise to faith the transcendent Word of God? Faith believes that the answer is yes. But outside of faith another answer is possible. Which of these two answers is correct? It is not possible to give an *independent* answer. It is only possible to speak in faith or unbelief.

If the language of the kerygma is read straightforwardly, the reader encounters the consistent affirmation that Jesus is the Son of God (Roberts, p. 96). Is this the key to the kerygma? Does it become kerygma by declaring that Jesus is the Son of God? Two questions are ignored by this approach. 1. What is meant by 'Son of God'? 2. How did the New Testament writers come by this knowledge? Roberts seems to accept the view that the Gospels provide historically verifiable evidence that Jesus was the Son of God. It is verifiable *if* a less sceptical and more reasonable approach to the New Testament is adopted than that of Bultmann. The evidence to which he refers is the miracles of Jesus, his resurrection in particular, but also his own claims concerning himself and the affirmations of the writers of the New Testament. Roberts suggests that we are to understand that Jesus is Son of God in the sense of 'the Chalcedonian formula', understood as a succinct if awkward way of recognizing that, according to the Jesus story, 'he behaved as both God and man' (Roberts, p. 120 n. 67). This interpretation takes somewhat of a liberty with the language of the formula with its affirmation 'in two natures' and its negations, not divided, not separate, and not mixed, not confused. Even so, those with sympathy for Bultmann's approach will feel encouraged by Roberts's 'demythologizing' of the Chalcedonian formula.

How, then, is a man to be recognized as acting as God? Roberts's answer, as we have seen, points to miracles, the resurrection, and to Jesus' claim to be Son of God. But do miracles (resurrection), even if they can be 'proved', demonstrate that Jesus is 'Son of God'? Even if Jesus claimed to be 'Son of God' what would that 'prove'? Further, the language of the New Testament is not unambiguous when it speaks of Jesus as the Son of God (see J.D.G. Dunn, *Christology*, pp. 12-64). Even so, Roberts's understanding of the formula suggests that the confession, 'Son of God', was a response to Jesus' action. If this is the case, it needs to be asked whether the confession of Jesus as Son of God emerged during Jesus' ministry, or only after his crucifixion. Not only Bultmann, but almost all New Testament scholars consider that the presentation of Jesus in the Gospels reflects the Easter faith. At this point, what separates Roberts from Bultmann is the claim that the 'objective' resurrection of Jesus is fundamental to the recognition of him as the Son of God. Bultmann differs from this:

> It is often said, most of the time in criticism, that according to my interpretation of the kerygma Jesus has risen in the kerygma. I accept this proposition. It is entirely correct, assuming that it is properly understood. It presupposes that the kerygma itself is an eschatological event, and it expresses the fact that Jesus is really present in the kerygma. If that is the case, then all speculation concerning the modes of being of the risen Jesus, all the narratives of the empty tomb and all the Easter legends, whatever elements of historical fact they may contain, and as true as they may be in their symbolic form, are of no consequence. To believe in Christ present in the kerygma is the meaning of the Easter faith ('PCKHJ', p. 42).

What is at stake in this debate? The one claims that the Easter faith is a consequence of the 'objective' resurrection of Jesus and his appearance to his disciples. It follows from this that, while the resurrection of Jesus does not 'prove' him to be Son of God, *there is a strong positive connection between the event and the belief*. Further, while the first believers had the advantage of the 'objective' evidence, all that successive generations of believers have is an 'authoritative witness' to the event. They believe because of the authority of the testimony, accepting the unproven claim that Jesus is Son of God that is made on the basis of the witness.

On the other hand, Bultmann asserts that, in principle, for the believer of today the situation is not different from that of the first believers. Those first believers came to believe in spite of the crucifixion. *Paradoxically*, they perceived God's act in that event and, through that perception, they found new life, and believed that Jesus, who had been crucified, was present with them. The new life that they found must be understood in existentialist terms. It was new, in relation to God, and to Jesus confessed as risen. The kerygma, then, arose out of the Easter faith. But the kerygma cannot be regarded as the creation of the Easter faith, because this would not account for the rise of the Easter faith.

Believers of all time encounter Jesus risen from the dead in the same way. Through his life and death those who came to believe in Jesus encountered him anew after his crucifixion. They encountered him as the one in whom God had acted to transform human existence. The evidence of God's act was to be found in their transformed existence, of which the believer was aware, but which is not objectively demonstrable as the authentic existence brought about by God's act. Nonetheless, the believer has the assurance of God's saving act, but only in as much as faith is understood as a response to that act. Here Bultmann appeals to the character of faith as both a necessity, a *must*, and as a free act. Faith, as a genuine faith, is possibly only in response to God's act. But God's act is not at man's disposal. Man can only believe or not. The kerygma is an expression of the 'rise' of faith, and also the ground of faith. In it, Bultmann claims, 'Jesus is really present'. But what is the relation of Jesus to the kerygma?

2. **Jesus and the Kerygma**

If we accept that the first disciples actually encountered Jesus physically risen from the dead, then he is to them what the kerygma is to subsequent believers. Through him the first believers found new life, authentic existence in faith. The same is true for those who believe in response to the kerygma. The same Jesus is encountered in the kerygma, though the mode of encounter differs. Bultmann differs from this point of view by asserting that the mode of encounter is the same, as there was no physical resurrection. Here we have a problem. The believer of today encounters the kerygma which calls him to faith. But if the kerygma is an expression of the Easter faith, how did that Easter faith arise? Bultmann leaves this unexplained. If it was a response to the risen Jesus some understanding is possible. But

Bultmann rejects the *physical* resurrection. That does not mean that he rejects the resurrection. Jesus really is risen and the disciples did encounter him, not as an objective event such as the physical resurrection, but in some other way. What that was it not clarified. They were convinced that he was risen because of the way believing in him transformed their lives and believing that he was risen is not regarded as believing in an illusion. Nor is it thought to be a demonstrable fact. This truth is available only in faith.

As much for Bultmann as those who assert the physical resurrection of Jesus, the risen Jesus is the ground of faith and authentic existence. The difference from those who believe in the physical resurrection is that Bultmann appeals to no 'objective' evidence as an adequate ground for faith. It is not only that faith goes way beyond what any objective evidence justifies. This is true even if it is granted that the resurrection of Jesus was a physical event. However, the paradoxical nature of faith is stronger for Bultmann because the cross is both the saving event and the basis of faith out of which came belief in the risen one, *in spite of* the cross. The physical resurrection does not justify belief, but it could be argued that belief is more continuous with the recognition of this event, more a trajectory on the basis of it, than faith on the basis of the cross which, in one sense, could be argued to be in spite of the cross. However, it is easy to see how the crucifixion followed by physical resurrection could be interpreted as a temporary setback followed by vindication. The early preaching of Acts seems to adopt this model (Acts 2.22-24). On the other hand, Paul understood the kerygma as the proclamation of the cross. This proclamation was opposed to faith based on human wisdom, the wisdom of this world, opposed to faith based on signs (1 Corinthians 1.18-25) The paradoxical nature of faith, 'We can only believe in God in spite of experience' (*JCM*, p. 84), is a consequence of the paradox of the revelation of God who is transcendent, not a part of this world. But does this paradox exclude the physical resurrection of Jesus. It did not for Paul for whom the physical resurrection did not involve the characteristic objectifying confusion of myth.

The paradoxical relation of Jesus to the kerygma has already been stated. The kerygma proclaims Jesus, and Bultmann affirms that Jesus is risen in the kerygma and is really present in it. But what the kerygma proclaims about Jesus is not self-evident in what we know of the historical Jesus. How are the two to be related? Clearly the

Easter faith proclaims truth about Jesus which was not evident during his earthly life. Is this truth an extension of the truth of his historical life or discontinuous with it, either as being simply unrelated, or perhaps even in contradiction to it?

What is the relation of the historical Jesus to the kerygma? First, it *was* the life of the historical Jesus that gave rise to the kerygma. About that there can be no serious doubt. Second, the kerygma proclaimed Jesus. In this we have the problem of the relation *in nuce*. In Bultmann's terms the problem can be stated in terms of 'the proclaimer became the proclaimed' ('PCKHJ', pp. 38f.; *FU*, pp. 83f.; *EF*, pp. 195f.; cf. Roberts, pp. 103ff.). This 'slogan' asserts both continuity and discontinuity between the kerygma and the historical Jesus. This complexity has led to the charge that the historical Jesus has no significance for Bultmann's understanding of the kerygma. The charge has taken various forms. Bultmann has frequently responded to such criticisms.

> I do not regard the factual character of history and of Jesus as in any way irrelevant for faith and for theology. I say, rather, Christian faith declares the paradox that an historical event (precisely, Jesus and his history) is at the same time an eschatological occurrence. If the historical fact were stricken out, then the paradox would be abandoned. There is no existentialist interpretation of history at all which ignores the factual occurrence. I can also say that the existentialist interpretation of history attempts to answer the questions that the factual history in which we are entangled poses for us ('AR', in Kegley, pp. 274f.).

According to Roberts (p. 121), Bultmann's appeal to the historical Jesus is an inconsistency due to sentimentality in relation to traditional Christianity. Bultmann says the historical Jesus is essential to his understanding of faith and theology, that the kerygma is a sober account of a human life possessing saving efficacy (*K&M*, p. 44). Roberts asserts that this is not really the case and that Bultmann is attempting to make his theology appear more traditional than it really is and that Jesus has no essential place in the kerygma in Bultmann's theology (Roberts, pp. 100 n. 29, 118).

Roberts argues that Jesus' relation to the kerygma is understood in two ways by Bultmann. 1. He refers to the *genetic* relation which recognizes that Jesus is the origin of the kerygma, that the kerygma arose out of the history of Jesus. 2. He recognizes a strange analogical relation between Jesus and the kerygma in that what Jesus was to the first disciples, the kerygma is to believers today. This would be a functional analogy recognizing both Jesus and the kerygma as 'events' which can 'trigger' faith and authentic existence. Roberts argued that Bultmann allowed for no relation between Jesus and the content of the kerygma.

The denial that there is any relation between Jesus and the content of the kerygma leads to the view that the genetic relation is arbitrary. It might just as well have been John Wesley as Jesus who gave rise to the kerygma; if not Jesus, someone else (Roberts, p. 116). Roberts's criticism on this point has some validity. Bultmann does refuse to say why it should be in Jesus, and not someone else, that the act of God occurs. This means that there is nothing apart from the act of God itself to provide assurance that God has acted in Jesus. But this does not mean that the act of God has nothing to do with the specific actuality of Jesus' life (*FU*, p. 64). It means only that his life does not *prove* that God *must* have acted in him.

The arbitrary nature of the relation is also apparent in the analogical relation postulated by Roberts. Anything that will 'trigger' the faith of authentic existence qualifies as kerygma and this could be constructed by some existentialist philosopher (Roberts, pp. 83f., 89ff.). This kerygma meets us as 'something utterly beyond our control or calculation'. Here Roberts is confused about the philosophers' ontological analysis, which can deal with such questions as what is involved in an act of decision, but does not prescribe the content of the decision. He has overlooked the specifically Christian character of authentic existence and consequently the circular relation between the kerygma and authentic existence.

His analysis of the analogical relation is also imprecise. He suggested that Jesus' relation to the first disciples is analogous to that of the kerygma to believers today. But the *Easter faith* is not in the Jesus of history and prior to the Easter faith there is no analogy with the believer today. The inexplicable miracle of the Easter faith has a relation to the historical Jesus which certainly qualifies as genetic, and the Easter faith gave rise to the kerygma as an expression of that faith. But the analogy is with whatever gave rise to the Easter faith and the kerygma. Whatever it was that gave rise to the Easter faith is unspecified and this emphasizes the miracle of faith.

While Bultmann distinguishes between the historical Jesus and the Christ of the kerygma—they are not identical—a continuity of identity is asserted and this is clear in the formula 'the proclaimer became the proclaimed' (*Th.N.T.*, I, pp. 3, 33; 'PCKHJ', pp. 38f.). But how is this to be understood? Certainly it means that there is a relation between the historical Jesus and the content of the kerygma. Even though Bultmann says that the arising of the Easter faith cannot be explained, this does not rule out some relation between Jesus and the content of the kerygma. Indeed, 'the proclaimer *became* the proclaimed' affirms continuity of identity while recognizing that the proclaimer, the historical Jesus, is not identical with the proclaimed, the Christ of faith. But 'Jesus really is risen in the kerygma'.

In order that Bultmann's position should not be misunderstood certain matters not strictly relevant to his answer to this question need to be set out to provide the context in which he gives his answer. Bultmann indicates that, because of the nature of the Gospels, little can be said with certainty about Jesus' life and personality' (*Jesus*, p. 14). However he was able to characterize the activities of Jesus (see 'PCKHJ', pp. 22f.). In the same place, the subject being the *life* of Jesus, he intimates something of what could be said about the preaching of Jesus ('PCKHJ', p. 23).

Bultmann clearly considered the teaching of Jesus to be more important than the *details* of his life because the purpose of one who worked through the medium of *word* 'can be comprehended only as teaching' (*Jesus*, p. 15). In fact Bultmann was of the opinion that a great deal could be said about the teaching of Jesus, as appears in outline in his *Th.N.T.*, I, pp. 3-32 and in some detail in his book on *Jesus*, which is a book on the teaching or proclamation of Jesus. The magnitude of that piece of work is not apparent unless it is seen in relation to his *History of the Synoptic Tradition* which deals with the critical analysis and considerations as the foundation for the writing of *Jesus* (p. 8).

However, this stress on the importance of the historical Jesus and his proclamation should not be allowed to hide the fact that neither is the subject matter of the kerygma. Bultmann is quite clear: Jesus was not a Christian ('PCKHJ', p. 19). He was a Jew, and his proclamation is to be understood in the context of Judaism, even if it is thought to be the overcoming of Judaism, and for this reason (his teaching is Jewish) modern Jewish scholars 'claim Jesus for themselves' (*ibid.*; see also G. Vermes, *Jesus the Jew*). Bultmann treats the historical Jesus and his proclamation as the presuppositions of New Testament Theology, the presuppositions of the kerygma. This approach raises the question of the relation of Jesus to the kerygma in an acute form (*Th.N.T.*, I, p. 3). Jesus' having come was the decisive event, the eschatological event through which the Easter faith came about and the eschatological congregation came into being (*Th.N.T.*, I, pp. 42f.). The Easter faith added nothing new in factual content to the historical Jesus and his teaching. But it did view him from a new perspective. From the perspective of the Easter faith everything appears in a new light.

Up until the early 1920s Bultmann spoke of that which gave unity to the Synoptic Gospels as the Christ myth, or the myth of the kerygma, and attributed to Mark the creation of the unity of traditional stories based on the myth of the kerygma (*HST*, p. 371). Even so, he was clear that this did not dissolve the figure of Jesus into myth. The myth provided the formal unity but the content was made up of the narratives from the older tradition ('MMNT', *RGG*, IV, p. 394). In his later work Bultmann spoke of the Christ-kerygma rather than the Christ myth ('PCKHJ', p. 42, etc.). Both of these designations were used to indicate that this perspective was not given by the historical Jesus, however much of the individual pieces of narrative might be derived from him. The stress on the kerygma was to bring out the definitive role of the Easter faith which is expressed in the kerygma. The Easter faith *in Jesus' resurrection* (*Th.N.T.*, I, p. 43) is expressed in the kerygma and at the same time Jesus is risen and really present in the kerygma ('PCKHJ', p. 42). The latter being true, Bultmann argues that speculation about the mode of Jesus' resurrection is of no consequence. While this is not an affirmation of a physical resurrection, the Easter faith proclaims that Jesus is really risen, and this faith opens up a new perspective on the understanding of the tradition.

Faith proclaims that it is really Jesus who is risen. What is the relation of the risen one to the historical Jesus? If Jesus is really risen in the kerygma then it is legitimate to speak of the continuity of *identity* between the historical Jesus and the Christ of the kerygma. In the Synoptics this is expressed by using the traditional stories and sayings of Jesus in the framework provided by the kerygma, thus throwing new light on the old tradition so that it was interpreted in the light of the Easter faith. In this process the belief in the continuity of *identity* is emphasized while revealing that the Jesus of history and the Christ of the kerygma are not *identical*. In the kerygma Jesus comes to be understood through the total achievement of his life and death. The continuity of identity is expressed in the kerygmatic confession '*Jesus* is the Christ', '*Jesus* is the Lord' ('PCKJH', p. 18), and is brought out in Bultmann's 'Reply' to Martin Stallmann where he says that the continuity between the historical Jesus and the Christ of the kerygma is the 'that' of his humanity which belongs to the kerygma (Kegley, p. 286). However, contrary to Roberts (p. 107), Bultmann does not assert that the only connection between Jesus and the kerygma 'must be the bare "that"'. Roberts's mistake is to be found in the '*must*'. In fact Bultmann asserts that, on the basis of the evidence of Paul and John we *need not* go beyond the 'that' ('PCKHJ', p. 20).

Many of the problems in understanding Bultmann are caused because his critics go a stage beyond him and then charge him with inconsistency. The kerygma arises from Jesus. He is the historical origin of the kerygma. Without him there would be no kerygma. Hence the existence of the kerygma bears witness to the 'that' of Jesus. The statement 'the proclaimer became the proclaimed' suggests that there is continuity between Jesus and the content of the kerygma. But Bultmann argues that, while Jesus is an historical figure, the Christ of the kerygma is not ('PCKHJ', p. 18). Hence, there can be no continuity between the 'what' and 'how' of Jesus and the kerygma, though there is a continuity of identity (that), it is Jesus who is risen in the kerygma. The use of the traditional material was not intended to give historical legitimacy to the kerygma. Rather, it is made messianic by viewing it in the light of the kerygmatic christology ('PCKHJ', pp. 24f.). In doing this the Synoptic Gospels affirm the continuity of identity between the proclaimer and the proclaimed. Yet the Christ of the kerygma is not identical with the historical Jesus.

Are there other ways in which Bultmann perceives the continuity between the historical Jesus and the kerygma? The historical continuity is between Jesus as proclaimer and those who proclaim the kerygma. But this continuity may only be seen in terms of a functional analogy. Jesus as proclaimer has a more central role than the proclaimer of the kerygma. In fact Bultmann perceived that the manner of Jesus' proclamation was implicitly christological (*Th.N.T.*, I, p. 43; 'PCKHJ', p. 28; *FU*, p. 283). Hence Roberts (p. 120 n. 70) is wrong in asserting that Jesus must be replaceable by the preacher. This is to overlook the fact that 'the proclaimer must become the proclaimed' (*FU*, p. 284), but the preacher does not preach himself.

That he was and is proclaimed signifies that he was the decisive act of God, the inaugurator of the new world (*FU*, p. 284).

In terms of the content of the preaching of Jesus and the kerygma Bultmann also affirms another point of continuity. In both, man is confronted with decision in the same way ('PCKHJ', pp. 36f.). In both faith perceives the ultimate and definitive address of God. However, in neither is it possible to *demonstrate* that God does so address man. Historical encounter is encounter with what is 'other'. In the historical event, which is the eschatological event, man is encountered by the transcendent Word of grace, but only faith perceives this.

Both in the preaching of Jesus and the kerygma we find the same understanding of God and of human existence ('PCKHJ', pp. 32, 36). This broad outline could be amplified in terms of grace, freedom, responsibility, sin, and so on. Hence there *is* a material unity between the proclamation of Jesus and the kerygma. However there is a significant difference as well. While the proclamation of Jesus called man to authentic existence and even proclaimed God's unqualified acceptance of the sinner, only in the kerygma, in the Easter faith, is the possibility of that proclamation realized. This is the significance of the proclamation of the resurrection, of Jesus risen in the kerygma, in the Easter faith. For this reason it was inevitable that the proclaimer should become the proclaimed ('PCKHJ', p. 4).

The relation between the historical Jesus and the Christ of the kerygma is further illuminated by the assertion of the paradox that an historical event is the eschatological event ('Reply', in Kegley, pp. 261, 286; *K&M*, I, p. 44). The event, as an historical event, entails Jesus life and work *as a whole*. However the eschatological character of that event is not discernible on the basis of historical-critical research. What is discernible on this basis is the *belief*, that in Jesus the eschatological event has occurred. Indeed, Bultmann argues that the Gospels—especially the Synoptics—are kerygmatic interpretations of the life of Jesus ('PCKHJ', pp. 24f.). This means that it is not possible for historical-critical research to demonstrate that God has acted in Jesus. The most it can do is to raise the question of whether perhaps this might not be so.

At this point it is convenient to discuss the relation between historically established facts concerning Jesus' life and the kerygma. It is clear that Bultmann does not think that historical-critical research can establish that what the kerygma says of Jesus is true of the historical Jesus. It is not possible to validate the kerygma *in this way*. However, the absence of evidence, the inability to prove the assertions of the kerygma, should not be taken to imply that the kerygma is impregnable to contradictory evidence. It could be that Bultmann does not sufficiently distinguish this point. But we again notice how quickly his critics take what he has said a stage further in order to criticize his argument. Speaking of Jesus' understanding of his impending death Bultmann says:

> We may not veil from ourselves the possibility that he suffered a collapse ('PCKHJ', p. 24).

Here Bultmann is discussing 'how Jesus understood his end, his death'. His own conclusion is 'that we cannot know' ('PCKHJ', p. 23). He argues that we cannot tell whether or how Jesus found meaning in his fate (*ibid*., p. 24), and in this context he says he might have suffered 'a collapse'. Certainly the historical-critical approach makes quite uncertain that Jesus interpreted his vocation in terms of suffering and death. This could be the way his vocation was interpreted after his suffering and death. Hence Bultmann refers to the possibility that Jesus suffered 'a collapse', a question that would seem to be justifiable on the basis of the words from the cross, 'My God, My God, Why have you forsaken me?'. While these words can be understood (in the context of Psalm 22) as implying trust in the face of suffering, the question remains legitimate. Did Jesus suffer 'a collapse'? Roberts refers to this statement and says that according to Bultmann

> we must reckon with the possibility that on the way to the cross Jesus suffered a moral break-down (Roberts, p. 121).

The assumption that 'a collapse' is 'a moral break-down' is unjustifiable, but essential to Roberts's argument that for Bultmann

> nothing that could be established about the historical Jesus could invalidate the kerygma (Roberts, p. 121).

Bultmann argues that nothing that could be established about the historical Jesus could *validate* the kerygma ('Reply', in Kegley, p. 262). That is altogether different from what would invalidate it. His point about validation is, the deficiency of the evidence; the fragmentary nature of the historical tradition, and the interpretation of it on the basis of the kerygma in our sources. He argues that the kerygma goes beyond what is historically verifiable. But this is not to say that, if Jesus were proved to be *altogether different* from the picture in the Gospels (a liar, cheat, murderer, etc.), it would make *no difference*. It is true that, whatever Jesus was actually like, his life gave rise to the kerygma and the kerygma goes on calling forth the life of faith. Of course it might well be questioned whether the kerygma would 'work' if historical criticism proved Jesus to be immoral, selfish and wicked. The discussion is quite hypothetical as Bultmann nowhere argues that the picture of Jesus is antithetical to the kerygma, only that it is not possible, on the basis of it, to validate the kerygma. He is also quite clear that the kerygmatic character of the text must not be separated from historical-critical questions ('Reply', in Kegley, p. 287).

How then is the kerygma to be validated? How is Christ to be known? Bultmann concurs with the young Melanchthon, 'to know Christ is to know the benefits he confers' (*FU*, pp. 279, 285; Kegley, p. 17; *K&M*, II, p. 92). This does not mean that Christ 'can only be what he is for me', as Thiselton (pp. 291f.) asserts. What is an epistemological problem for Bultmann is here mistaken for an ontological problem. The question is not whether Christ *is* apart from the believer, but whether Christ is known by the believer and secondly, how he knows. Christ is known as God's saving action in and through the new self-understanding which has its origin in the event of Jesus' ministry and fate and is fulfilled constantly in the encounter brought about through the kerygma ('Reply', in Kegley, p. 261).

3. **The Kerygma as God's Saving Act**

The kerygma is God's act, which Bultmann understands analogically and distinguishes from symbols or images. God's action is understood as an analogue to the actions between men (*JCM*, p. 68). Bultmann distinguishes analogical speech of God's action from myth because myth (as he defines it) speaks of God's action as intervening in worldly events, interrupting them, while he speaks of God's action hidden within worldly events (*JCM*, pp. 60ff.). While the definition of myth is not important to him, it is important to recognize that when he speaks of God as acting this does not involve the objectifying confusion which is fundamental to his understanding of myth (*JCM*, p. 62; Kegley, p. 261).

Bultmann opposes the claim inherent in myth, that God's action is visible as God's action in the midst of worldly phenomena. Hence he asks what there is about the historical Jesus that lifts his incognito, what are the objective criteria for recognizing an act of God ('Reply', in Kegley, p. 262). When faith perceives God acting in hidden ways within worldly events it acknowledges the inadequacy of 'the scientific world-view', not in order to establish another world-view, but to assert another dimension of reality perceived only by faith (*JCM*, pp. 65f.). However, mythological language can be used as the language of faith if it is understood in terms of symbols and images. In this way God is spoken of as creator. Such symbols or images are necessary for the language of Christian faith (*JCM*, p. 67).

This symbolic use of mythological language is distinguished from the analogical language of God acting, which 'must be able to convey the full, direct meaning' (*JCM*, p. 68). Yet it is not mythological language. Hence it is distinguished from myth and from symbol and image. The distinction from myth is clear. God's act is not spoken of as an objective act visible as God's act in the world as it is in myth. Analogical speech of God's act is possible where the speaker is drawn into the act so that

> to speak of God as acting involves the events of personal existence ... here and now, since man lives within the limits of space and time ... we mean that we are confronted by God, addressed, asked, judged, or blessed by God. Therefore to speak in this manner is not to speak in symbols or images, but to speak analogically. For when we speak in this manner of God as acting, we conceive God's action as an analogue to the actions taking place between men (*JCM*, p. 68).

How then does Bultmann distinguish the analogical language concerning God's act from symbols and images? When he says that analogical language must convey the 'full, direct meaning' the implication seems to be that symbols and images do not. Evidently to speak of God as creator is to use mythological language as symbol or image (*JCM*, p. 67), but to speak of God as Father is to use mythological language analogically because this expression of God's love and care involves 'real experiences of God as acting here and now ... it expresses a purely personal relationship' (*JCM*, p. 69).

From this Bultmann concludes that only the language about God which expresses 'the existential relation between God and man' is legitimate. Symbolic language about God as creator should be interpreted existentially to the effect that 'I understand myself to be a creature which owes its existence to God' (*JCM*, p. 69). Evidently the action of God can be spoken of fully, directly, in analogical language, or less directly in symbolic language. To speak of God's action 'as cultic action' is not legitimate unless understood symbolically (*JCM*, pp. 69f.). Such symbols are legitimate only as affirmation that 'God is a personal being acting on persons' (*JCM*, p. 70). Symbols and images can qualify as analogy when mythological ideas are left behind and when the language is directly existential as in the case of speaking of God as Father (*JCM*, p. 69). Here, as with the problem of the definition of myth, Bultmann's clarification of the distinction between analogy, images and symbols lacks detailed treatment and many problems remain unresolved. However, his development of the notion of analogy is probably a response to the criticism that symbolic language is meaningless unless it can be related to a full and direct assertion of meaning.

To speak of God it is necessary to speak of God's act and language concerning God's act is existential language. Speech of God's act means 'we are confronted with God, addressed . . . ' (*JCM*, p. 68). To speak of God means to speak of our own personal existence, not because God does not exist outside of our own personal existence, but because we *know* him only in as much as he impinges on our existence (*JCM*, pp. 70, 72). For the believer, his faith is a consequence of such an encounter, though he cannot prove that this is not the consequence of an illusion (*JCM*, p. 71). The paradox of faith is that the object of faith is the ground of faith and is 'apprehended as such only by the eye of faith' (*JCM*, p. 72). The launching of Jesus' ministry and his death constitute God's act which gives rise to faith ('Reply', in Kegley, p. 261; cf. *K&M*, I, p. 44; 'PCKHJ', p. 20), and this is the basis of the kerygma in which God addresses man. Just as there is nothing in the historical Jesus which lifts his incognito ('Reply', in Kegley, p. 262), 'God's Word is hidden in the Scriptures as each action of God is hidden everywhere' (*JCM*, p. 71).

God's action is eschatological in the sense defined by Bultmann. Though occurring in space and time *in the life and death of Jesus* it is not restricted to that time. It is this paradox which constitutes an historical event as the eschatological event. However, what God has done is not open to historical proof. Faith perceives in God's action the gift of a new understanding of existence (*JCM*, pp. 73, 80ff.) which arises out of the life and death of Jesus and goes on as a possibility in the kerygma. This new understanding of existence, that is, new self-understanding, involves a total transformation. The whole world appears in a new light so that it has become a new world to the believer (*JCM*, p. 75; cf. *GJ*, pp. 317ff.). Consequently the kerygma proclaims that God's act in Jesus is 'once for all', and this is understood in the sense that God's act is always present in the kerygma (*JCM*, p. 82). As God's action this word is not only a word, it is an event, an action. It is an action in which God speaks, a word in which God acts (*EF*, p. 87). The historical ground of faith in Jesus Christ and his life and death, as perceived by faith, are a revelation of God's grace, God's love. In this event God's free and gracious acceptance of man is revealed, not as a timeless word but as an event in space and time. In the kerygma that event is present, and faith is the ever new response to that event by means of which the new self-understanding is renewed (*JCM*, p. 76). This new self-understanding is evidence of God's act because faith understands that forgiveness is God's act (*FU*, p. 276).

Is it not true that God *is* gracious and loving, and that this truth is given in creation? If this is true, what need is there of a particular act of God? What need is there for the kerygma? The problem is that, even though God meets us always and everywhere, we do not recognize him, he does not become real to us apart from his Word (the kerygma) spoken here and now (*JCM*, pp. 78f.). What is potential must become actual in the Word spoken in the kerygma. This is the word which 'rises up in history', which has its 'origin in an historical event', the life and death of Jesus (*JCM*, pp. 79f.). While the kerygma brings back the lost possibility which was given in creation (*GJ*, pp. 35, 39f., 342 n. 2, 521) and that possibility is perceived as an understanding of existence, it is not an eternal idea. That understanding is only given in an event (*EF*, pp. 80ff.).

Paradoxically, Christian faith perceives the revelation of God hidden in the world as God's creation and proclaims that the world is God's creation but also affirms that the truth of this proclamation lies hidden apart from the kerygma ('Reply', in Kegley, pp. 265, 268). What does it mean to say that the world becomes visible as creation only in the light of the cross as God's act? Is this what Bultmann means when he says that we can only believe in God in spite of experience? For him faith in response to God's act is not thought of as an 'experience', which is understood by him in a purely psychological sense. Faith is a response to what is beyond man, not just an experience. The paradox is that the world is God's creation, but is perceptible as such only by faith in response to the event of Jesus' life and death, and the kerygma is part of that event (*FU*, p. 308). While some scholars today would follow Bultmann in his assertion that creation is perceptible only in the light of the cross (E.F. Osborn, *TBCP*), this is sometimes done in the context of an understanding of the world as being in the process of creation. Because the process is not complete, only in the light of the cross is it visible as such. This is an ontological explanation of the problem. Bultmann's response is in terms of epistemology, declaring the problem to be with man. The revelation is given in creation, but apart from the cross man fails to see, and indeed obscures the revelation. Only in the event, of which the kerygma forms part, does the possible revelation become actual. For this reason it is important to understand the nature of the event and the understanding of existence which actually came about through it.

4. **God's Act of Revelation**

Bultmann's understanding of God is bound to his understanding of revelation. It is for this reason that he asserts that man who speaks of God must speak of himself, the man who has been encountered by the revelation. He uses the language of personal analogy to speak of God and his act. Analogically it is appropriate to speak of God as 'personal' in the language of personal relationships so that 'every assertion about God is simultaneously an assertion about man and vice versa' (*Th.N.T.*, I, p. 191; cf. Ogden, 'GAIH?', p. 170). Ogden argues that Bultmann's anthropological/existentialist approach is one sided in that he might just as well have presented Paul's theology as the doctrine of God, as is implied by the 'vice versa'. But Bultmann refused to do this. What Ogden seems not to recognize in this criticism is the epistemological problem implied in dealing with everything in terms of a doctrine of God. It implies speaking of everything from God's point of view. But how can a *man* do this? It is because God can be spoken of only by the believer who has been encountered by the revelation that Bultmann insists that theology is best treated as anthropology, or better, existentially. Such anthropology includes what the believer has to say of God and of the revelation, in relation to which he is a believer. However, it might be true that Bultmann does not say as much as he might about God, even allowing for his own perspectives. This is not the point of Ogden's criticism though later he is at pains to show that he in no way *intends* to abandon the position that *all* theological statements are existential statements ('GAIH?', p. 172).

Ogden's position appears to involve a different understanding of God from what we find in Bultmann's writings, a philosophical theology which Bultmann did not think possible (Kegley, p. 272). The question is, how can there be an existentialist anthropology in terms of theology? Surely that means speaking of man from God's point of view. Perhaps we could understand this to mean that in man's coming to knowledge of the truth of existence it is God coming to consciousness and self-realization.[95] Certainly such a theology is quite different from Bultmann's and there was no misunderstanding when he said that he did not think such a theology to be possible.

While Bultmann did not give any detailed discussion of what he meant by speaking of God's act in terms of analogy, he intended to speak *directly* of God and his action, analogically representing God as 'a personal being acting on persons' (*JCM*, p. 70; cf. p. 68).[96] Ogden has argued that Bultmann's existentialist interpretation can be justified only if it is 'supplemented by something like Hartshorne's dipolar theism' ('GAIH?', p. 172). The different understanding of God emerges in Ogden's discussion of Jesus as God's act. He argues that Bultmann's interpretation of analogy has been shown to be untenable (*ibid.*, p. 174) but that Hartshorne's understanding of the interrelation between God and the world on the analogy of the interaction between our minds and bodies is viable (*ibid.*, p. 178). Thus statements can and do refer directly to God and his action as creator and redeemer (*ibid.*, p. 179). The direct speaking of God, to which Ogden refers, is what it is possible to say of the *final destiny* of all creatures who contribute to the self-creation of God, who accepts his creatures into the security of his own eternal life (*ibid.*, pp. 178f.). Consequently, Ogden speaks of God also in terms of potentiality, or possibility. God, as well as man, is a temporal and historical being, though he is not simply identifiable with the historical process (*ibid.*, p. 180).

For Ogden there are two senses in which God may be said to act *in history*. 1. If God's relation to the world is analogous to our own relation to our bodies every creature is to some extent God's act (*ibid.*, p. 180). 2. Human being not only is, but also has the capacity to understand. Man is therefore the creature of meaning and the various historical religions are attempts to grasp the meaning of existence. Speech and action arising from this awareness actually *are*

God's action (*ibid.*, p. 181). Some of our actions are peculiarly our own, especially in relation to other people, when we reveal ourselves in our actions. While every creature is an act of God, certain creaturely happenings can be said to be his act in a *special sense* when they manifest his characteristic action as creator and redeemer. Because man has the possibility of grasping the truth about life, his words and deeds carry the possibility of becoming an act of God. The various historical religions display different understandings of existence which cannot all be true. Where religious symbols 're-present' God's action as creator and redeemer they become God's acts in the special sense. However, any event can become an act of God when it is perceived as a symbol of God's creative and redemptive action. Because man is distinctively the creature of meaning there is no event which cannot become such a symbol. It is the event which evokes the understanding in man by means of which the events are understood as symbols. However, because man is the creature of meaning he expresses himself through words and acts which are *intentionally* symbolic. In such words and actions the characteristic action of the creator and redeemer is revealed. They are acts of God just as our outer acts 're-present' our own characteristic decisions.

Ogden takes one further step. He recognizes that, for the Christian community, the history of Jesus, as presented in the Gospels, is the decisive act of God. In it is revealed an understanding of human existence which reveals that Jesus *is* God's decisive act (*ibid.*, p. 186). In this interpretation the transcendence of God is affirmed while his decisive act in the historical event of Jesus' ministry is also recognized.

The relation of this approach to Bultmann's understanding is quite close. Both interpret the 'act' of God as the revelation event. Both see this decisively identified with the 'Christ event'. Both see this act of God in terms of the analogy of human action. However, Ogden's interpretation departs from Bultmann's where Bultmann interprets the Christ event not only as the decisive act of God but also as the only effective act of God (*ibid.*, p. 173). On the contrary, Ogden argues:

> The claim 'only in Jesus Christ' must be interpreted to mean, not that God acts to redeem only in the history of Jesus and in no other history, but that the only God who redeems any history—*although he in fact redeems every history*—is the God whose redemptive

> action is decisively re-presented in the word that Jesus speaks and is (*ibid.*, p. 173).

This decisive revelation is not *absolutely necessary* as the revelation is to be received elsewhere. But the decisive revelation is the touchstone of revelation because not all claims to revelation in fact are revelations of God as creator and redeemer. Not all of the historical religions have the same understanding of existence and they cannot all be right. However, true responses to the revelation are to be found apart from the 'Christ event' and the kerygma. Here Ogden is on firmer ground from the point of view of existentialism. But what about the intention of the New Testament? Is it not true that for Paul and John Jesus is not only the *decisive* act of God, he is *the* act of God?

Bultmann is not far from Ogden when he asserts that God's acts are hidden everywhere in the world just as his Word is hidden everywhere in Scripture (*JCM*, pp. 71, 78f.). This could allow for a development of the idea of analogy along lines suggested by Ogden. But Bultmann asserts that, apart from the kerygma, and the response of faith it evokes, God's actions in the world are not recognized. His refusal to be moved on this point might have created difficulties, but given his commitment to the intention of the New Testament it is both intelligible and defensible.

From an empirical point of view the claim that the revelation is communicated in the Christ-kerygma can also be defended. Christian faith and understanding are communicated in this way. But can it be asserted that this is exclusively the only way? It would be hard to defend the claim that only Christians love one another. However, the life of which we speak here is love which arises from the faith evoked by the kerygma. By definition this makes the Christ event not only the decisive act of God but the exclusive act of God in that only this act actually frees man from himself and opens up new life for him. It could still be questioned whether anything significant is added when it is said of a life or action 'and he was a Christian believer'. Bultmann wrote:

> Perhaps one may say that faith and love are made manifest only in so far as there are Christians who, acting in faith and love and guided by their reason, take upon themselves responsibility for the world ('Reply', in Kegley, p. 280).

However this question is decided, with Ogden, as the *decisive* act of

God, or with Bultmann, as the *unique* and decisive act of God, each of these ways is a significant and serious attempt to understand faith today in the context of a pluralistic world.

Ogden argues that by making the history of Jesus Christ the only act of God to redeem mankind Bultmann has fallen back into mythology, into objectifying categories of space and time (*ibid.*, p. 173). But this criticism is not based on Bultmann's understanding of myth. (1) The history of Jesus is not to be understood as an objective display of divine power in action. His history can be understood as the history of a man, a Jew, who was executed. (2) The revelation event is not bound by space and time. Beginning with Jesus, it goes on in the world in the proclamation in which 'the proclaimer became the proclaimed'. Only faith perceives the act of God in the kerygma, just as only faith perceived an act of God in the crucifixion of Jesus.

Bultmann's insistence that the revelation event is bound exclusively to the Christ event, into which the kerygma is caught up, involves the acceptance, according to Ogden, of the distinction between ontological and ontic possibilities. His own view, that the Christ event is the *decisive* act of God, but not exclusively the act of God, is intended to avoid this problematical distinction. But is this really the case? Unless Ogden argues that the act of God *is always and everywhere perceived*, he also must allow for the possibility of perception, which at any given moment is not fulfilled, as distinct from actual perception. Bultmann's distinction is based on the conviction that to be human is to have this possibility, so that when the revelation occurs, the believer fulfils the genuinely human possibility. However, that possibility could not be fulfilled without the revelation. But the revelation does not make man other than human. The ontic presupposes the ontological. An analogy might be hunger, which is satisfied by food. Unless man was ontologically capable of eating and being satisfied, food would be irrelevant. Thus Ogden also appears to accept, against his intention, the reality which Bultmann speaks of in terms of ontological and ontic possibility. It would only be otherwise if there were no distinction between possibility and actuality, that is, if human freedom, in this matter, were denied. Bultmann certainly is not willing to abandon this. It might be that Ogden is and that the realization of the revelation is for him a determined process. His perception of the relation between God and the world in terms of an analogy between the mind and the body suggests that such a deterministic view might be held. However I doubt this.

Ogden, like Bultmann, is not willing to allow that all religions are equally valid. Bultmann insists that, apart from the revelation in the Christ event, all men are searchers whose knowledge of God and themselves is distorted. Ogden allows for revelation elsewhere, and thus authentic perception of God and the nature of existence are not bound to the Christ event. However, the decisive act of God is in the Christ event. Therefore, it would seem that this event has the character of a criterion for recognizing God's acts elsewhere.

5. **Kerygma, Tradition, Scripture and Church**

The kerygma takes its rise from the life and death of Jesus which evoke interpretation leading to the decision which bears responsibility for the future ('Reply', in Kegley, p. 265). Interpretation is not an addition but a continuation. It is evoked by the event. Hence the kerygma, as faith's interpretation of the life and death of Jesus, and the event which it interprets are intimately related. Indeed, it is faith which perceived the hidden meaning in Jesus' life and death and in the light of that, 'the hidden meaning of all history in the presence of God' (*ibid.*). However, both the historical Jesus and the kerygma are accessible only in the tradition which contains such information about Jesus that survives in the framework of kerygmatic interpretation.

In his preface to Schmithals's book on Bultmann's theology John Bowden drew attention to Bultmann's concentration on the Bible suggesting that he does not adequately justify basing his theology on the 'canon' (Schmithals, p. xiv). Bowden has drawn attention to one of the most difficult problems for contemporary Christian thought. Why the canon, and if the canon, what is its place and authority?

The problem of the canon has been treated in a number of ways by Bultmann. To begin with we need to separate the two Testaments. The Old Testament is not a Christian book. How could it be? It is an Israelite/Jewish book. In it there are many of the fundamental issues which separate Judaism from Christianity. The Old Testament gives expression to national/cultural racism. In this framework food and purity laws, amongst other things, separate the Jews from the nations and from Christianity. Of course this should not be allowed to obscure the fact that the 'pure prophetic' faith finds its continuity in Jesus. Indeed, Jesus would be quite unintelligible apart from

Judaism, even if he is seen both as the fulfilment of the prophetic tradition and the overcoming of Judaism. In this overthrowal he can only be understood in terms of elements within Judaism which arise to bring about its overthrowal.

Both Jesus and the Old Testament belong to Judaism though both are also presuppositions for Christianity and the theology of the New Testament. However, Jesus' life and death are the events which evoke the interpretation of faith. For this the Old Testament is not an adequate presupposition to determine the interpretation. The intelligibility of Jesus depends on the Old Testament but the interpretation in the kerygma goes beyond this intelligibility.

While the Old Testament stands alone, there is no *account* of the historical Jesus which is not taken up into the understanding of faith. Fragments of information about Jesus in the works of Tacitus, Josephus and the Talmud in no way invalidate this observation. The historical Jesus, as distinct from the Christ of faith, is only known through the work of the historian who seeks to separate what we can know of Jesus from what faith confesses concerning him. What the Gospels teach concerning Jesus belongs to the understanding of faith and the theology of the New Testament. It is at this point that one considerable weakness can be found in Bultmann's *Th.N.T.*: he gives no account of the theology of the Synoptic evangelists.[97] Their works are used only as quarries from which to recover the proclamation of Jesus, the theology of Earliest Christianity, and the theology of Hellenistic Christianity.

Though it is true that the Christ of the kerygma is an expression of Christian faith rather than the Jesus of history, the latter has vital importance for understanding Christian faith. Only when we know what actual historical events gave rise to Christian faith is it possible to understand the nature of faith. This is not to suggest that historical-critical research can even begin to establish faith. However, the nature of faith can only be understood when its ground/object is recognized.

If it is true that Jesus called men to authentic existence, it is also true that the tradition claims that this call was not realized until Jesus' ministry had concluded in death. The kerygma goes on in the tradition, handed on by the community of faith. This continuity raises the problem of the canon of the New Testament in acute form. Given that faith begins in response to Jesus, that is, the interpretation which his life and death evokes ('Reply', in Kegley, p. 265), the case for beginning the canon with the beginning of the confession of faith in Jesus appears reasonable enough. But why should the canon be closed if Jesus continues to be present in the kerygma? Does not this give a continuing authority to the tradition which embodies the kerygma and the faith which it evokes as a response? Bultmann's answer to this question is complex.

First, it should be recognized that Bultmann's *Th.N.T.* does not simply accept the traditional canon of the New Testament. His cut-off point is temporal rather than one of supposed authority. It is this that gives the clue to Bultmann's approach. In this selection of tradition is included all of the authentic independent tradition concerning the historical Jesus and the earliest kerygmatic faith responses to his historic life and death.

Second, the canon of the New Testament is not seen as the scope of the kerygma. The kerygma lives in the tradition as the ground/object of the faith and life of the believing community. The role of the canon is not to limit the kerygma. As far as Bultmann is concerned, Jesus is present in the kerygma and where he is present the call to faith is heard. The point of the canon is to ensure that the kerygma continues to be heard. In the New Testament we discover how faith arose, how the kerygma arose in response to Jesus. In this context Bultmann argues that it is possible to understand the christological confessions of Earliest Christianity and Hellenistic Christianity as the explanation of faith's understanding of the new being (*FU*, p. 285).[98] Christ really is known and confessed in the new life he confers. Hence, the canon stands for the primacy of the event which gave rise to the kerygma, on the basis of which alone is the kerygma perceived and thus maintained in perpetuity. The aim of the interpretation of the New Testament is to ensure that the Church's preaching corresponds to the content of the kerygma ('Reply', in Kegley, pp. 281f., 287). In addition, the New Testament provides a precedent for stating the kerygma in different conceptual frameworks, first in terms of Jewish apocalyptic and then in terms of an Hellenistic Gnostic framework. This is a precedent for further restatement.

Two important themes have emerged here for further discussion.
1. What is the relation of the church to the tradition, to the kerygma?
2. What is the relation of the kerygma to christology?

Critics of Bultmann have frequently charged him with individualism and overlooking the 'doctrine' of the church (e.g. Macquarrie,

AET, pp. 202ff.). In 1929 Bultmann published an article entitled 'Church and Teaching in the New Testament' (*FU*, pp. 184–219). The paradoxical relation between the church and the kerygma is clear in this essay. Church and word belong together. *The church is constituted by the kerygma and the word is constituted by the church*. The one cannot be played off against the other (*FU*, pp. 212f.). This same theme is present in other essays of the same period such as 'The Concept of the Word of God in the New Testament' (*FU*, pp. 286-312, esp. pp 307f.). The believing community, the church, is the *Sitz im Leben* of the tradition which transmits the kerygma. In fact the 'proclamation lives from the historical tradition' ('Reply', in Kegley, p. 277). The kerygma is taken up into the eschatological event and, as the bearer of the kerygma, the church is the eschatological community ('Reply', in Kegley, pp. 276f.). It lives from the kerygma and its faith expresses or confesses the kerygma. The kerygma, as an event which rises up in history, evoked by the life and death of Jesus, survives because the church survives by transmitting the tradition in which the kerygma is embedded. But can the tradition obscure the kerygma rather than transmitting it?

6. **Kerygma and Christology**

Without christology there would be no Christian kerygma ('PCKHJ', p. 28). But how are we to understand the christology of the kerygma? One clue to the answer of this question is to be found in the variety of kerygmatic forms in the New Testament. Not only do we find a variety of christological titles, but their significance seems to be understood variously in the contexts of pre-existence, incarnation, virgin birth, baptismal adoption, resurrection adoption, and eschatological judgment. The variety of christological forms appears to be a consequence of a variety of conceptual frameworks. The christological formulae are *a way* of saying something. But what is it that they say? 'What is asserted is that in Jesus God is acting, that in Jesus and in him only is God to be found' (*FU*, p. 282). Christology is a way of speaking about God acting. The kerygma proclaims that, in Jesus, God has acted and that here the action of God is still to be known. We have already noted that the christological kerygma is to be distinguished from the proclamation of Jesus, recognizing the problem of how and why the proclaimer became the proclaimed (*FU*, p. 283).

Bultmann says that this enigma is solved when it is realized that what is decisive is '*that* he proclaimed'. What is decisive is his person because 'he was the decisive event, the act of God, the inaugurator of the new world' (*FU*, p. 284). The titles are confessions of faith in Jesus as God's act. These confessions of faith, embodied in the kerygma, are expressions of the Easter faith. The Easter faith is inseparably linked with the 'that' of Jesus, that is, the total event of his life and mission. The Easter faith arises out of that event, and the new self-understanding it brings is an act of God ('Reply', in Kegley, p. 261). Only in the word which proclaims this event is God accessible to men (*FU*, p. 283), because Jesus is really risen in the kerygma ('PCKHJ', p. 42). It could also be said that christology arises in the kerygma. Given Bultmann's understanding of the resurrection, it is not surprising to find that christology, as a way of speaking of God's act, is not understood as a self-evident 'world' event. It rises up in the kerygma as an eschatological event which calls forth both belief and unbelief (*EPT*, pp. 286f.). Christology is the believing response to the event so that it can be said that Paul's teaching of justification is his real christology, that Christ is known by his benefits (*FU*, p. 279). Christology speaks of Jesus, not the benefits, because he is the bringer of the benefits. Justification makes explicit what kind of new understanding of existence is given in faith (*FU*, p. 279) and the christological titles proclaim Jesus as the eschatological bringer of salvation (*FU*, p. 285).

Roberts raised the question of the identity of Jesus, asserting that this question is central to the New Testament and that the unanimous answer is 'Son of God' (p. 96). He argues that Paul assumes the identity of the earthly Jesus and the exalted Christ (p. 97). Against this background he asserts that, as a consequence of Bultmann's work, 'the identity of Jesus is lost' (p. 97), and that he deprives Jesus of the identity which the New Testament writers ascribe to him (pp. 97ff.) This criticism is central to Roberts's criticism of Bultmann's understanding of the kerygma (see also pp. 105ff., 108f., 116ff.). At the heart of this criticism is a confusion and misunderstanding of Bultmann's distinction of the person of Jesus from his personality (*EPT*, p. 288; *FU*, p. 284). Roberts says that Bultmann uses words eccentricly (p. 116). Evidently the distinction seemed to be 'nonsense' to Roberts.

Bultmann argues that the New Testament writers were not at all concerned about the personality of Jesus. Was he an extrovert or an introvert? for example. The New Testament writers were concerned with what *he* taught and what *he* did. That it was Jesus who taught and acted was decisive for them. This decisiveness is referred to by Bultmann as the 'that' of Jesus, and he has argued that Paul and John have taught us that we *need* no more than the 'that'. However Roberts has gone too far in his assertion that Bultmann *cannot* accept more than 'the bare that' (Roberts, p. 108 n. 44). Bultmann has done a great deal to show what can be said with probability about the historical Jesus (see 'PCKHJ', pp. 22f.). However, he argues that such knowledge is not the basis of faith. His reference to the 'that' draws attention to what is decisive, and focuses on the *uniqueness* of Jesus, what is uniquely decisive about him. Bultmann says that to adhere to his *person* includes the recognition of his death as an essential part of God's saving act which decisively determines everything else (*FU*, p. 238). Thus, from the perspective of faith, the 'that' of Jesus is his 'person', including his death, as God's saving act.

The question is, can historical criticism demonstrate, from what can be known of Jesus life, that God has acted decisively in Jesus' life and death? Roberts appears to argue that an affirmative answer is to be given to this question (p. 98). Bultmann argued that only the arising of faith as a response to Jesus' life and death can know that God has acted in him. Thus, 'to know Christ is to know his benefits' (*FU*, p. 279). Roberts says that this approach collapses the person of Christ into his work; it is to speak of Christ's work without his person so that Jesus has no identity except as revealer, justifier (pp. 108f.). Jesus' identity is destroyed, it is argued, by excising miracles, and those other elements in his life which show him to be Son of God (Roberts, p. 98). But surely this criticism misses the point. If through his death Jesus of Nazareth becomes the revealer of God and the justifier of man can anything more revealing of his person be said of him than that he is revealer and justifier? It is not that anything else is of no interest but that this is what is decisive about him. Hence it is not anomalous (*pace* Roberts, p. 118) that, for Bultmann, to ignore the connection of faith and the cross of Christ as a past event would sunder the confession of faith and the kerygma (*K&M*, p. 110).

The *identity* of Jesus is essential to the kerygma both as its origin—it was his life and death which gave rise to it—and as its content. The kerygma proclaims the life and death of Jesus, but with a difference. It proclaims this event *as God's saving act*, and, as such, proclaims that Jesus is really risen in the Easter faith ('PCKHJ', p. 42). Hence,

Roberts (p. 99) is wrong when he says that for Bultmann the resurrection is 'only' the way unsophisticated disciples expressed their new-found authenticity. What is wrong with this statement is the use of 'only'. It is doubly wrong. 1. It is wrong because it tends to devalue the significance of the new-found authenticity. 2. More importantly, it is wrong because it suggests that the new-found authenticity was a totally subjective experience without reference to anything or anyone but those who experienced it. On the contrary, Bultmann affirms that Jesus really is risen in the Easter faith. Thus Roberts (pp. 116-17) is again wrong when he asserts that Bultmann cannot mean that Jesus, as a 'person', is present in the kerygma. This is precisely the paradox that Bultmann asserts again and again ('Reply', in Kegley, pp. 274f.; 'PCKHJ', p. 18; *K&M*, pp. 44, 209; cf. Roberts, pp. 110f., 113f.), when he speaks of the historical event, which belongs to the past, as an eschatological event, an event ever new, ever becoming present in the kerygma which is taken up into the eschatological event for no other reason than Jesus is present in the kerygma. It is no accident that the kerygma proclaims the life and death of Jesus as God's saving act (*K&M*, p. 115). As the life of Jesus, this aspect of the kerygma is open to historical criticism, but the truth of the affirmation that this event is God's act is not. And that is the paradox, that an historical event is experienced and proclaimed as the eschatological saving act of God.

We now come to Roberts's claim that the New Testament writers answer the question of the identity of Jesus in terms of Son of God (pp. 96f.). His argument is, therefore, that Bultmann contradicts the unanimous teaching of the New Testament. Two questions need to be asked and answered before this problem can be settled. 1. What did the New Testament writers mean by Son of God? 2. How did they know what they assert? Roberts seems to think that the meaning of this language is straightforward—Jesus' identity is Son of God. But New Testament research shows that this designation can be understood variously (see J.G. Dunn, *Christology*, pp. 12-64). The various conceptual frameworks within which the designation 'Son of God' operates suggest that the meaning in the New Testament might become clear when we know *why* the New Testament authors proclaimed Jesus as Son of God. Bultmann argues that those who experienced him as revealer and justifier proclaimed him as Lord and Son of God ('PCKHJ', p. 18).

Bultmann has stressed the paradox that a genuine historical event is the eschatological event ('PCKHJ', p. 18; 'Reply', in Kegley, pp. 274f.; *K&M*, p. 44). He insists that not to take the historical element seriously would destroy the paradox, yet Roberts insists that the contradiction must be dealt with by treating the appeal to the historical as an inconsistency due to Bultmann's 'tender sentiments towards traditional Christianity' (p. 121). It is not only the paradox which leads Roberts astray, it is also Bultmann's language about the eschatological character of the kerygma. From this perspective the kerygma is to be understood as God's address spoken anew (*JR*, p. 85). As God's forgiving word it is not historical narrative but address. However, the *form* of this word is the sober factual account of a human life (*K&M*, p. 44). Roberts assumes that Bultmann cannot mean this. But how could it be otherwise? The kerygma *is* the proclamation of Jesus' life and death. Bultmann did not prescribe the contents of the kerygma. It is given in the record of the New Testament which is the expression of the Easter faith. While Bultmann's language is at times ambiguous, Roberts has assumed the worst, and where it is not ambiguous, he has argued that Bultmann cannot mean what he has said. What has been argued here is that the paradox is genuinely necessary for Bultmann's theology. The invisibility of God demands this paradox when the transcendent Word of God encounters man. Thus the truly human character of the historical event is crucial. But it is not its historicity which constitutes it as the eschatological event. It is God who addresses man in the event. The kerygma, like Jesus, is historical. Both are taken up into the eschatological event in which God addresses man. In the kerygma God calls man to give up his claim to his own life and to submit to the claim of God in the kerygma. That claim is made actual in the encounters of the moment which involve love to the neighbour and obedience to God in whatever fate brings.

Roberts (p. 119) is not wrong in seeing Bultmann's understanding of christology as an existentialist interpretation of the doctrine of the 'two natures' of the Chalcedonian formula. But Bultmann expresses his attitude to this formula in terms of opposition and rejection. He does this, according to Roberts (p. 120 n. 67) because he assumes that the 'two natures' refer to 'quasi-physical properties'. He argues

> we can hold another reading at least possible . . . it might be taken as a succinct and perhaps somewhat awkward way of highlighting master features of Jesus' story: that he behaved as both God and man (Roberts, p. 120 n. 67).

We must ask Roberts, 'for whom is this reading of the Chalcedonian formula possible?' Surely not for those who produce the formula! Were they not working with a different conceptual framework than Bultmann, or Roberts for that matter? While Roberts has rejected the approach to hermeneutical translation (Roberts, pp. 217ff., 221ff., 230f.), which Bultmann sees as necessary (*K&M*, II, p. 186; see my 'Note', *ABR*, 19, pp. 26ff.), he inadvertently acknowledges it here in his re-interpretation of the Chalcedonian formula. It is something of a Bultmannian interpretation at that. The formula is a succinct and awkward way of indicating that Jesus 'behaved as both God and man'. He *behaved*, acted, as both God and man. From his actions he is known. Bultmann also is prepared to speak of God's action in Jesus. However, at this point, there is probably some difference of opinion between Roberts and Bultmann. While Roberts does not say so explicitly, it seems probable that, in Jesus' story, when he *behaved* as both God and man, some acts were viewed as acts of God, and others as acts of man, for he says that, in excising miracles, Bultmann has deprived Jesus of his identity as Son of God (Roberts, pp. 97ff.). In terms of the ancient formulae, this seems like a modern form of Nestorianism.

Contrary to Roberts, Bultmann asserts that the historical event *is* the eschatological event. This is the paradox, that in the life and death of Jesus as a whole, the revealing and saving act of God has occurred. The kerygma is caught up into that event, and Jesus is caught up into the kerygma. The historical and the eschatological are inextricably bound together. The eschatological lies hidden in the historical. The original eschatological event was the life and death of Jesus, not Jesus' preaching, as Roberts asserts (p. 116). Because it is the eschatological event, it is ever new, and Jesus, who arose in the Easter faith, is present in the kerygma. He is God's word to man, before whom man is addressed and encountered by God. But the word of the kerygma is also a human word, proclaimed by human preachers. Hence, in the kerygma the paradox of historical and eschatological is preserved. With this understanding of christology Paul's understanding of justification by faith has been applied epistemologically to the sphere of knowledge and thought (*JCM*, p. 84; *K&M*, I, pp. 210f.). This is a reminder of the centrality of the problem of epistemology for Bultmann, for whom the problem is not so much the question of the being of God as it is with how to know and speak of him.

The experience of faith in response to God's act in Jesus was expressed in christology. How far is christology justified on the basis of the Easter faith which claims to know Christ's benefits? There are those who understand the Christian tradition in terms of the unfolding of that initial faith in Jesus, which came to know his benefits. There are others who would stop where the New Testament stops. Bultmann argues that the New Testament confession must be understood kerygmatically and not christologically. That is, what is said of Christ is said because he is the salvation-bringer. Consequently he is confessed in the language concerning the salvation-bringer appropriate to Judaism and Gnosticism. Such confessions should not be understood dogmatically. The problem with the later christological development was that it took these confessions dogmatically.

The christological problem is an historical-theological problem. The evidence is complex, perhaps even contradictory. How is the complexity to be understood? For those who think that meaning is self-evident in historical facts the way ahead is to be found in the new quest of the historical Jesus. By establishing the historical facts of the life, teaching, death and resurrection of Jesus it is thought that the christological problems can be solved. While Bultmann did not argue that nothing of value could be said on these matters he did set out to demonstrate the difficulties involved in the task and the uncertainties which must remain in the end. More importantly, for him, he argued that, whatever could be known, it was inconclusive as evidence for the validity of faith. Without that history there would be no faith but that history was not the sort of evidence that could be used to demonstrate the necessity and validity of faith. Even if Bultmann is wrong in rejecting the physical resurrection of Jesus, he is right to reject the view that the factual history of Jesus necessitates faith. Historical-critical reconstruction of the historical Jesus will not provide a solution to the christological problems. That is not to deny the validity, even the necessity, of such historical work. It is to recognize the limits to its possible achievements (see Tracy, *TAI*, pp. 238ff. and notes).

The history of Jesus raises the christological question. In itself it cannot answer this question. It, however, is because the question has been raised that there are answers to be found. The New Testament bears witness to a large variety of answers. There were those who concluded, 'This man is a sinner, he does not keep the law' (John 9.16, 24). Others concluded that he was a teacher come from God

(John 3.2), a prophet (John 9.17), the Messiah (John 1.41, 49). The Fourth Evangelist proclaimed Jesus as the one in whom God was present and acting (John 1.1-18). The history of Jesus poses a question to which is given a variety of answers. How is this variety to be interpreted?

Thus far we have seen that the history of Jesus poses a question to which both faith and unbelief are possible answers. With this recognition we might possibly clarify Bultmann's position. While the history of Jesus cannot prove the validity of faith, in principle it is possible that historical research might invalidate the basis of faith. Historical criticism can be seen as a negative criterion, destroying views that are unjustifiable on the basis of the evidence. But whether faith or unbelief is valid such an approach is not competent to judge. It is not that there is no relation between the history, with which historical criticism deals, and faith or unbelief, but the evaluation of the relation is not demonstrable. Even if it is allowed that the question raised by the history of Jesus is adequately answered only by faith we are faced with the diversity of responses which have been made by faith. Faith responses are christological responses. Are there limits to the extent of acceptable diversity and how is the diversity to be understood?

Given the diversity of expression a number of interpretations are possible. It could be argued that all expressions are partial and equally valid. Because of the assumed mystery of God, for which christology stands as a symbol of revelation, it could be argued that the variety maintains the sense of mystery. Alternatively, it might be argued that the variety arises from the human situation, that the various christological symbols arise from Jewish, Hellenistic, and other cultural contexts. In this context it might be argued that the variety of forms all, more or less adequately, express the experience of salvation wrought through the Christ event. This is Bultmann's position, and in this he has been followed by many other scholars (see Ogden, *Point*, pp. 76ff.).

This variety of positions raises the question of the relative adequacy of the various expressions. For Bultmann the most adequate expression is the Christ kerygma found in the writings of Paul and John. This kerygma is the key for understanding all kerygmatic expressions. More recently attention has been drawn to the fact that, in addition to the historical Jesus and the Christ kerygma, the New Testament provides evidence of the Jesus kerygma. Because this is attested in Q and the early Markan material it is argued that it has a priority over the Christ kerygma of Paul and John. However, even if the criterion of the earliest tradition is valid, Q and Mark are not self-evidently earlier than the tradition in Paul. The establishment of the *earliest* kerygma as the criterion is itself of doubtful value and involves what has been called a 'genetic fallacy' (*JTSA* 39, pp. 27, 35f.). The earliest perception need not be the clearest and most adequate. With regard to christology, however, the genetic argument is unlikely to be totally irrelevant. The genetic argument is that truth can be detected by means of the route travelled in acquiring it or 'because of the circumstances under which it was born' (*JTSA* 39, p. 35). Truth can be arrived at by many routes, even inadvertently by means of a mistake. However, unless the truth were self-evident, or demonstrable by some other means, the mistakes en route would not convey a sense of confidence in the truth of the inquiry when dealing with history. Because we do not have a neutral and objective criterion our problem is not ontological but epistemological. It is possible, in theory, that someone without any knowledge of the tradition of Jesus might develop a true christology. But this is hardly likely. Further, it would be impossible to test the adequacy of the christology without referring to the tradition. Only if christology were a symbol for true humanity, which is somehow accessible generally in human existence, would it be valid to dispense with the genetic criterion.

While the earliest christology is not necessarily the most adequate, in that reflection may bring clarification and remove misunderstanding,[99] if the Christ event is the norm, christology remains bound to the Christ event. The event of Jesus' life gave rise to the faith which is expressed in the various kerygmatic forms, and they in turn continue to evoke faith. But it remains genuine Christian faith only as long as the event which gave rise to faith continues to be proclaimed. Hence the history of Jesus, and the faith that he evoked, do have some sort of normative role. This could look like a defence of both the normative role of the historical Jesus and the earliest expressions of faith, such as the Jesus kerygma. Bultmann, however, has argued that, in the Jesus kerygma, elements of Jewish apocalyptic are retained side by side with genuine kerygmatic elements although they conflict with them. Partially in Paul, and radically in John, this conflict has been overcome by reinterpreting the apocalyptic elements in a way in keeping with genuine kerygmatic insights.

Thus, in the Jesus kerygma the genuine kerygmatic insights are recognized as the genuinely new elements alongside traditional Jewish ideas, but the implications of the new have not yet been fully perceived. Thus the transformation from Judaism to Christian faith is incomplete.

The strength of Bultmann's position is that he is able to argue that the perception which he finds most adequately in the Christ kerygma of Paul and John is also to be found, though inconsistently, in the Jesus kerygma. It is this that gives his argument cogency, together with the plausible suggestion that the full implications of this perception were not immediately plain because of the pervasive influence of Jewish apocalyptic. Ogden shares Bultmann's view that the various kerygmatic forms express the belief that God has acted in Jesus (*Point*, p. 76). He departs from Bultmann's commitment to the Christ kerygma, however, in favour of Marxsen's Jesus kerygma (*Point*, pp. 51ff.). He is critical of Marxsen, however, because the latter falls back into the quest for the *empirical*-historical Jesus while Ogden asserts that the earliest kerygma must only be used christologically to identify the *existential*-historical Jesus (*Point*, p. 56). On this point he is in agreement with Bultmann. I doubt, however, that Ogden is really committed to the apocalyptic elements in this tradition. If he is not, then it would seem that he has been seduced by the idea that the earliest form of the kerygma must be normative.

Insight can come with reflection, though in the case of christology the original event does have normative status. The question is, how best are we to recognize and make use of that normative status given that perception can be clarified with reflection? An alternative to this position is offered by David Tracy. Like Ogden, he appeals to the Jesus kerygma, but not as the canon within the canon. He prefers to refer to this as 'the major internal corrective' because he seeks to allow for the diversity of the New Testament. Diversity is for him a virtue. Hence there are other correctives besides the major internal corrective. He argues that apocalyptic and the doctrines of Early Catholicism are correctives (*TAI*, pp. 265f.). In recognizing the positive place of apocalyptic Tracy is consistent with his preference for the Jesus kerygma as the major internal corrective. Further, by treating the doctrines of Early Catholicism as a corrective he has begun to indicate his attitude to tradition as 'primary mediator' along with his defence of the fuller scriptural witness as a basis to his attitude to diversity (*TAI*, p. 243 n. 13).

Bultmann's view of both scripture and tradition is that they need to be treated critically because of inconsistencies and contradictions. It is here that his use of the Christ kerygma comes into play. Tracy binds scripture and tradition together in a way that makes it difficult for his major internal corrective to work effectively. If this corrective already involves a contradiction as Bultmann argues, his treatment of the christological diversity can only end in confusion.

The christological tradition reaches some sort of finality in the Chalcedonian definition. In Bultmann's essay on 'The Christology of the New Testament', it becomes clear that he considered the problem of the relation of the two natures of Christ to be a side track leading nowhere (*FU*, pp. 262ff.; *EPT*, pp. 273ff.). Certainly, it could be argued that Bultmann's treatment of this tradition was unsympathetic. He nowhere asks, as he does in his treatment of Paul and John, what might have been *intended* by those who framed the definition. Because of this he sees a marked difference between the New Testament and the patristic doctrine.

> The New Testament indeed holds unmistakenly fast to the humanity of Jesus over against all gnostic doctrine, naturally with a naîveté for which the problems of 'very God and very man' have not yet arisen—those problems which the ancient Church doubtless saw, but sought to solve in an inadequate way by means of Greek thought with its objectivizing nature; a solution which indeed found an expression that is now impossible for our thought, in the Chalcedonian formula ('The Christological Confession of the World Council of Churches', *EPT*, p. 286).

Robert Roberts has argued that a more sympathetic interpretation might understand the formula differently.

> For if it is kept in close association with the biblical narrative, it might be taken as a succinct and perhaps somewhat awkward way of highlighting master features of Jesus' *story*: that he behaved as both God and a man. The non-biblical vocabulary, taken in this way, would not be worrisome (Roberts, p. 120 n. 67).

Two points of interest emerge from this comment. 1. Roberts advocates the demythologizing of the Chalcedonian formula, and in a Bultmannian fashion. He uses the term 'behaved' where Bultmann characteristically uses the analogical language of action. If Bultmann's use of the language of analogy to speak of God's act calls for systematic treatment, the same must be said of Roberts's statement, which does not even begin to indicate how the word 'behaved' is to be understood when used of God. In relation to this problem Bultmann does appeal to the language of analogy and to the work of the philosopher Erich Frank for an exposition of his understanding of this, inadequate though this appeal is. 2. If demythologizing the New Testament is justifiable, indeed necessary, should not the same practice be followed in the interpretation of dogma? Such an approach has been suggested by Hans Jonas.[100] It is therefore somewhat strange that Bultmann, the advocate of demythologizing the New Testament, did not advocate the interpretation of dogma by means of demythologizing. Such an approach might have led to a more sympathetic understanding of dogma. Certainly there have been more sympathetic treatments of the Chalcedonian formula.

Duncan Watson[101] has argued that, far from expressing themselves in a self-contradictory fashion, the fathers of Chalcedon intended to avoid 'squaring the circle', being well aware of the difference between God and man, but believing that God and man had come together in a unique way in Jesus. This conviction was given to them by their reading of scripture and by the tradition of the earlier fathers. Watson rightly recognized the intention of the Chalcedonian fathers and argued that what they have said is to be interpreted in the light of their intention. He also notes that their intention had been formed by scripture and the tradition of the earlier fathers. Perhaps he should have said that their intention was formed by *their reading* of scripture *in the light of the earlier fathers*. What the fathers appear not to have done is to ask about the intention of the New Testament authors. Rather, they appear to have read the New Testament books as source books for dogma. Apparently their intention (the Chalcedonian fathers) was dogmatic. But if we ask of the New Testament authors, concerning their intention, what was the basis of their statements, what motivated them, then Ogden's assessment appears to come close to the point. Ogden says that the most diverse concepts and symbols are used (in the New Testament) 'to identify Jesus as the decisive representation of God' (*Point*, p. 76). Bultmann did not demythologize the Chalcedonian formula because such an interpretation does not express the intention of the fathers. They really did intend to speak about the natures of Christ. Their statements were based on a deductive reading of scripture in the light of the earlier fathers. From this perspective it appears that demythologizing would not be a legitimate form of interpretation.

This objection to the demythologizing of dogma, *as an approach to interpretation*, appears to be decisive. Naturally, demythologizing could be used critically to show how and why the fathers came to false conclusions because of mythological presuppositions. But this is not interpretation; it is criticism. However, the problem is not quite so straightforward. The Chalcedonian formula was not drawn up as a positive statement of belief but as a form which would exclude wrong beliefs. When it is read in its opposition to the heresies of the time it is not so strange that we should conclude that the formula asserts that Jesus acted as both God and a man. Even so, Bultmann's primary justification for not demythologizing the dogma of the early Church has a reasonable basis in the intention of the fathers.

Further, Bultmann saw no reason to regard the Chalcedonian formula, or any other dogmatic statement from the early Church, as essential to the life of the Church. In its own day it was a necessary weapon in a particular situation, but today it is 'an expression that is impossible for our thought' (*EPT*, pp. 273, 286). Demythologizing the New Testament differs from this both because of the intention of the New Testament writers, naive though they may have been, and because of the nature of the New Testament as the *primary* witness to the Christ event.

How then is the christology of the New Testament to be interpreted? Bultmann correctly notes that the New Testament, speaking from faith, speaks of Jesus in terms of the benefits he brings. However, the New Testament goes beyond this. It not only speaks of him as the one who has brought salvation to believers, it declares him to be the only bringer of salvation. Such a confession goes beyond speaking of him from the perspective of his 'benefits'. Bultmann follows the New Testament writers here but will not follow their '*compulsive*' christological affirmations. Both evaluations spring from the knowledge of the salvation brought by Jesus. From this knowledge is it valid to *project* a confession of faith in him as the *only* saviour and if such a projection is valid is not a christological confession also justifiable, perhaps even demanded?

Given the importance of the Fourth Gospel for Bultmann it is relevant to note the argument concerning the implications of the *function* of christology in that Gospel. Both J. Riedl and H. Schlier have argued that the clue to Jesus' person is in his works, that what he does implies who he is, reveals his person. It can hardly be doubted that the evangelist was interested in the metaphysical status of Jesus (John 10.30) as well as his functional significance. Studies attempting to highlight the functional significance of the christology of the Fourth Gospel have recognized this. It could be that this recognition is not only exegetically necessary but logically implied by the function.

Chapter Five

Faith and Understanding

Synopsis

The understanding of faith is the key to Bultmann's theology because the theologian has access to God through the revelation which is known as revelation only in faith. What the revelation reveals of God, faith, and the world, is understood and spoken of from the perspective of faith. From this perspective it becomes clear that the central problem for theology, as far as Bultmann is concerned, is not 'Does God exist?' but 'Can we know him?', 'Can we speak of him?' If we can know him, 'What is the basis and mode of this knowledge?' Such questions provide the setting for contemporary theology.

Evocative Epigram

> It is not enough nor is it Christian, to preach the works, life, and words of Christ as historical facts, as if the knowledge of these would suffice for the conduct of life, although this is the fashion of those who must today be regarded as our best preachers. Far less is it enough or Christian to say nothing at all about Christ and to teach instead the laws of men and the decrees of the fathers . . . Rather ought Christ to be preached to the end that faith in him may be established, that he may not only be Christ, but be Christ for you and me, and that what his name denotes may be effectual in us. Such faith is produced and preserved in us by preaching why Christ came, what he brought and bestowed, what benefit it is to us to accept him. This is done when that Christian freedom that he bestows is rightly taught, and we are told how we Christians are all kings and priests and therefore lords of all, and may firmly believe that whatever we have done is pleasing and acceptable in the sight of God . . .

MARTIN LUTHER, *Tractatus de libertate christiana*

Chapter Five

FAITH AND UNDERSTANDING

The centrality of the theme to Bultmann's theology is indicated by the title he chose for his multi-volume collected essays, *Glauben und Verstehen*. Indeed, the theme is so central that it is not possible to discuss any theme of significance without taking account of his approach to faith and understanding.

1. **Faith and Fact**

How is it that the proclamation of 'the sober facts' of Jesus' life and death can be God's transcendent Word of grace to man? Yet this is Bultmann's understanding as is expressed in the paradox that the historical event is the eschatological event. This affirmation has two roots. 1. The awareness that God is not accessible everywhere but that he is encountered and known in the revelation event. 2. The understanding of the transcendence of God as invisibility and utter difference from this world. Given God's transcendence how can he encounter man in the world? Given God's utter difference from everything in this world, how would man understand him even if such an encounter were possible? These questions set the context within which the complex relation of faith and understanding in Bultmann's thought can be understood.

The 'sober facts' are accessible in the sources collected in the New Testament. Historical-critical methods bring to light what we can know, with some probability, about the life and death of Jesus. These methods, applied to the same sources, also enable us to know what the first Christians *believed* had taken place in and through Jesus' life and death. In various ways they affirmed that God had 'acted' in Jesus to save the world and that Jesus had been raised from the dead. The proclamation of Jesus' life and death was a proclamation of 'sober facts' but the affirmation that God had 'acted' in his life and death goes beyond 'sober facts' and is bound up with the proclamation of the resurrection. The proclamation of the resurrection is not 'sober facts', according to Bultmann. It is the way the first Christians proclaimed that the life and death of Jesus was the eschatological event. Yet, at the same time, Jesus is really risen, and the evidence for this is to be found in the arising of faith as expressed in the kerygma, not in an empty tomb, which is a mythical way of expressing eschatological faith.

Anyone who takes the trouble can learn of Jesus' life and death by approaching the sources with appropriate methods. Anyone can learn what the first Christians believed about him. That is not to suggest that either of these tasks is simple. It is rather to recognize that this knowledge is publicly accessible. Nor does it imply that such reconstructions of past understanding find universal acceptance in terms of fine detail. But the most serious disagreements emerge over the questions of whether the form in which the first Christians proclaimed their faith was mythological and whether their faith corresponds to reality or not. Bultmann's position is weakened by the fact that the New Testament writers really intended to assert that Jesus was physically risen from the dead, and this is admitted by him. There is no indication that the 'resurrection' faith was an expression of new life rather than a reference to the physical resurrection of Jesus. Without this clear indication Bultmann is forced to depend only on the recognition that the *Weltbild* of the first-century Christians was mythical. Such a way of thinking is no longer acceptable. This need not be the case.

Given that it is possible to understand the 'sober facts' and that what the first Christians believed had occurred in and through them it is important to recognize that such understanding does not involve sharing that faith. It is, however, the precondition to sharing it. The distinction has two bases. (1) The faith is based on presuppositions which are not generally accepted. (2) The evidence in which the truth claims of faith is expressed is itself problematical. The fragmentary and conflicting nature of the evidence is accentuated by the presuppositions peculiar to faith.

2. **Understanding God's Act**

What is the difference between faith and understanding? Is it possible to understand *what* faith proclaims without actually believing? In as much as faith proclaims the life and death of Jesus as events which are evident in accessible data this much can be understood by anyone who cares to take the effort to understand. Further, when it is proclaimed that in these events God has 'acted', this is also open to understanding *if* those who proclaim it explain what they mean. Certainly an act of God is not visible as an act of God in these events. How then does faith perceive an act of God in these events? Can this perception be communicated? In fact the kerygma is the communication of this perception with one addition. It is the proclamation that the God who acted in Jesus' life and death continues to act in the proclamation of that life and death. This means that God's 'act' is bound to Jesus' life and death and the proclamation of it.

How, then, is the life and death of Jesus to be understood as the 'act' of God? Bultmann's interpretation is set out in his commentary on the *Fourth Gospel*, especially in the double interpretation of the Footwashing (John 13.1-20; *GJ*, p. 468). Here, as elsewhere, Bultmann emphasizes that Jesus' work is complete in his coming and going.

The cross overcomes the epistemological problem. Through it the believer comes to understand Jesus' work as God's act, and God's act as Jesus' loving service to his own. His death illustrates what had been true 'since his incarnation'. The 'footwashing' symbolizes the cross, and Peter's response (13.8) represents the basic way men think, refusing to see God's saving act in what is lowly, God in the form of a slave. The 'footwashing' symbolizes Jesus' cleansing work, which he performs by his word (15.3). He himself is encountered in his word and the service he performs is spoken of in terms of cleansing, or freedom, in other words, as salvation (*GJ*, p. 470).

Jesus' saving work was complete except that the disciples had to experience or know that work performed on themselves (13.7, 10; *GJ*, pp. 473f.). The footwashing is seen as a symbolic act, representative of his loving service. This work is not objectively visible, not a piece of world history, but is known when his service is received. Only the person whom Jesus has served perceives the significance of his work, for what he is becomes apparent in each new situation. In each new situation the disciple knows that he has been served by Jesus, that he is loved. What is more, the service of Jesus is perceived as God's act grounded in God's love.

3. Understanding and Faith

Anyone who takes the trouble can discover that those who believe assert that, in Jesus, God's loving action of service has been performed, and that, in it, God's saving act is to be known. But knowing that this is what believers understand is not the same thing as having the understanding of faith. It is not the same as believing. This is to leave aside the question of precisely what is meant when it is said that Jesus' life and death is God's act. Here all that needs to be said is that such a statement can be understood in various ways, some more satisfactory than others. Understanding what is asserted is the possibility and responsibility of any man. It is a necessary presupposition of faith but is not to be equated with faith itself. The understanding which precedes faith is what makes the kerygma intelligible. It is the understanding of what the kerygma proclaims. This can be compared with the distinction of speaking *about* God and speaking *from* God. It is not in man's power to speak from God. Only if God graciously enables man, who speaks about God, to speak from God does what is humanly impossible actually occur. It is then that the kerygma, which is speech about God's act, becomes itself God's act, and man knows himself to be addressed by God.

When man knows himself to be addressed by God then, in faith, he knows he is loved by God. From another point of view it can be said that, for the believer, the world has become God's creation once more. According to this understanding man knows that his life is a gracious gift God. He no longer has any need to establish his own existence because he has it as a gift from God. But he only knows this when he is addressed by God in the kerygma. The address of the kerygma is not something that can be demonstrated, but it is recognized as such only by faith. Paradoxically, only faith perceives God's address in the kerygma and without that address there would be no faith. Through it man is drawn by the Father.

> It occurs when man abandons his own judgement and 'hears' and 'learns' from the Father, when he allows God to speak to him. The 'drawing' by the Father occurs not, as it were, *behind* man's decision of faith but *in* it (*GJ*, pp. 231f.).

4. **The Revelation of Faith**

Bultmann's interpretation seems to be related to what has traditionally been called the doctrine of election. Certainly the occurrence of God's address to man is outside man's control. Not even the proclamation of the kerygma guarantees that address. Its occurrence is a mystery, dependent on God. When that address does occur a response is necessary. That response need not be faith. It must be faith or unbelief in response to the question of the divine *love*. Faith and unbelief are responsible *deeds*, in which it becomes manifest what man is (*GJ*, p. 156). This is a boldly paradoxical way of saying that in man's decision in the encounter with the Revealer it becomes apparent what he really is (*GJ*, p. 159). Here the idea of the determination of man by his origin, which (according to Bultmann) the evangelist has taken over from Gnosticism, has been radically interpreted so that in the decision of faith or unbelief man definitively *chooses* his origin. Before the encounter with the Revealer all men are 'blind', in the 'darkness', that is, without authentic life and knowledge of God. But through encounter with the revelation men definitively choose light and life or darkness and death. This is the paradox of the revelation, that to be grace it must reveal sin and for those who reject the revelation sin becomes definitive for the first time (*GJ*, pp. 341f.).

From what has been said it could appear that deterministic language is a form of *hyperbole* to bring out the miraculous nature of faith in response to the revelation. The response is not determined as is shown by the stress on man's responsibility to decide in faith or unbelief. However, the matter is more complex than is at first apparent. The revelation presupposes a certain pre-understanding if it is to be intelligible. Because the revelation calls man into question it will be unintelligible to the man who is unaware of his own questionableness. All understanding is grounded on self-understanding and it is this that is put in question by the revelation. A changed self-understanding involves a new understanding of everything. Paradoxically, apart from faith it is impossible to understand what the revelation says. At the same time faith is a process of understanding.

> For the being of the unbeliever is constituted by the will to unbelief. What he *wills* is determined by this *being*, and he *cannot* will any differently. Can he then *be* different? Yes, for the question of the Revealer puts his very being in question; the Revealer calls on him to decide... Confronted by the revelation man, by his decision, chooses his origin; and this origin which he chooses is unambiguous: God or the Devil (*GJ*, p. 317).

Hidden within this discussion are important distinctions. Bultmann is not saying that the revelation or the language of the kerygma is meaningless in the sense that such a man cannot understand what is being said at all. Rather his point is that such a man will not see how the message could have anything to do with him. It is for this reason that the revelation specifically confronts man with his own questionableness. What seems to be impossible in fact occurs. Man, confronted by the challenge of the revelation, decides for or against it. By all accounts his decision would be expected to be a rejection of the revelation. Miraculously, this is not always the case. Confronted by the revelation some men recognize their questionableness and respond in faith. When this is done the believer is no longer determined by his past, by his own past self-understanding. This can be described as the gaining of a new origin, a 'new birth' or as the decision by means of which the 'world' is tilted off its axis so that it again becomes the creation of God (*FU*, p. 64). Two matters need further discussion. How is this impossible possibility of faith to be understood? Is not talk of the 'world' becoming creation going too far as an interpretation of the coming of faith?

Because faith comes where it seems to be impossible, Bultmann has some justification in arguing that without faith the revelation is unintelligible in the sense described above. How then can man pass from unbelief to faith? How can he be different? Confronted with the revelation man must decide and in decision some men do in fact believe. This view of revelation has something in common with what Ian Ramsey called 'a disclosure situation' and the resulting conviction could be compared with the 'blik' of R. Hare. Bultmann wished to emphasize the unpredictable effectiveness of the revelation and the absolute assurance of believer as a consequence of his experience. That assurance of faith is not based on objective evidence, it goes beyond evidence and can even be in spite of the evidence. Bultmann differs from both Ramsey and Hare in asserting that the conviction of which he speaks is a consequence of a particular disclosure event, the encounter with the Revealer through the transcendent Word of grace in the kerygma.

Only the encounter with the Revealer can make man other than he is. The question why more men, or all men, do not believe can only be answered by saying that, in order to bring grace, the revelation must also give offence, because the Word of grace is qualitatively other than this world of darkness. It can only be present as a challenge which overcomes this world. Those who are committed to this world can only be judged by the Word of grace. However, it would be a mistake to understand the priority of grace as an explanation of why some believe and others do not. This would be to misunderstand Bultmann's intention which was to make clear the nature of man's freedom and responsibility in response to the goodness of God.

5. **The Significance of Faith**

The coming of faith is the dawn of a new self-understanding and the dawn of the new creation because the new self-understanding transforms the vision of all else (*GJ*, p. 317). Because man's self understanding is changed the world becomes a new place to him, it is seen in a new light. That light, from the perspective of faith, is the light of God's creation. Thus faith is the Archimedean point from which the world is moved off its axis and is transformed from the world of sin into God's world (*FU*, p. 64; cf. Kegley, p. 268). This is the fulfilment of the original possibility given with creation (*GJ*, pp. 40ff.). But the world is not visible as creation apart from faith because such a vision has its basis in 'faith in redemption' (*EF*, p. 224). This is faith in Jesus

> in whose destiny God is at work, in whose Word God speaks. He has died on the cross—for us; and now he lives in eternity—for us! And only when we understand this do we understand that God is the creator; and so it is through him that the world becomes creation—for us (*EF*, pp. 179f.).

Only faith recognizes the claim of the revelation and understands itself in the light of the revelation. This new understanding corresponds to the reality of God's creation—the world of sin becomes God's creation.

Perhaps this stress on the significance of faith throws light on the tendency among Bultmann's critics to label him as a Lutheran as if such a label put him in his place so that he need no longer trouble us. Bultmann was a Lutheran and for him justification by faith was central. However, the contexts in which this teaching was understood are quite different for Bultmann and Luther. For Luther the problem was the burden of a guilty conscience before God (*EPT*, p. 40) while Bultmann dealt with the problem of human insecurity in the modern world (*JCM*, p. 84; cf. Johnson, pp. 196-200). Hence, for him, the problem should be seen in terms of epistemology. He saw one of his tasks as applying the teaching of justification by faith to epistemology (*JCM*, p. 84; *K&M*, II, p. 191), a task quite different from Luther's. While he was not uninfluenced by Luther it was to Paul (and John) that he appealed as the real source of both his understanding and also of Luther's (*JCM*, p. 94; *K&M*, I, pp. 210f.). He refused to base his understanding of Paul on Luther because this would only complicate the task (*FU*, p. 154). He also saw the need of dialogue with Catholic exegesis (*EF*, pp. 296, 351). This critical dialogue was a safeguard against a biased reading of Paul.

Paul's teaching of justification by faith alone is understood as the rejection of every human attempt to *secure* man's life before God, whether on the basis of the works of the law or on the basis of knowledge. In this regard this teaching is the counterpart of the kerygma understood as the preaching of the cross of Christ as God's saving act. Bultmann has argued that events and their interpretations are *inseparable*. The event evokes interpretation (Kegley, p. 265). In the case of the cross of *Christ* it evoked the interpretation of faith. It is pointless to ask if God might not have used some other event. The fact is that the cross is the saving event because through it faith and life have dawned in the world.

6. **Faith as Perception**

While a degree of understanding is a precondition of faith—for this reason Bultmann has worked to make the gospel intelligible to modern man at the level of concepts—such understanding is not faith. Faith involves a *perception* which goes beyond what is apparent in the world of nature or history.[102] Indeed, it can be said that faith is the hidden meaning in history (Kegley, p. 265). But this hiddenness is not something which can be uncovered once and for all. It is something perceptible only to faith. In one sense it is true to say that God is revealed in the world and in history. But it must be said immediately that such revelation can only be seen by one who believes. Anyone can learn that Christians claim that the cross of Christ is God's saving act, but only the believer actually *sees it as such*. The further mystery that Bultmann asserts is that once this has been seen the hidden meaning in the world and history can also be seen (*FU*, p. 64; *EPT*, pp. 114ff., 118,; *EF*, pp. 179ff., 224). It can even be said that the world, and history, and man's own life raise the question of God. But in these realms alone God is not to be found. Only man living in history in the world, confronted by God's call in the kerygma, can discover the faith in which to live with others before God in this world. The world and world history do not in themselves reveal God. They are enigmatic and much that happens there is clamorous, confusing and inimitable of God. For this situation the cross of Christ appears as the appropriate Word of God to man in a world in which God's Word, if it is heard at all, appears distorted. Is this perhaps what Bultmann meant when he asserted that we can believe in God only in spite of experience? (*JCM*, p. 84). Neither the world, nor world history, in itself is an adequate basis for faith. But in the light of the faith which arises from the kerygmna, the word of the cross, God's action is perceptible in both the world of creation and of history. This is not thought of as a 'worldview' that belongs to faith once and for all. It is a possibility to be realized again and again in the decision of the moment.

7. **Faith as Decision**

Faith is the perception of God's act in Christ. This perception opens the believer's eyes to the world as God's creation. But faith is more than this perception. Faith is also a *decision*. There is no need to argue that the element of decision is central to Bultmann's understanding of faith. This is generally recognized. What has not been properly noted is that, for him, the decision of faith is *submissive* rather than assertive.[103] The believer is overcome by the revelation and submits to it. The believer willingly allows his life to be determined by the revelation. This is how the decision is to be understood. Thus, from Bultmann's point of view it is the unbeliever who is *self-assertive* in refusing to submit to the revelation. Faith is also seen as a gift of the revelation, not a human work. While it is an act in which the believer is fully and freely involved, it is not a work because the believer knows that the gift comes from God, life comes from God and can only be received or rejected. Because faith is caught up in the revelation event it can be said that life is revealed and that the word of proclamation and faith are revealed (*EF*, p. 78).

8. **Faith and Self-Understanding**

What the revelation brings is *not* new conceptual knowledge otherwise inaccessible to man. The conceptions used arise from the pre-understanding given with man's life in the world and developed in tradition. But in the revelation this understanding is radicalized and corrected (*EF*, p. 88). What is achieved in this? The revelation of faith involves a *new self-understanding* for the believer (*EF*, p. 85). This sounds self-centred. The reverse is actually true. The old self-understanding is what was self-centred. In the new self-understanding the believer's world has been tipped off its axis, the axis which made man himself the centre. It is this centre which made that world the world of sin. The revelation of faith brings a new Archimedean point so that the world of sin becomes God's world (*FU*, p. 64). All of this is bound up with the understanding that belongs to faith. It is crucial to recognize that, for Bultmann, understanding is relational. The new self-understanding is the consequence of the believer finding himself in a new relationship which transforms all relationships and also his self-understanding. For faith, this new self-understanding is brought about by God's act, his revelation (Kegley, p. 261).

9. **Love for the Neighbour**

Faith has its rise in the Christ event for which the cross of Christ is central. Understood as God's saving act the cross reveals God's love for man which can be expressed in terms of forgiveness. In John the 'footwashing' has become symbolic of that event. In addition to demonstrating Christ's act of loving service Bultmann appeals to a second interpretation. For those who know themselves as those who have been served by Jesus, his act becomes the paradigm for life. But it is not *simply* a matter of following his example. Knowing themselves to be loved by God they know themselves to be both called and free to love one another (*GJ*, p. 475). Consequently faith involves a new understanding of the neighbour as the one the believer is called to love and in fact is able to love. This transformation is a consequence of the revelation event and it is an evidence of faith.

But what will be involved by faith in relation to the neighbour? According to Bultmann this cannot be laid down in advance. All that can be said is that the response of faith will involve the believer in love for the neighbour and obedience to God's demand which meets him in the claim of the moment (*EPT*, p. 309). Thus it can be said in advance that love will be required and that we know what love is on the basis of God's forgiving love revealed in Christ ('TLYN', pp. 53ff.). While this gives a clue as to what might be involved, in fact only time can reveal what love will demand. It will involve the good of the neighbour, which is not a limited liability. But nothing is laid down specifically. The believer is not relieved of his responsibility. What he is given is the actual possibility of loving in whatever way the situation demands. However, that possibility is actual only in faith, when the believer responds believingly out of his own awareness of being loved by God.

Given this stress on faith expressed in love for the neighbour, it is difficult to understand how Bultmann could be charged with an individualistic understanding of faith. Faith involves the neighbour, it is a reality within the community of faith. Faith presupposes and involves the Church. The Church is the historical bearer of the kerygma without which there would be no faith (Kegley, p. 260). The purpose of Church order is to serve the proclamation. But awareness of this cannot determine Church order. Bultmann says that church order has not been the focus of his work (Kegley, pp. 277f.). This is not because he denied the importance of such work. Rather he has left the reflection on this subject to those who bear specific responsibility for the task. Hence he acknowledges 'this lack in my work' (Kegley, p. 278). The 'lack' is not evidence of a rejection or a view of the insignificance of the subject. Rather it is to be seen as a consequence of the task appropriate to Bultmann as a 'scientific' interpreter of the New Testament writings. Here Bultmann's stress on faith, which finds expression in love for the neighbour, is clear and constant. Naturally, what love will mean cannot be treated systematically because this can be discovered only in the claim of the moment.

10. **Responsibility for the World**

The claim of the moment goes beyond love for the neighbour; it involves obedience to God's demand in all situations. Man's relation to the world must be considered because the believer is called to be responsible for the world (Kegley, pp. 279f.). What does this mean? It involves no Christian world view, as if Christians had a blueprint for the future. The possibilities for the world are opened up by science and technology, and the believer, as much as any man, must take note of all this. What the believer knows is that the world is God's creation and he is God's creature, that his life has been given to him and that he is responsible for the life of his neighbour and for the life of the world. This is involved in the obedience man owes to God and is included in 'the love command'. But the love command gives no specific directions. For this purpose the believer, as all men, has the faculty of reason.

> He is, therefore, also responsible for institutions in which a life of freedom and responsibility is possible, and for the ordering of social existence through justice and righteousness ... it is equally true that these demands are, as such, not specifically Christian, but are

> rather general human demands . . . Perhaps one may say that faith and love are made manifest only in so far as there are Christians who, acting in faith and love and guided by their reason, take upon themselves responsibility for the world (Kegley, p. 280).

What distinguishes the Christian from others is not the knowledge of what is good and just and loving. The faculty of reason is the means by which all have to work out such questions. What distinguishes Christians is the realization of faith and love, of authentic existence (Kegley, p. 260).

When the believer takes responsibility for the world he does so from the perspective of the relationship of faith. His relationship to the world has a dialectical character which Bultmann describes as 'having as though he did not have' (1 Corinthians 7.29-31; *EF*, pp. 84f., 221; *EPT*, pp. 112, 131; *FU*, pp. 74f.). From this perspective the world is seen as 'provisional', not of ultimate concern. Consequently the man of faith does not surrender to the world. In this sense, 'he is not of the world'. Yet the world is of value, it is God's creation, his gift, and the man of faith has responsibility for it, not because he is a believer, but because he is a man. As a believer what is different is that the world is seen as creation, as provisional, and of value, but not of ultimate concern. The believer knows he has responsibility for the world. It is not to be plundered and exploited by him. How the believer should act can only be spoken of generally in terms of love and obedience to God. What this will actually mean can only be discovered through the reasoned exercise of faith and love in the situation in which the believer finds himself. But he is not left without some guidance. Not only does he know he is loved and that, because his life is given to him, he is freed from the world and free to love, he knows quite concretely what love is. God's love in Christ is the basis and paradigm for the believer's obedience in love (John 13.34f.; 15.9-14; Rom. 5.8; 1 John 4.9-19; *EF*, p. 85).

Such faith and love are understood as the response to the transcendent Word. Bultmann stresses the responsive nature of faith. The new life of faith is possibly only through the Word of revelation. Here Bultmann has run into conflict with those who are in general agreement with him, e.g. Schubert Ogden (Kegley, pp. 271-73). The believer proclaims the reality of the *Other* encountered in the Word though this cannot be proved outside of faith. Faith is a decision for that reality, that is, the believer has been overcome by the *One* who encounters him in the Word. To be overcome in this way is to be made *free from* the determining power of the past and *free to* obey the call of God in whatever might come, although this cannot be foreseen or predicted. The call of God becomes clear in the challenge of the moment. All that can be said in advance is that love will be required and that what is required is given, that in Christ the believer has been made free to love because he knows he is loved by God.

Surprisingly and mistakenly it is sometimes argued that all that matters for Bultmann is that man decide and that what he decides is irrelevant (thus Roberts, p. 26 n. 22). It would be difficult to find an interpretation of Bultmann more wrong than this one. What Roberts has said might be true of some existentialists. It is not true of Bultmann. The fact is, according to Bultmann, that man *is* 'potentiality to be'. He chooses himself in his choices. This is inevitable. But *what he chooses* is crucial. Will he choose faith or unbelief, life or death, love or hate, the world or God? In each of these choices man chooses himself in the sense of choosing what he will be. It is here that Roberts has been beguiled by language. For Bultmann 'the choice of one's self' is a byproduct of every decision. What one is to be is settled in the decision. Each decision is critical, whether it will be in faith and love or not. The choice of one's self is a consequence, a byproduct of the decision of faith or unbelief. To suggest that the decision for one's self is a direct 'choice of one's self' would be, in Bultmann's terms, a decision of unbelief which, as a consequence, gives up the possibility of authentic existence. The decision of faith is always for God and for the neighbour and in responsibility for the world. Indeed it can be said that the believer accepts responsibility for the world with a new urgency. Though Bultmann does not elaborate the theme, he has said enough to show that the Christian's responsibility for the world also involves concerns for institutions which will provide structures to safeguard human freedom and responsibility, justice and righteousness. That is, theology provides a guide to the goal of political activity though it prescribes nothing that could be seen as a party-political programme.

11. Theology as Hermeneutics

Bultmann is also at pains to insist that no *ethical programme* can be derived from his theology. His theology reveals the motivation for the development of ethics on the basis of faith and love. He has emphasized the urgency for Christians to take their responsibility for the world seriously. The world is not to be given up, it is God's creation. Existence in faith is to be lived out in the world and for the sake of the world. While Bultmann did not write about ecology and conservation—in this his writings reflect the time of his work and his preoccupation with the New Testament—from our perspective these implications are clearly in his theology. Here, as elsewhere, the believer is to respond to the problems and challenges of his situation in the faith and love which are the response to the transcendent Word of grace. Theology has to understand that Word and the response which it evokes (Kegley, p. xxiv; *Letters*, p. 160). Understanding involves the problems and questions of each new age. Our new age is quite different from that in which Bultmann stood and by which his questions were formed. He recognized that this would happen and that each new age must do its own theology. The task of interpreting the New Testament—which Bultmann understood as the task of theology—is *never* done definitively. That is not to say that there are no gains on the basis of the endeavour of those who have gone before us. But, however much we may build on their work, it can never take the place of our own endeavour to understand God's transcendent Word of grace and what it means to hear and to believe.

From Bultmann we may learn that the transcendent Word of grace, the revelation, can only be known when it encounters man in his existence. Theology is, therefore, the attempt to understand that Word as it is known and believed. Theology has the task of explicating believing *understanding* of the Word, the revelation which gives rise to faith, and faith itself (Kegley, p. xxiv). Taken seriously the implications are far-reaching. Whatever the dogmas, they have their origin, in so far as they have meaning, in the existence of believers, which gave rise to these statements. In terms of the history of dogma, dogmas often developed in a very different fashion. The Bible was 'mined' with a view to constructing dogmas concerning God, man and the world. This was often done without regard for what gave rise to the biblical statements and what these statements meant in their historical contexts. Rather the Bible was used to answer questions and problems of later times when 'orthodoxy' of beliefs, understood as dogmas, had become important. The existential basis of the language of faith was not maintained as central. The development of dogmas along these lines was possible on the basis of the belief that God had revealed truths about 'the other world', this world, man and the future. Such truths could be given only by the communication of conceptual knowledge in language, in words that could be passed on. Did the prophets communicate such supernatural truths? Did Jesus bring information from heaven? Perhaps it is not impossible to defend some such position. Few scholars would wish to do so. What is the alternative, at least an alternative, for faith?

Bultmann regards the idea of revelation as the communication of information inaccessible to man except by supernatural means as mythological. Nor did he think that the New Testament actually communicates this understanding, at least not when it is read critically taking account of the intention of the New Testament writers. The reader of today can be misled about *what* was intended by the *way* in which it was expressed. It is a truism to say that the New Testament writers expressed themselves in the *language* of their day: not merely the words, but the language. Hence the interpreter is caught up with the conceptuality of the first century *as well* as of the twentieth century.

But where does theology begin? It can only begin with faith and that means faith as it is. What faith is today is the consequence of the tradition which joins the believer of today with the origin of faith. That tradition is bound up with the believing community, the Church, without which there would be no faith. Methodologically the correct way for theology to operate is from the present through the past back to the origin of faith, because the theologian cannot and should not attempt to strip away his own understanding in order to learn from the past. He can only learn from the past on the basis of what he knows. The tour through the past has, initially, the purpose of illuminating his understanding and showing how understanding came to be what it is. However, present understanding has, as its ground and object, an event of the past. The reason for this can be summed up in the slogan 'the proclaimer became the proclaimed'. The one who first, through his life and death, gave rise to faith continues to be proclaimed as the ground of faith. What is 'special' about the New Testament is that it is the witness to the faith to which the life and death of Jesus actually gave rise. From that point on, all faith is dependent on the proclamation arising out of the faith evoked by the life and death of Jesus.

The Word that is proclaimed is first made known to us in the New Testament. The life of the Church down through the ages is dependent on that kerygma. In this sense *theology is hermeneutics*, the critical understanding of the kerygma as it finds expression in the New Testament. Because the kerygma there is expressed in a variety of historical-cultural forms and varying degrees of perception the task is both demanding and critical. It is demanding because of the complexity of the historical data with inherent problems of gaps in our knowledge of situations, authors, literary techniques and conventions, not to mention the different worlds of thought. It is necessarily critical because, in Bultmann's view, the kerygma was not understood by all writers with the same clarity and consistency. Even a writer like Paul could himself fall away from the new understanding involved in the kerygma back into the old world of thought of Judaism.

Faith has understood the Christ event as the event which reconciles man to God. Bultmann does not doubt this; it is the given with which theology works. Not every theologian would agree. There is a growing tendency to recognize other religions as authentic ways to God. For such an approach the New Testament need not be normative in the way that it was for Bultmann. For him the purity of the kerygma is safeguarded by the critical interpretation of the New Testament. Theology does not have the liberty to work outside the kerygma. Theology is the understanding of faith and the Word which gives rise to faith. As the interpretation of the Word it is the interpretation of faith's understanding of the Word.

Because theology is always an expression of faith's understanding, hermeneutics involves the interpretation of this understanding. Theology which deals with the interpretation of the New Testament involves also the understanding of the believer who brings his questions and problems to the work of interpretation. If we are to build on the work of Bultmann this will be done *not only* in critical discussion with his work in its own terms but also in critical discussion on our terms.

12. **Faith in a Pluralistic Age**

Living in a pluralistic age, perhaps more accurately described as an age which recognizes pluralism, has produced a situation of crisis for the claim that Christ is *the way* to God. Frequently this has led to the reduction of the claim from *the* way to *a* way, even if for some it is a way which is decisively significant for the recognition of other ways and evaluating their relative adequacy. But Bultmann is not one of those who has moved in this direction. Two important questions arise in response to his position. (1) What is the fate of those who have never heard of Christ? (2) What is the fate of those who lived before Christ; in particular, what about the Old Testament?

Recognition of the unique act of God in Christ as *the* saving act of God does not necessarily mean that *salvation* is restricted to those who believe in Christ. Bultmann recognized the importance of the distinction between those who reject the revelation and those who have never heard (*GJ*, p. 257 n. 3). Consequently, while ultimate salvation might not be bound to the response of faith to the revelation in the Christ event, authentic existence certainly is. Existence in faith is authentic existence. For those who, like Ogden, would distinguish between Christian existence and authentic existence the question needs to be asked, 'What difference does faith in Christ make?' If it makes no difference, why bother? If it is one authentic way amongst others why choose it rather than one of the other ways? According to Bultmann existence in faith is decisively different from all other modes of human existence and is justifiably called 'authentic existence'.

From this perspective Bultmann recognized the complex question concerning the relation of the Old Testament to the New. While the Old Testament is not a Christian book, to abandon the Old is to abandon the New ('SOTCF', p. 21). However, the ethnic nationalism, marked by particular cultic practices which separate this people from all others, is enough to show that the Old Testament is not a Christian book. Yet in the Old Testament there is to be found the same understanding of God, creation and human existence as we find in the New, at least in the teaching of the great prophets. But is this understanding of authentic existence shared only as an unrealized ideal? Is the life of faith actually achieved in Old Testament times? Does not Bultmann teach that the life of faith is realized only in the faith of the kerygma which had its origin in the historical Jesus? That the Old Testament should teach an understanding of what constitutes authentic existence is not a problem. Philosophy might do this also. There is a problem for his theology only if authentic existence is attainable apart from the faith of the kerygma. For Bultmann asserts that with the arising of the kerygma there is a new history, the history of the revelation, the history of faith (*GJ*, pp. 615f.).

While the kerygma arose from the history of Jesus, he was not a Christian but a Jew standing in the line of the great prophets. Only in the proclamation of the early church did 'the proclaimer become the proclaimed'. This marks the distinctive development of Christian faith. The Christian kerygma and faith have a christological orientation without which they would not be Christian. Does this mean that Jesus, while proclaiming the promises of God and the possibility of authentic existence, did not himself realize authentic existence? And what are we to make of the faith of such Old Testament figures as Abraham? According to Paul, Abraham was the archetypal believer (Romans 4). Bultmann regarded such faith as atypical.

> It must be recognized, however, that the *relation of the Church to Israel's history* is a peculiarly paradoxical one because the course of events from Jacob–Israel down to the present is not a continuous history but one broken by the eschatological occurrence in Christ. That is, the eschatological congregation is not simply the historical successor and heir of the empirical Israel of history but the heir of the ideal Israel, so to say, the people of God which the historical Israel was indeed called to be, but which, in point of fact, it never actually was. For it was indeed the elect People of God; but its election always hovered above and ahead of it, so to say, as a goal and promise. Israel's election determined its history in consequence of divine guidance in bane and blessing. Still the election never came to realization—or, when it did, only in exceptions like Abraham, the strong in faith (Rom. 4, Heb. 11.8ff., etc.), David in whom God was pleased (Acts 13.22) and in whom the Spirit spoke (Acts 1.16, Rom. 4.6, etc.), the prophets and men of faith who now serve as models to the Church (*Th.N.T.*, I, p. 97).

Are such exceptional responses to the promises of God prior to the arising of the kerygma to be thought of as the realization of authentic faith, authentic existence? For Israel generally authentic existence is to be seen as an unfulfilled ideal, a hope. But Abraham, David, and the prophets were exceptions to this rule. Should not Jesus also be included in this exceptional group? Against all probability and without continuity these individuals responded in faith to the promises of God. As such, the exceptional faith of such individuals is testimony to the power of the grace of God to encounter man in his situation and to free him from his past.

What is said here about the exceptional breakthrough of the grace of God in human history is also applicable to the 'pagan' world outside the circle where the sound of the gospel is to be heard. There also, from time to time there are those who manifest the grace of God in their lives in the way that is true of the response of faith. But as in the Old Testament, such responses might lack the clarity and fullness of the life of faith in response to the gospel. Also lacking outside the circle where the gospel is to be heard is the continuing community where such faith and life are the norm rather than the exception. Perhaps one should say that, in the continuing community, they ought to be and often are to be found and that there the continuity of the gospel guarantees the continuity of the response of faith. Thus it would seem that Bultmann makes the faith of the kerygma the norm of authentic existence though he allows for exceptions outside this tradition because the grace of God cannot be bound, that is, restricted, to it. In another sense the grace of God is bound (not restricted) to this tradition and because of this the continuity of faith is maintained. If this reading of Bultmann is correct his position is closer to Schubert Ogden than is generally recognized.

Hermeneutical theology is the interpretation of the New Testament (as a document from the past) in the light of our contemporary self-understanding, with the questions and the problem that raises. In the past theology has been allowed to develop a degree of independence from the New Testament and to work philosophically. In the new theological movement there was the awareness that theology had to be rooted in the New Testament. The birth of that movement was announced by the publication of Barth's *Romans*, and he continued to publish works concerned with the interpretation of the New Testament, both as monographs and as long excursuses in his *CD*. But Barth's methodology failed to take sufficient account of the New Testament as a collection of documents from the past. Bultmann, more than anyone else in that movement, was concerned to understand the New Testament on the basis of a scientific historical approach. Today it is increasingly being recognized that theology must work with the New Testament and wrestle with the difficult historical problems it involves and not merely take over the results which suit.[104]

But theology is not only the scientific historical interpretation of the New Testament. Theology is concerned with what the New Testament has to say *to us today* and for this it is necessary for us to understand ourselves at this point of history. Our situation in world history is expressly relevant for this task. Hermeneutical theology can only be done where the theologian is as fully conscious as possible of the two horizons—the past conceptuality and the present conceptuality.

Understanding the kerygma in our age of pluralism of values, cultures and religions constitutes a major crisis for our day. Theology as hermeneutics self-consciously attempts to understand the kerygma in relation to these problems. Ours is a world which has seen an incredible development of technology over the past one hundred years. Such developments have placed previously undreamt-of powers in the hands of the few, the technocrats, multinational corporations and political institutions. Ours is a nuclear age. Never before has man had at his disposal such powers for good or evil, and since Hiroshima, August 6th, 1945, the world has lived in the shadow and threat of nuclear holocaust.

What the gospel will mean in a nuclear age is a question that might well, more than ever before, and more urgently, call believers to exercise responsibility for those institutions which open up freedom, justice and righteousness for the world in the face of the threat of institutional tyranny and destruction. However, the gospel gives no blueprint for the future, no party-political programme. What it does is to call man to responsibility for the world, to alert him to the nature of that responsibility in terms of the structures which make possible freedom, justice and righteousness, and to alert him to the real source of the world's problems, man. The real problem is human sinfulness, self centredness, the lust for power. Thus, the believer who understands that he is called to take on this responsibility knows the goal for which he works and, guided by reason, can work for this with all other men of goodwill. The believer shares this responsibility with all men and participates in this work with all who share his vision.

However, the institutions which can provide structures for freedom, justice and righteousness are not the Kingdom of God. What is more, no institution is free from exploitation and injustice. That is not to say that exploitation and injustice are inevitably institutionalized. There is a difference. But man, who is turned in on himself, will find means of exploitation and injustice in any social institution. The problem lies with man. It is for this reason that Bultmann was preoccupied with the gospel which calls man to faith and understanding. Only in response to the gospel can this world of sin, which is already for some a veritable hell, and is potentially that for us all in this nuclear age, become again God's creation. If Bultmann was right the task of theology is more urgent today than ever before. That task involves understanding the kerygma of the

New Testament. For this the most stringent and demanding historical work on the New Testament is required. But this is not enough. When we can understand the kerygma in the terms of the first century we then must struggle with the questions of our own day in relation to that understanding. This is the task of theology in every age.

NOTES

Notes to Introduction

1. See Hans Jonas, 'Is Faith Still Possible? Memories of Rudolf Bultmann and Reflections on the Philosophical Aspects of His Work', *HTR* 75/1 (1982), pp. 1-23; and also 'A Retrospective View', in *Proceedings of the International Colloquium on Gnosticism* (Leiden: Brill, 1977), pp. 1-15.

2. See for example O. Betz, *What do we know about Jesus?* (London: SCM, 1968), pp. 12ff.

3. Thus Macquarrie (*AET*, p. ix, etc.). Johnson, p. 19 n. l, notes the influence of Macquarrie's book in establishing the thesis of Bultmann's dependence on Heidegger in English language theology.

4. For Bultmann's relation to existentialism prior to his meeting with Heidegger, see Schmithals, pp. 18f., and *Letters*, p. 6. See also Karl Barth in *K&M*, II, p. 123. James Richmond, *Ritschl's Theology*, pp. 41f., rightly argues that the emphasis on the influence of Kierkegaard and Heidegger is too narrow. He emphasizes the importance of the Ritschlian school.

5. Johnson, pp. 34f.; Thiselton, pp. 210f.; Richmond, pp. 41f., 296ff.

6. The letter is dated December 31st, 1922. Bultmann thought that Barth's opposition to Schleiermacher was based on Rudolf Otto's edition of the *Reden*. Bultmann's conflict with Otto is documented in 'AR' (Kegley, p. xxii). Barth's misunderstanding was also a consequence of seeing Herrmann and Otto together (*Letters*, p. 50) as well as interpreting Herrmann in terms of Feuerbach (*EPT*, p. 260).

7. *Letters*, p. 2. The debate about conceptual clarity continued to be raised with Barth by Bultmann throughout their correspondence. See *Letters*, nos. 23, 29, 31, 45, 46, 47, 48 and his essay 'The Problem of Hermeneutics', *EPT*, pp. 260f.

8. *Letters*, pp. 4f.; *Osborn*, *TBCP*, pp. 10-17.

9. *The Honest to God Debate* (London: SCM, 1977), p. 134.

10. *CWM*, pp. 111-26; *TRG*, pp. 172-74, 184-87; Kegley, pp. 120-23; *TAI*, pp. 13, 162, including nn. 28, 29, and pp. 248-338.

11. Both Schubert Ogden and David Tracy argue that the Christ event is decisive but not exclusive and absolute. In the case of Tracy the argument is explicitly presented in the context of the recognition of the plurality of religions. This is true to a lesser extent for Ogden. See note 10 above.

12. Karl Barth, *K&M*, II, pp. 121ff.

13. Bultmann refers to his commentary in a letter dated September 16th, 1923, and Barth refers to the manuscript in a letter dated August 11th, 1925 (*Letters*, pp. 7, 23).

14. Ogden's approach is dependent on the work of Charles Hartshorne, whose work is in the tradition of A.N. Whitehead. The resulting 'panentheism' has its roots in the philosophy of Hegel, for whom history is the history of Spirit becoming increasingly self-conscious. This provides us with an evolutionary understanding, not only of the world, but also of God. Spirit is active in all of history though this need not be perceived. This appears to be the model for Ogden's understanding of God's relation to the world which he expresses in terms of the relation of soul to body. Hence everything that happens is God's action, though it need not be perceived as such. The decisive significance of the Christ event is that God's action is consistently perceived there. In Ogden's theology the perception of God's actions in the world does seem to provide the basis for a theistic worldview. Bultmann's thought cannot easily be reconciled with this aspect. Nor would he have agreed that God was coming to self-consciousness in the process of world becoming. In spite of these differences Ogden's position remains close to Bultmann's, perhaps closer than either of them realized.

Notes to Chapter One

1. Franz Kafka, *The Great Wall of China: Stories and Reflections* (New York: Schocken Books, 1970), pp. 178f. Bultmann's position differs from Kafka's in that, for him, it is not the visible world but man's *use* of his 'worldview', whether scientific or mythological, which expresses his will to find peace for a moment. In this regard Kafka appears to give expression to the Neo-Kantianism with which Bultmann is wrongly charged.

2. By 'existentialism' attention is drawn to a movement so diverse as to include Sören Kierkegaard, Martin Heidegger, Jean-Paul Sartre, Albert Camus, Karl Jaspers, Martin Buber, Gabriel Marcel, Nicholas Berdyaev, etc. Hence the movement includes Jews, Christians of Protestant, Catholic and Orthodox persuasion, atheists and agnostics. The authors do not necessarily claim to be 'existentialists' but they obviously belong to a common *movement*. Perhaps the one common feature which makes speaking of this possible is the stress on the significance of man as a knowing, thinking, willing, acting *subject*, so that each person is unique, and not simply one of a class or group. Throughout this study the German terms *existential* will be translated existentialist (existentialist philosophy) and *existentiell* will be translated existential (an existential decision). Bultmann's distinction between *ontological* and *ontic* is relevant to this distinction. Existentialist philosophy is concerned with the *ontological* analysis of *human being* for which Bultmann uses the word *Dasein*. Human being is a concept which covers all the possibilities which can be actualized in any human life. For the actuality of human life in which the individual makes actual decisions Bultmann used the term *Existenz*. Thus Thiselton, p. 152, is wrong to assert

that *Dasein* is synonymous with *Existenz* by definition. See *EF*, pp. 92ff., and *EPT*, p. 236n. It is a pity that the English translation of *EF*, pp. 92ff., 'The Historicity of Man (*Dasein*) and Faith' obscures the distinction between *Dasein* and *Existenz* which is clear in the original essay.

3. See also Karl Barth's 'Rudolf Bultmann - An Attempt to Understand Him', *K&M*, II, pp. 83ff.

4. Where Bultmann has made use of Heidegger he has 'made no mistake whatever' (Malet, p. 326 n. 17; Schmithals, p. 18).

5. Thus Macquarrie, *AET*, p. 12; see my 'A Note on the Hermeneutical Theology of Rudolf Bultmann', *ABR* (October 1981), pp. 26-31. The conceptual framework is determined by and gives expression to the operative understanding of 'reality', whether expressed or hidden. See *Letters*, pp. 87f.

6. *EF*, p. 288; and 'the concept of "existence" must be the methodical starting-point for theology, since the latter's theme is existence in faith . . . ' (*EF*, p. 92); also 'Theology can have its basis only in the man of faith' (*EF*, p. 97). Naturally this assumes man *in relation* to God.

7. Thus it is ironical that Bultmann should be accused of ignoring Heidegger's ontology. See Bultmann's comment in 'The Historicity of Man and Faith' (*EF*, p. 93 n. 4, which is printed on pp. 302-303).

8. '*Dasein*' refers to man ontologically. See 'The Historicity of Man (*Dasein*) and Faith', *EF*, pp. 92-110. It is a pity that the English translation does not make this clear. Thus '*das Dasein des Menschen*' has the same meaning as '*das Sein des Menschen*', and this is clearly the case in *FU*, p. 149 (*GV*, I, p. 118).

9. On *Dasein* as 'Being-in-the world' in Heidegger see *Being and Time*, pp. 78ff., and Thiselton, pp. 154ff.

10. 'For Heidegger man is limited by death; for Gogarten' (as for Bultmann) 'he is limited by the thou' ('The Historicity of Man (*Daseins*) and Faith', *EF*, p. 103).

11. *EPT*, p. 309; *FU*, p. 149; and see Malet, pp. 7, 10f.; Roberts, pp. 31, 37f.

12. 'TLYN', p. 44=*GV*, I, p. 231; and 'OTPD', in Batey, especially in p. 37. Part of the confusion appears to be due to the ambiguous use of 'world' in Bultmann's writings, as in the Gospel of John.

13. *JCM*, pp. 35-38, 85; *FU*, p. 59; *K&M*, I, pp. 2, 10; II, pp. 181, 210; Johnson, p. 158; Malet, pp. 44f.; and recognized by Barth in *K&M*, II, p. 118, and clarified further by *Letters*, p. 99.

14. Dustjacket to *This World and the Beyond: Marburg Sermons*, London: Lutterworth Press, 1960). Cf. the views of C.J. Jung. This aspect of the role of 'Science' in Bultmann's thought has been largely overlooked. What is in principle 'correct' becomes an instrument of tyranny in the hands of man who lives 'according to the flesh'.

15. 'TLYN', *Scottish Periodical* 1 (1947), p. 44=*GV*, I, p. 231. 'Vielmehr

ist mein Sein von vornherein ein Sein mit Anderen; menschliches Sein ist Miteinandersein, und damit ist es *geschichtliches* Sein im Unterschied vom Sein der Natur.' The use of '*Sein*' in this quotation alerts us to the fact that this is an ontological discussion of human being as such, for which the use of *Dasein* is also appropriate. See the interchange of *Dasein* with *Sein* in the quotation from *FU*, p. 149=*GV*, I, p.118, below. See also *EPT*, pp. 257ff.= *GV*, II, pp. 231f.; *EF*, p. 98 *ZTK*, n.s. 11 (1930), pp. 349f.

16. Macquarrie, *AET*, pp. 202ff., wrongly charges Bultmann with individualism and as evidence draws attention to the absence of *Koinonia* from the list of Greek words in *Th.N.T.* This is hardly a fair test as *Koinonia* is not a word frequently used in the New Testament and where it appears it does not always connote the fellowship between believers to which Macquarrie refers. More to the point is Bultmann's treatment of authentic existence in terms of the eschatological community and love for the neighbour. See *EF*, pp. 92ff., and 'TLYN'.

17. *EF*, pp. 102, 105f., 107; *FU*, p. 149; *EPT*, p. 309. See especially 'The Historicity of Man (*Dasein*) and Faith', *EF*, n. 10 on pp. 303f. For Heidegger's views see *Being and Time*, p. 183. But Bultmann indicates that this approach to history and the historicity (*Geschichtlichkeit*) of man had already been introduced to him by Wilhelm Herrmann (see Thiselton, pp. 207f.).

18. See Johnson, pp. 57, 78, 181; Roberts, p. 57.

19. *FU*, p. 149=*GV*, I. p. 118; and see *FU*, p. 150; Malet, pp. 7, 10f.; Roberts, pp. 31, 37f. 'Man *is* at all times himself possibility, that his being is potentiality-to-be' (*FU*, p. 170).

20. *EF*, pp. 101f., and p. 306 n. 26, 'The essence of *Dasein* is his *Existenz*.' But it is wrong to conclude as Thiselton (pp. 152f.) does, that *Dasein* is synonymous with *Existenz* by definition. *Dasein* always exists, but all the possibilities of *Dasein* are not fulfilled in the actual *existence* of every person.

21. *EF*, pp. 62f., cf. p. 65; *FU*, p. 192 n. 4. It belongs to *our* life because of the common *structure* of human existence and consciousness (see *EF*, pp. 94, 101); and 'we share the basic humanity' (Thiselton, pp. 53, 69).

22. *EPT*, p. 137, and *GJ*, p. 317. Hence E. Beti is wrong in supposing that, for Bultmann, the text merely confirms pre-understanding. See R.E. Palmer, *Hermeneutics*, p. 58.

23. Thiselton, p. xx quotes Gerhard Ebeling: 'According to Luther, the Word of God always comes as *adversarius noster*, our adversary. It does not simply confirm and strengthen us in what we think we are and as what we wish to be taken for.' As for Bultmann the conflict must be the contact.

24. C. Braaten, *History and Hermeneutics*, pp. 140f.; and Macquarrie, *AET*, pp. 200ff.

25. Thus both G.N. Stanton and J.D.G. Dunn, in *New Testament Interpretation*, ed. by I. H. Marshall, pp. 67f., 259f. See also Thiselton, p. 113.

26. *JCM*, pp. 37f. See also *K&M*, I, pp. 3, 10; II, pp. 118, 210; *FU*, p. 59; Johnson, p. 158.

27. N.J. Young, p. 49; D.M. Smith, pp. 238-48. In opposition to this view see Malet, p. 83, and Bultmann, in *GJ*, pp. 308, 393.

28. This is the criticism of Thiselton, pp. 40, 290ff. John Macquarrie rightly refutes such views in Kegley, p. 140: 'Such critics have failed to grasp the concept of existence, which is never the existence of a bare subject, but always refers to the concrete encounters of the self with the world, with other selves, and with God.'

29. J.D.G. Dunn, *Christology in the Making*, p. 254.

Notes to Chapter Two

30. On this theme see *FU*, p. 177, and Roberts, p. 51.

31. On Hermeneutics from Schleiermacher to Gadamer see R. E. Palmer, *Hermeneutics*.

32. See *HE*, pp. 117f. This is the reverse of the assertion of Michael Polanyi, *Personal Knowledge* (New York: Harper Torchbooks, 1964), p. x, 'we can know more than we can tell and we can tell nothing without relying on our awareness of things we may not be able to tell'.

On 'meaning' see 'The Meaning of Meaning', in G.B. Caird, *The Language and Imagery of the Bible*, (London: Duckworth, 1980).

33. *Th.N.T.*, II, pp. 237-44, especially pp. 240 2f. and p. 244 1; and see also *GJ*, p. 566.

34. SOTCF, p. 13 n. 2. Obviously hermeneutical translation is concerned with the primary task of understanding. See *EF*, p. 292, and *K&M*, II, p. 186.

35. See *FU*, pp. 31f., 132, 263. The 'so-called' *historical method* is in fact a complex of methods bound together by the attitude or presupposition that history is intelligible in terms of its own internal causes. This attitude is crucial for Bultmann's historical approach and his own theology might be seen as a response to the problems raised by such an approach.

36. *The So-Called Historical Jesus and the Historic Biblical Christ* (Philadelphia: Fortress Press, 1964), p. 66 (ET of 1896 German edition).

37. See John Drane, *Paul: Libertine or Legalist* and my review in *JTSA* 18 (1977), pp. 58f.

38. See my 'A Note on the Hermeneutical Theology of Rudolf Bultmann', *ABR* 29 (1981), pp. 26-31, esp. p. 26.

39. See 'Das Problem einer theologischen Exegese des Neuen Testaments', *Zwischen den Zeiten* 3 (1925), p. 340.

40. *The Interpretation of the Fourth Gospel* (Cambridge: CUP, 1953).

41. *NTS* 1 (1954-1955), p. 91 (ET in *Harvard Divinity Bulletin* 27 [1963], p. 22).

42. See Ernst Käsemann, 'The Canon of the New Testament and the Unity of the Church' and 'An Apologia for Primitive Christian Eschatology', in *Essays on New Testament Themes*; 'Unity and Multiplicity in the New Testament Doctrine of the Church' and 'Paul and Early Catholicism', in *New Testament Questions of Today*. For a critique of his views see Hans Küng, 'Early Catholicism in the New Testament as a Problem in Controversial Theology', in *The Council in Action: Theological Reflections on the Second Vatican Council* (New York: Sheed and Ward, 1963), pp. 233-92; *Structures of the Church* (London: Burns and Oats, 1965), pp. 135-51; J.H. Elliott, 'A Catholic Gospel: Reflections on "Early Catholicism" in the New Testament', *CBQ* 31 (1969), pp. 213-33. See also Ernst Troeltsch, *The Social Teaching of the Christian Churches* (London: Allen and Unwin, 1931), pp. 89-200.

43. G.E. Ladd, 'The Role of Jesus in Bultmann's Theology', *SJT* 18/1 (1955), p. 66. Compare Roberts (p. 116) who asks why the historical John Wesley should not be regarded as the eschatological event rather than Jesus. Roberts suggests that as 'both Jesus and the present-day preaching are the Eschatological Event' it can only be because 'Jesus' preaching was the original Eschatological Event'. But this completely overlooks the fact that 'the proclaimer became the proclaimed'. Jesus as the Christ is not only the origin of the kerygma. He is the kerygma.

44. See M. Hengel, *Acts and the History of Earliest Christianity*, pp. 129f.

45. *EF*, pp. 291-92; and see *JCM*, pp. 15f.; *FU*, pp. 247ff.; Kegley, pp. 266f.; Johnson, pp. 131, 145; Roberts, p. 98. The criteria by which evidence is evaluated and judged are part of the pre-understanding brought to the text. See Geoffrey Turner, 'Pre-understanding and New Testament Interpretation', *SJT* 28/3 (1975), pp. 233-35.

46. Miracles in this sense do not happen, according to Bultmann. See *K&M*, II, p. 184; *EF*, p. 292; *FU*, pp. 247ff.; *JCM*, pp. 15, 37f. Early attempts to *explain* the resurrection narratives did so on the basis of alternative hypotheses concerning what actually happened, for example, the 'swoon' theory, body-snatchers, mistaken identity, hallucination, etc. More recent approaches attempt to reconstruct the development of the resurrection narratives, assuming that the event did not happen as described in the New Testament. The conflicting evidence in the Gospels, Acts, and the Epistles of Paul, suggests that the task of historical reconstruction needs to be undertaken. If the event did not happen as described, some explanatory hypothesis needs to be offered, indicating how whatever happened could come to be proclaimed in terms of the resurrection of Jesus. This is true of Bultmann's hypothesis. The culture and tradition of the time, especially Jewish apocalyptic, provide a framework within which the Easter faith becomes intelligible in terms of the proclamation of the resurrection. The resurrection was an eschatological hope and the early Christians believed that, through Jesus' life and death, they had entered into the fulfilment of the

eschatological hope. For attempts to deal with the development of the resurrection narratives see Norman Perrin, *Resurrection*; R.H. Fuller, *Resurrection*. Notable recent attempts to argue that the resurrection is an event in which God vindicates Jesus, and not *merely* an expression of the Easter faith, have been made by Edward Schillebeeckx, *Jesus*, pp. 320-90, 516-45, 640-50; Hans Küng, *On Being a Christian*, pp. 343-411; Langdon Gilkey, *Message and Existence*, pp. 178-94. However, it would be a mistake, and a distortion of Bultmann's position, to suggest that, for him, the resurrection is *merely* an expression of the Easter faith. The Easter faith is the real evidence of the resurrection rather than the empty tomb.

47. 'We can believe in God only in spite of experience' (*JCM*, p. 84). Obviously what is meant by 'experience' concerns the nature of life in the world. Perhaps Bultmann's experience of Nazi Germany influenced his judgment in this 'pessimistic' direction so that the 'horrors' of worldly experience were clearer to him than to many 'Western Christians' today. But there are still many for whom the world is more a kind of hell, a chaos, than appears to be the case for 'the privileged' who are likely to read this book. But what continuity is there between *this world* and God, except in the light of the cross?

48. Julius Schniewind, in *K&M*, I, p. 82. This definition is noted by Norman Young (pp. 22ff.) and specifically identified with Bultmann's use of language. Young adds that Bultmann preferred the use of the adjectives and of his own choice did not use the nouns *Historie* and *Geschichte*.

49. Richard Batey and Jerry H. Gill, 'Fact, Language and Hermeneutics', *SJT* 23/1 (1970), p. 13. For a criticism of the inadequacies of the categories usually used by language philosophers for the discussion of religion see W.F. Zuurdeeg, pp. 16f.

50. Thus both G.N. Stanton and J.D.G. Dunn in *New Testament Interpretation* (ed. by I.H. Marshall), pp. 67f., 259f. See also Thiselton, p. 113.

51. *GJ*, p. 52(32). For other instances of this use see pp. 70(46, twice), 167(121), 199(147), 200(148, five times), 213(157), 252(189), 308(233) (translated 'course of events'), 361(275), 364(277), 414(316), 424(325), 428(328), 439(337, three times), 441(331, eight times), 475(362), 492(376, three times), 493(377, three times), 496(379, twice), 500(383), 501(383), 508(389), 514(394, four times), 520(399, three times), 526(404), 527(404), 536(412), 562(433), 565(436), 566(436, twice), 589(454), 607(469, twice), 616(476, three times). In each case the reference given in brackets is to the German *EJ*.

52. *GJ*, p. 99 n. 1(p. 69 n. 1). For other examples see pp. 175(128, three times), 187(138), 203(149f., four times), 206(150, four times), 207(153), 208(154), 210(155, twice), 211(156), 212(157), 213(157), 216(160), 237(177, three times), 238(178, twice), 239(178, twice), 246(184), 276(208), 313(237, twice), 326(247), 329(250), 330(250, twice), 331(251), 333(253, twice),

339(258), 392(299), 393(299), 398(303), 399(304), 402(306, twice), 406(310), 409(313), 412(315), 413(315f., three times), 414(316), 416(318, twice), 419(320), 444(340), 465(354), 466(354), 648(502, twice), 675(523), 681ff. (528ff., fifteen times), 688(533, twice), 690(534, three times), 691(536), 693f.(537, three times), 698(541), 702(543), 704f.(545f., five times), 706f.(547, twice), 710f.(550, three times), 713(551., twice).

53. *GJ*, p. 361(275); see also p. 419(320).

54. In *GJ*, *historisch* is used to qualify situation, sense or meaning, notes (*Notiz*), fact (*Factum*), narrative, account, tradition, interest, Jesus, the perspective, scenery (*Szenerie*), revelation, event (*Ereignis*), reminiscence, figure (*Gestalt*), virtuoso, contemporaneity, occurrences (*Vorkommnisse*), disciples, characteristic, occasion, phenomenon, interpretation, scene, achievement, time/place, reconstruction. See *GJ*, pp. 57(31), 69(45), 86(58), 94(65), 108(76, three times), 195(144), 197(145), 198(146), 199(147), 200(148), 297(223), 307(232), 308(232f., three times), 379(289), 423(324), 424(324), 473(360), 485(370), 493(377, three times), 504(386), 512(392), 522(401, twice), 525(403), 527(404), 554(427), 558(430, twice), 559(431, twice), 563(434), 566(437), 589(454), 592(456), 610(472, twice), 626(485, twice), 630(487), 637(493).

55. The adjective *geschichtlich* is used to qualify Jesus, event (*Geschehen*) revealer, revelation, figure (*Gestalt*), Man, tradition, event (*Ereignis*), event (*Vorgang*), separation (*Scheidung*), reality, person, situation? (*Notwendigkeit*), appearance, ministry, situation (*Situation*), entity, church, consideration, existence (*Existenz*), existence (*Sein*, better 'being'), decision, possibility, actions, life, sphere, fact, action (*Wirkung*), Word of Jesus, existence (*Existieren*). *GJ*, pp. 17(4), 35(18, three times), 49(29), 54(33), 56(33), 56(35), 65(41), 65(42), 70(46), 99(69), 108 nn. 4,5(76 nn. 4,5), 203(149), 229(170), 233(173f., twice), 252(189, three times), 254(190), 255(191), 270(203), 308(233), 328(249), 275(285, twice), 426(326, twice), 473(361), 475(362), 501(383, three times), 514(394), 520(399, twice), 522(401), 559(431), 562(433, three times), 566(436), 567(437), 578(446), 606(468, twice), 607(469, twice), 620f.(480), 628(486), 629(487), 630(487f.).

56. *GJ*, p. 203. This sentence is missing from the English translation at the end of the first paragraph. See the German original *EJ*, p. 149.

57. There are some overlaps which might suggest a confusion between *historisch* and *geschichtlich*. Both words are used to qualify the following nouns: (1) 'situation' (*historisch*, *GJ*, pp. 51, 504, 512, 592, 630 three times and *geschichtlich*, p. 255 twice. On p. 252 *Notwendigkeit* is translated 'situation' and qualified by *geschichtlich* but the meaning is different from *Situation*, having the sense of 'urgency' or 'necessity'.); (2) 'event' (a number of different words are translated thus: *Ereignis* is qualified by *historisch*, pp. 308, 493, *geschichtlich*, pp. 70, 233, 252, 566, and *weltgeschichtlich*, p. 589; *Geschehen* qualified by *geschichtlich*, p. 35; as is also *Vorgang*, pp. 99, 108 n. 5; while *Vorkommnisse* is qualified by *historisch*, p. 473.); (3)

'revelation' (*historisch*, p. 307, *geschichtlich*, p. 35, *Geschichte*, p. 500); (4) 'Jesus' (qualified by *historisch*, pp. 198, 200, 423, 493 twice, 522, 525, 558, *geschichtlich*, pp. 17, 229, 630, and *Geschichte*, pp. 361, 419); (5) 'figure' (*Gestalt* is qualified by *historisch*, pp. 376, 493, 525 and *geschichtlich*, pp. 49, 475); (6) 'tradition' (*historisch*, p. 108 and *geschichtlich*, P. 65); (7) 'fact' (*Faktum*, qualified by *Historisch*, pp. 94, 563 and *Weltgeschichtlich*; *Tatsache* is qualified by *Geschichtlich*, pp. 1008 n. 4, 562. Possibly *Tatsache* should be distinguished from *Faktum*.); (8) 'person' and 'figure' (*Person* is qualified by *geschichtlich*, pp. 229, 252, 270, and *historisch*, p. 308; *Gestalt* is qualified by *geschichtlich*, pp. 49, 475, and *historisch*, pp. 376, 493, 525). But a detailed examination of the overlap between *historisch* and *geschichtlich* confirms the distinction which appears where there is no overlap. The former qualifies *Faktum* (*GJ*, pp. 94, 563) while the latter qualifies *Tatsachen* (*GJ*, pp. 108 n. 4, 562). Both are translated 'fact' but *Faktum* means more the fact established by evidence while *Tatsachen* takes account of the event. The distinction is implied also in the context.

Situation is normally qualified by *historisch* (*GJ*, pp. 51, 504, 512, 592, 630) but in one statement it is used twice with *geschichtlich* (*GJ*, p. 255). Used with *historisch*, a situation *located* in the past is in view but *geschichtlich* qualifies the situation brought about by the eschatological word of revelation for which *historisch* would be inappropriate. The same location in the past is in view when an historical event (*historische Vorkommnisse*) is mentioned whereas an event (*Geschehen* or *Ereignis*) qualified by *geschichtlich* emphasizes the dynamics of the event as a happening. (*Geschehen* is also qualified by *geschichtlich*, p. 35, as is *Ereignis*, pp. 70, 233, 252, 566, which is also qualified by *historisch*, pp. 308, 493 and *weltgeschichtlich*, p. 589.) When *geschichtlich* is used it is the reality of the event rather than its place in the circle of inner-historical causality that is in view. The event is stressed as eschatological. When *Ereignis* is used with *historisch* or *weltgeschichtlich* the stress has moved to the place of the event in inner-historical causality. While the Revealer and revelation are normally spoken of using *geschichtlich* (*GJ*, pp. 35, 54, 56, 233) and *Geschichte* (*GJ*, pp. 213, 234), *historisch* is used to speak of 'the historical contingency of the revelation' (*GJ*, p. 307). The use of *historisch* brings out the point that the revelation is restricted to certain times and places. It is not always and everywhere available. This is also the point of the reference to the revelation as an historically limited event (*als historisch begrenztes Ereignis*; *GJ*, p. 308). The eschatological event is *paradoxically* identified with this historical event located in the past. But its eschatological character does not reside in its location in the past. The past event has the power to become present. Thus, as an historical event (*historisches Ereignis*) Jesus' life falls into the past. The historical (*historisch*) Jesus can be reconstructed by historical recollection (*historische Erinnerung*) but this reconstruction is not the revelation, which is not a chapter of world history (*Weltgeschichte*), but is constantly future (*GJ*, p. 493). The same is true of the founding of the believing community. It is not a chapter of world history (*Weltgeschichte*) or the historical (*historisch*) achievement of a great man. It is the revelation event sent into the world by God but without becoming a factor in the inner-historical causality of the world (*GJ*, p. 589). However, such a relation to inner-historical causality is indicated by such events (*Ereignis*) as are qualified by *historisch* or *weltgeschichtlich*. From this perspective Jesus is a Palestinian Jew of the first century whose life and message are intelligible in terms of this context.

Bultmann's discussion of Jesus is qualified by *historisch* (pp. 198, 200, 423, 493, 522, 525, 558), *geschichtlich* (pp. 17, 229, 630) and in terms of *Geschichte* (pp. 234, 361, 419). He speaks of an expression of the revelation given by the historical Jesus (*geschichtlich*). This historical reality is not dependent on the historian's ability to reconstruct history nor on inner-historical causality. The eschatological event of the revelation is a paradox in the context of inner-historical causality, a paradox perceived only by faith. Yet the paradox is tied to an historical event which really occurred and is shown to be eschatological by the way the revelation continues to occur through it.

However, when the *historisch* Jesus is spoken of it is the Jesus known by historical reconstruction in his context of inner-historical causality. While the *historisch* Jesus belongs to the past his work goes on (see *EJ*, p. 146, for which *GJ*, p. 198, is an inadequate translation). Placing Jesus in an historical succession is also the point of *historisch* in *GJ*, p. 200.

They all stand in a *Geschichte* (not 'an historical tradition') which had its beginning in the *historisch* Jesus (*GJ*, p. 200). Thus the *historisch* Jesus is Jesus firmly located in historical context (see also *GJ*, p. 423) as an event that falls into the past (*GJ*, p. 493). Yet it is this figure, located in the past, who became the eschatological event. Concerning the farewell prayer of Jesus Bultmann says that from an *historisch* point of view it was not Jesus but the community speaking. Yet the evangelist portrays it as the prayer of Jesus because he believed that the glorified Jesus continued to speak in the community (*GJ*, p. 522, cf. p. 558). The same contrast between *geschichtlich* and *historisch* is to be found in their use to qualify both *Person* and *Gestalt*. Hence the Revealer was an actual historical (*geschichtlich*) person (*GJ*, pp. 229, 252). The point is neither the ability to reconstruct knowledge on the basis of evidence nor to assert inner-historical causality. Inner-historical causality is in view in reference to the *historisch* person of Jesus which would have cultural and intellectual effects but cannot be identified with the eschatological presence of Jesus (*GJ*, p. 308).

58. *Weltgeschichte*, pp. 199(147), 366(278), 428(328), 475(362), 493(377), 508(389), 513(393), 514(394), 520(399), 529(406), 536(412), 562(433), 565(436), 589(454), 616(476, twice); *heilsgeschichtlich*, pp. 326, 424(247, 325); *geistergeschichtlich*, pp. 308, 576 n. 2(233, 444); *dogmensgeschichtlich*, p. 576 n. 2 (444 n. 1).

59. See Bultmann's 'The Problem of Hermeneutics', *EPT*, pp. 259ff.,

where he discussed Barth's views as expressed in *KD* 3/2 (1948), pp. 534ff. For a discussion of development in Barth's understanding of the resurrection see G. O'Collins, 'Karl Barth on Christ's Resurrection', *SJT*, 26/1 (1973), pp. 85-99. See also Barth's clarification of categories in *Letters*, pp. 143ff.

60. See D.E. Nineham in *The Myth of God Incarnate*, ed. by John Hick, pp. 186ff.

61. New York: Abingdon, 1970 (= ET of the 1913 German original). Bultmann's high opinion of *this work* is evident in his preface and in comments elsewhere (e.g. *JCM*, p. 48). However, he nowhere suggests that he thinks Bousset's work on Judaism to be of great importance.

62. *NTS* 1 (1954-1955), pp. 77-91; ET in *Harvard Divinity Bulletin* 27 (1963), pp. 9-22. See p. 22 for the comment on Bauer.

63. See *Martin Luther: Selections from his Writings*, ed. by John Dillenberger, pp. 18-19, and the 'Preface to James', pp. 35-36.

64. For the thesis concerning the Jesus-kerygma see Willi Marxsen, *Introduction to the New Testament: An Approach to Its Problems*; *Mark the Evangelist*; Edward Schillebeeckx, *Jesus*, pp. 105-107; J.D. Kingsbury, 'The Gospel of Mark in Recent Research', *RSR* (1979), pp. 101-107.

65. See E.P. Sanders, pp. 12ff., for an account of 'holism'.

66. See Howard Marshall, 'Palestinian and Hellenistic Christianity: Some Critical Comments', *NTS* 19/3 (1973), pp. 271-87. M. Hengel, *Judaism and Hellenism*, has attempted to provide a detailed criticism of the distinction between Palestinian and diaspora Judaism upon which Bultmann's analysis of Christianity was based.

67. Points of contact between his criticism of Bultmann's *PC* and criticisms of the same work by Jacob Neusner suggest that Sanders was aware of Neusner's critique, which is to be found in his *The Rabbinic Traditions About the Pharisees Before 70* (Leiden: Brill, 1971), pp. 362f.

68. The quotations appear in Sanders, pp. 44f. and are quoted from the American edition of *PC*, pp. 60-71, which is pp. 70-84 of the Fontana edition.

69. *Jesus and the Word* (= *Jesus*), translated from the German original of 1926. Sanders quotes from p. 22 of my edition. *Jesus* deals with Palestinian Judaism, the matter being summarized in a mere 40 pages in *PC*, which does not modify the earlier treatment in any significant way.

70. John Macquarrie in Kegley, pp. 141f., and see Bultmann's 'Reply', in Kegley, pp. 274f.

71. O. Betz, *What do we Know about Jesus?* pp. 12ff.

72. *Gnosticism at Corinth*, especially p. 71. Bultmann explicitly notes that Paul was probably influenced by Gnosticism via his Jewish heritage as well as encountering it directly himself at a later stage (*Th.N.T.*, I, p. 173).

73. R. Bultmann, 'Die Bedeutung der neuerschlossenen mandäischen und manichäischen Quellen für das Verständnis des Johannesevangeliums', in *ZNW* 24 (1925), pp. 142-43; cf. J.M. Robinson, 'Gnosticism and the New

Testament', in *Gnosis: Festschrift für Hans Jonas*, ed. by B. Aland et al., p. 127.

74. See S.G. Wilson, *Luke and the Pastoral Epistles*; and C.K. Barrett, 'Pauline Controversies in the Post-Pauline Period', *NTS* 20 (1974), pp. 229-45; and see note 42 above.

Notes to Chapter Three

75. *On Religion: Speeches to its Cultured Despisers*; *The Christian Faith*. On Schleiermacher see R.R. Niebuhr, *Schleiermacher on Christ and Religion*; J. Fortsman, *A Romantic Triangle: Schleiermacher and Early Germanic Romanticism*; M. Redeker, *Schleiermacher: Life and Thought*; A. Garish, 'Continuity and Change: Friederich Schleiermacher on "The Task of Theology"', in *Tradition and the Modern World*.

76. On Schleiermacher's use of 'feeling' see Schubert Ogden, 'On Revelation', pp. 288f., n. 3; and Niebuhr (see n. 75 above), pp. 116-34. In *GJ*, p. 44 n. 2, Bultmann, with obvious reference to Schleiermacher, says, 'man's knowledge of his creatureliness is neither a theory nor "an emotion of creatureliness", grounded in some kind of "numinous" experience; it is, rather, existential self-understanding, whatever the thoughts or feelings may be in which it becomes explicit'.

77. See Ogden 'On Revelation', pp. 268, 276-88; *Reality*, pp. 172ff. While Bultmann speaks of the 'original revelation' as an unfulfilled *possibility*, Ogden sees it as effective in all human life. This leads to a different evaluation of the religions of the world. See also Tracy, *TAI*, for the view that all life is already 'graced', implying that this can be recognized apart from the decisive 'special' revelation.

78. *The Idea of the Holy*.

79. Paul Tillich, *What is Religion?*; *The Protestant Era*.

80. See my 'Johannine Symbols: A Case Study in Epistemology', *JTSA* 27 (1979), pp. 26-41, especially pp. 32-37, for a more detailed exposition. More recently see my 'John 9 and the Interpretation of the Fourth Gospel' in *JSNT* 28 (October 1986) pp. 31-61. For Bultmann's discussion of the significance of man's search see *GJ*, pp. 44ff., 52f., 62, 81, 100, 107 n. 2, 141, 143, 149, 156, 158f., 167, 180f., 189, 192f., 222f., 225, 227ff., 237, 268, 271, 296, 317, 327; *Th.NT*, II, pp. 27ff., 67ff.; *K&M*, I, p. 192; *JCM*, p. 52; *HE*, p. 109.

81. Ogden, 'On Revelation', p. 276, notes that Bultmann identifies the revelation in Christ with the universal revelation. 'There is no other light shining in Jesus than has always already shined in creation ...' (*EF*, p. 86; see also *GJ*, pp. 40ff. and *JCM*, pp. 71, 78f., where Bultmann refers to God's action 'hidden everywhere' and says that 'God meets us always and everywhere' but we do not recognize him outside the circle of kerygma). Ogden rejects Bultmann's distinction between the ontological possibility

given in creation and the actualization of that possibility in the Christ event. For Ogden, this approach is incompatible with the Christian understanding of God, which implied his universal revelation, not only as a possibility, but actually. The revelation is at work in the world generally and the Christ event, while necessary for Christian existence, is not necessary for authentic existence as such. See Ogden, 'On Revelation', pp. 276-88, especially 281. But for Bultmann authentic existence is existence in the faith which is a response to the Christ event. The question Ogden needs to answer concerns whether the Christ event and faith make any difference to human existence. If it makes no difference it is doubtful whether distinguishing Christian existence is significant at all. If it is significant perhaps it is justifiably called authentic existence. Bultmann not only distinguishes authentic existence as existence in faith from unbelieving existence, he also distinguishes unbelieving existence from those who have never heard and hence have not rejected the revelation. There is a finality about the inauthenticity of those who have rejected the revelation while those who have never heard are characterized more by an openness to the revelation.

82. The literature on myth is vast. For example see H.W. Bartsch, *Kerygma und Mythos*, I-VI (ET of some of the articles I-II); G. Stählin, *Mythos*, *TDNT*, IV, pp. 762-95; A. Cunningham (ed.), *The Theory of Myth* (London: Sheed & Ward, 1973); G.S. Kirk, *Myth: Its Meaning and Functions in Ancient and Other Cultures* (London: OUP, 1970); *The Nature of Greek Myths* (Harmondsworth: Penguin, 1974); E. Cassirer, *Language and Myth* (New York: Harper & Bros., 1946); Alasdair MacIntyre, 'Myth', in P. Edwards (ed.), *Encyclopedia of Philosophy*, V; F.W. Dillistone (ed.), *Myth and Symbol* (London: SPCK, 1966); Ian G. Barbour, *Myths, Models and Paradigms* (London: SCM, 1974); Thomas Fawcett, *The Symbolic Language of Religion* (London: SCM, 1970); *Hebrew Myth and Christian Gospel* (London: SCM, 1973); and see notes 83-87 below.

83. Karl Jaspers, *Myth and Christianity*, especially pp. 16ff.; and see Bultmann's comment on p. 61 n. 1 (=*K&M*, II, p. 185 n. 1).

84. C.G. Jung, *The Collected Works*, IX/1, *The Archetypes and the Collective Unconscious* (New York: Pantheon, 1959); II, *Psychology and Religion* (New York: Pantheon, 1963); *Memories, Dreams, Reflections* (New York: Random, 1961); C.G. Jung and C. Kerenyi, *Essays on a Science of Mythology* (Princeton: Princeton University Press, 1969). Jung's own interest in mythology is apparent in these works which have had a considerable influence on other studies, not least on the work of Mircea Eliade.

85. Martin Heidegger, *Being and Time* (Oxford: Blackwell, 1962); *An Introduction to Megaphysics* (New Haven: Yale University Press, 1959); *Existence and Being* (London: Vision Press, 1968); *On Time and Being* (New York: Harper & Row, 1972). Heidegger's positive evaluation of myth and his critique of the malaise of Western society suggest that a comparison with the

work of Jung on myth and the crisis for modern Western man might be illuminating.

86. Mircea Eliade, *Patterns in Comparative Religion* (London: Sheed & Ward, 1958); *The Quest* (Chicago: University of Chicago Press, 1969); *Images and Symbols* (New York: Sheed & Ward, 1969); *Myths, Dreams and Mysteries: The Encounter between Contemporary Faiths and Archaic Realities* (New York: Harper, 1960); *The Sacred and the Profane: The Nature of Religion* (New York: Harper, 1961); *The Myth of the Eternal Return* (Princeton: Princeton University Press, 1954). The importance of myth as a paradigmatic perception of reality is stressed in Eliade's writings. His use of 'archetypes' calls for study in relation to the works of Jung. This relation is perhaps suggested in Eliade's choice of *Myths, Dreams and Mysteries* as the title of one of his important studies on myth, a title that can hardly have been chosen without awareness of Jung's *Memories, Dreams, Reflections*. However, Eliade does not indicate how his own understanding of the 'archetypes' relates to Jung. On the work of Eliade see Guildford Dudley, *Religion on Trial: Mircea Eliade and his Critics* (Philadelphia: Temple University Press, 1977); Douglas Allen, *Structure and Creativity in Religion: Hermeneutics in Mircea Eliade's Phenomenology* (The Hague: Mouton, 1978)

87. Paul Tillich, 'The Religious Symbol', in *Myth and Symbol*, ed. by F.W. Dillistone; 'Myth and Mythology: The Concept and the Religious Psychology of Myth' from *RGG* (2nd edn, 1927) reprinted in English in *Twentieth Century Theology in the Making*, II, ed. by Jaroslav Pelikan.

88. Hans Hübner, *Politische Theologie und existentiale Interpretation* (Witten: Luther Verlag, 1973), p. 31 n. 64, adds the weight of a letter from Bultmann confirming that his existentialist interpretation of the New Testament was independent of Heidegger and that this is true of his book on *Jesus*. The research for this book was done while writing *HST* (1921), though *Jesus* was not published until 1926.

89. See Johnson, pp. 114f., 124f.; and for the basic literature criticizing Reitzenstein's position see R.P. Casey, 'Gnosis, Gnosticism and the New Testament' in *The Background of the New Testament and its Eschatology*, ed. by W.D. Davies and D. Daube (Cambridge: CUP, 1956), pp. 52-80; C. Colpe, 'New Testament and Gnostic Christology', *Studies in the History of* Religions 14, ed. J. Neusner (Leiden: Brill, 1968), pp. 227-43; *Die religionsgeschichtliche Schule: Darstellung und Kritik ihres Bildes vom gnostischen Erlösermythus* (Göttingen: Vandenhoeck and Ruprecht, 1961); C.H. Dodd, *The Interpretation of the Fourth Gospel* (Cambridge: CUP, 1953); R.M. Grant, *Gnosticism and Early Christianity* (New York: Colombia University Press, 1959); R.McL. Wilson, *The Gnostic Problem* (London: Mowbrays, 1958); *Gnosis and the New Testament* (Oxford: Blackwells, 1968). For a summary treatment of the problem see Edwin Yamauchi, *Pre-Christian Gnosticism* (London: Tyndale Press, 1973), and especially the bibliographical

material pp. 187-94. For an alternative understanding of Gnosticism see R. Bultmann, *PC*; 'Die Bedeutung der neuerschlossenen mandäischen und manichäischen Quellen für das Verständnis des Johannesevangeliums', *ZNW* 24 (1925), pp. 100-46; Hans Jonas, *Gnosis und spätantiker Geist* (2 vols.) (Göttingen: Vandenhoeck and Ruprecht, 1934, 1954); *The Gnostic Religion* (Boston: Beacon Press, 1958). For collections of the Gnostic texts see Werner Foerster, *Gnosis: A Selection of Gnostic Texts* (2 vols.) (Oxford: OUP, 1972, 1974); R.M. Grant, *Gnosticism: An Anthology* (London: Collins, 1961); Robert Haardt, *Gnosis: Character and Testimony* (Leiden: Brill, 1971). For the Nag Hammadi Library see, James M. Robinson, *The Nag Hammadi Library* (New York: Harper & Row, 1977); 'The Coptic Gnostic Library Today', *NTS* 14 (1968), pp. 356-401; John Dart, *The Laughing Saviour* (New York: Harper & Row, 1976).

90. Jonas had used both *entmythisiert* and *entmythologisiert* (J.M. Robinson, *Interpretation* 20 [1966], p. 71) in the introduction to his second volume on Gnosticism which appeared in 1954 though the introduction formed part of his 1928 thesis written under Bultmann so that the words in question probably go back to that time. This is confirmed by Johnson's note that Jonas used the term in his 1930 study on Augustine (Johnson, p. 3 n. 4). But Barth attributed the invention of the term to Bultmann (*K&M*, II, p. 102), and in 1958 Bultmann referred to the method of interpretation 'I call demythologizing—an unsatisfactory word to be sure' (*JCM*, p. 18). This would suggest that Jonas derived the term from his teacher, Bultmann. However, in the final paragraph of his 'AR', originally written in 1956, Bultmann said he first used the term in his lecture of 1941 (Kegley, p. xxv). Given that Bultmann freely acknowledged his debts it is puzzling that he did not acknowledge Jonas at this point if the term was derived from him as seems probable. Alternatively the comment in 'AR' might refer to Bultmann's first published use of the term and need not preclude his invention of it. For a more detailed discussion see my 'The Origins of Demythologizing Revisited', *ABR* 33 (1985), pp. 2-14.

91. The following quotation is from Bultmann's 'The Meaning of the Christian Faith in Creation' (*EF*, pp. 223f.), which was first published in 1936. Many of the same themes appeared in his sermon 'Faith in God the Creator' (*EF*, pp. 171-82), which was delivered in the academic worship service at Marburg on July 1st, 1934.

> And the Christian doctrine of the state may not attempt to reduce the latter to a *humanitas* that is determined by eternal principles or to a nationality that is constituted by the divine powers of blood and soil. Rather in the knowledge of the power of evil, it must affirm the authority of the state with its justice and coercion.
>
> However, the "ordinances of creation" and, to be sure, the "direct" ones as well as the "indirect" ones are *ambiguous* in consequence of sin. It is impossible to read off unambiguous demands as demands of God from the natural conditions that determine our immediate situation ...

> ... No nation is so unambiguous an entity that one can explain every stirring of the national will as a demand of a divine ordinance. Nor is nationality a purely natural thing that is given in one's blood; rather it is something that, though it has a natural basis, arises in history; and through history every nation is given the possibility of evil as well as of good. What is to be considered the law of a nation in a particular case is in fact left to the responsible decision of the individuals who belong to it. And in a day when nationality has again appeared as an ordinance of creation, the Christian faith has to prove its critical power by also insisting that the nation as something simply given is ambiguous and that, precisely for the sake of obedience to the nation as an ordinance of creation, the question must continue to be asked what is and what is not the nation's true demand. Just as faith in creation is only possible on the basis of faith in redemption, so also can a man truly serve his nation only if he has been set free to love by receiving the love of God in Christ.

It is difficult to believe that this comment is unrelated to the situation in Nazi Germany subsequent to Hitler's rise to power in 1933. The Nazi ideology was strengthened by appeal to a mythical understanding of the Gospel/Bible as a basis for racism (anti-Semitism) and the supremacy of the German people.

92. See also F. Buri, *Wie können wir heute noch verantwortlich von Gott reden?* (Tübingen, 1967), p. 28; and more recently Don Cupitt, *Taking Leave of God* (London: SCM, 1980).

93. Roberts (p. 17) adopted a critical approach to Bultmann assuming that he was to be understood in terms of Heidegger, which is a dubious assumption. He rightly recognized ambiguities in Bultmann's writings (cf. Barth's view, *K&M*, II, pp. 83f.) but also argued that he was a clear writer so that we know what he was saying (Roberts, p. 10). He concludes from the clarity that there are three Bultmanns (Roberts, p. 14). Or did Roberts misunderstand the ambiguity? Many of his criticisms ignore Bultmann's 'Reply' to his critics in the Kegley volume. Hence, Roberts failed to clarify ambiguities and used them to 'set up' Bultmann for his criticism. The criticisms manifest an antagonistic 'tone' which contributed to his misunderstanding of Bultmann. While Roberts (p. 15) formally acknowledged Bultmann's stature as a scholar his criticisms seem to deny this. For example, he argued (pp. 80f.) that Bultmann 'does not read the New Testament "naturally"' but uses the 'ploy' of hermeneutical translation to find his own meaning in the text. The word 'ploy' is emotive, ignoring the problems involved in interpretation and suggesting that the method was just a contrived tactic to get his own way. (Cf. Roberts, p. 143.) He refers to 'the ambiguous way Bultmann uses language ... to slip through the groping fingers of his critics' (Roberts, p. 114) suggesting a studied ambiguity to lead the critics astray. In dealing with Bultmann on Paul he referred to 'Bultmann's tendentious exegesis' and asserted 'Paul was not a Kantian' and 'Bultmann's notion that modern man *is* a Kantian' (Roberts, p. 152). Does

such a comment do justice to Bultmann's work on Paul? The Kantian imputation is a total misunderstanding of Bultmann's existentialism. Having summarized what *he thought* Bultmann's view was on a subject Roberts (pp. 174f.) asks 'what Bultmann seems to be getting at through all this messy logic'. The 'tone' of these words is obvious. Further, 'the messy logic' is a consequence of Roberts's reconstruction, not Bultmann's argument. The same 'tone' is to be found in his comments that existentialist analysis is 'an odd hybrid', that the language of faith is '*only* interpretation' (Roberts, p. 188). Why 'only'? He referred to 'Bultmann's crude distinction' (Roberts, p. 196). He asserted that 'preunderstanding' was 'tailored (if somewhat grossly)' to meet a difficulty (Roberts, p. 205). He said that Bultmann's notion of scientific exegesis is 'arbitrary' and that exegetes who have 'learned...most from philosophers have often been amongst the worst. Origen comes to mind' (Roberts, p. 213). Is Bultmann amongst the worst? Origen was theologian *par excellence* in his own day. What are we to make of that? Finally, Roberts likened Bultmann's hermeneutical approach to a surgeon performing a brain operation with a dull axe—we could hardly expect the patient to live (Roberts, p. 238). Roberts's 'tone' reflects an attitude which excluded the possibility of real understanding. His approach was also limited by the attitude to language criticized by W.F. Zuurdeeg (pp. 16f.).

94. Naturally 'world' is used here in the evaluative sense without any intention of questioning the objective reality of the natural order. But as 'world' that order is understood by man as being at his disposal, rather than, as God's creation, that which lays claim on him. This understanding of the 'world' is to be found in the Fourth Gospel (*Th.N.T.*, II, pp. 26ff.) and Paul (*Th.N.T.*, I, pp. 255ff.) where the 'world', created by the Logos, does not know him. Bultmann's critics have picked up this negative evaluation but have not noticed that here the 'world' is distinguished from God's creation and have concluded that Bultmann devalues human life in the world in favour of some kind of 'otherworldliness'. This tendency has been encouraged by Bultmann's stress on transcendence, as for example, in the title of his Marburg sermons, *This World and the Beyond*. Criticism of Bultmann along such lines is to be found in a recent article by Keith Clements, 'Worldliness or Unwordliness? The Issue between Bonhoeffer and Bultmann as seen by Ronald Gregor Smith', *SJT* 34/6 (1981), pp. 531-44. While recognizing the value of Bultmann's position Clements argues that it is inferior to Bonhoeffer's in that it undervalues man's life in the world and is over-individualistic (p. 547). Both criticisms can be treated together. First, the stress on transcendence in no way devalues the 'world'. Rather, in this way the 'world' is revalued as *creation*. It is valued, but not mistaken for God. Because it is God's creation it is possible for his word to address the believer in and through it. Second, the believer's response in the world involves love to the neighbour and obedience to God in all that he commands (*EPT*, p. 309). Whatever else, love is always required (*TLYN*, pp. 53ff.). What love

to the neighbour will mean cannot be set out in advance. It can be known only in the claim of the moment. But what love means is not arbitrary. The paradigm of love has been expressed in the Christ event. What this will mean can only be known in a concrete situation. Such obedience and love are not only to be expressed spontaneously and to individuals. The believer is also responsible for the world (Kegley, pp. 279f.), a responsibility which is shared with all human beings, but is accepted by the believer with a new urgency. Such responsibility must take account of what we call ecology and the provision of institutional frameworks which maximize the realization of human freedom. Bultmann's failure to do more than offer hints along these lines is not a consequence of his theological position but is due rather to his vocation as a New Testament scholar. The tasks of ecology and the development of socio-political institutions were to be worked out by others. But it would be wrong to see his theology as an impediment to these tasks. Rather, it should be seen as a potential basis for approaching these problems.

Notes to Chapter Four

95. In Process Theology, which is probably dependent on Hegel, not only is the world in process, so also is God. Perceiving God's action in the world in this tradition is the basis of a 'worldview'.

96. While the problem is not discussed by Bultmann, he appears to be aware of the criticism that if symbolic discourse about God is to be meaningful it must be based on a *direct*, non-symbolic statement (see R.W. Hepburn in *New Essays in Philosophical Theology* [London: SCM, 1955], pp. 238f.).

97. Bultmann has given detailed attention to the theology of the Fourth Evangelist and this highlights his failure to do so in the case of each of the Synoptic Gospels. However, his failure cannot be seen as a consequence of not recognizing the editorial techniques of the Synoptic evangelists because this is a fundamental aspect of his analysis in *HST*. It appears to be the consequence of using the Synoptics as source material for the reconstruction of the historical Jesus, Earliest Christianity and Hellenistic Christianity which forms the matrix for Paul and John. It is because of his critical use of the canon within the canon that the christological kerygma of Paul and John is his point of focus, and the kerygmatic forms which find expression in the Synoptics appear to be inconsistent and inadequate. Whether such an analysis is adequate could only be demonstrated on the basis of a detailed exposition of each of the Synoptic evangelists. While Bultmann himself did not provide such a study, his work reminds us that it is not enough to speak of the diversity of New Testament christologies, or kerygmas, without raising the question of the relative adequacy of the variety of forms. For Bultmann,

the Christ kerygma of Paul and John is taken to be the most adequate expression of the faith evoked by the Christ event and becomes his canon within the canon. This problem can perhaps be solved in other ways (see Tracy, *TAI*, pp. 308ff.).

98. See Ogden, *Point*, pp. 75ff., where Ogden argues that the various symbols of christology assert that Jesus is the re-presentation of God through whom we have authentic understanding of ourselves. He argues that the diverse concepts and symbols are functionally interchangeable in identifying Jesus as the decisive re-presentation of God.

99. Both C.F.D. Moule, *The Origin of Christology* (Cambridge: CUP, 1977), and J.D.G. Dunn, *Christology in the Making* (London: SCM, 1980), argue for the legitimacy of the development of christological perception within the New Testament. Perhaps the case needs to be argued more cogently for stopping development with the New Testament. However, both appear to assert that there are grounds in the Christ event itself to justify the development of perception within the New Testament.

100. See Hans Jonas, *Augustin und das paulinische Freiheitsproblem: Eine philosophische Studie zum pelagienischen Streit* (Göttingen: Vandenhoeck und Ruprecht, 1965), especially the Appendix 'The Hermeneutical Structure of Dogma'.

101. Duncan Watson, 'Why Chalcedon?', *JTSA* 39 (1982), pp. 3-22, esp. 3ff.

Notes to Chapter Five

102. Discovering the meaning of events is a complex task because events have a ripple effect so that their significance can be viewed from different vantage points. Secondly, the meaning or significance of events is not always *self-evident* in the events themselves. This need not imply a dualism of fact and value. It is a recognition that the meaning or significance of history is an epistemological problem.

103. Johnson, p. 181 n. 7, appears to recognize this. In that note he wrote 'In an essay written two years later (1927), "Zur Frage der Christologie", he brings the two (*freie Tat* and *Entscheidung*) together, speaking of "*freie Tat der Entscheidung*" (*GV*, I, p. 101, cf. p. 110). Bultmann's point is that, while faith is a free act, it is not self-assertive as a work is. Rather, faith is the free submission involved in obedience. Whether Johnson has adequately appreciated this point is unclear, since elsewhere he speaks of Bultmann's change from 'the passive *Erlebnis*' to 'the more active *Entscheidung*' (Johnson, p. 78). This is not an inconsistency because the *Entscheidung* of faith is an active decision to submit to the claim of God encountered in the moment of decision.

104. See, for example, the two massive volumes by the systematic theologian Edward Schillebeeckx entitled *Jesus* and *Christ*.

BIBLIOGRAPHY

Achtemeier, Paul J. 'How Adequate is the New Hermeneutic?', *ThT* 23 (1966), pp. 105-11.

—*An Introduction to the New Hermeneutic*, Philadelphia: Westminster Press, 1969.

Aland, B., et al. *Gnosis: Festschrift für Hans Jonas*, Göttingen: Vandenhoeck und Ruprecht, 1978.

Allen, Douglas *Structure and Creativity in Religion: Hermeneutics in Mircea Eliade's Phenomenology*, The Hague: Mouton, 1978.

Anderson, B.W. (ed.) *The Old Testament and Christian Faith*, London: SCM, 1964.

Barbour, I.G. *Issues in Science and Religion*, London: SCM, 1966.

—*Myths, Models and Paradigms: The Nature of Scientific and Religious Language*, London: SCM, 1974.

Barrett, C.K. 'Myth and the New Testament', I & II, *ExpTim* 68 (1957), pp. 345-48, 359-62.

—'Pauline Controversies in the Post-Pauline Period', *NTS* 20 (1974), pp. 229-45.

Barrett, Wm *What is Existentialism?*, New York: Grove Press, 1964.

Barth, Karl *The Word of God and the Word of Man* (ET) London: Hodder and Stoughton, 1928.

—*The Epistle to the Romans* (ET) Oxford: OUP, 1933, 1968.

—*Protestant Theology in the Nineteenth Century* (ET) London: SCM, 1959 (revised).

—*Church Dogmatics* (ET) Edinburgh: T. & T. Clark, 1956 onwards.

—'Rudolf Bultmann: An Attempt to Understand Him' in *K&M*, II, pp. 83-132.

Bartsch, H.W. (ed.) *Kerygma und Mythos: Ein theologisches Gespräch* (6 vols. with supplements) Hamburg: Reich & Heidrich, Evangelischer Verlag, 1948 onwards; Selections in English in *Kerygma and Myth* (2 vols.) London: SPCK, 1962 and 1964.

Batey, R. (ed.) *New Testament Issues*, London: SCM, 1970.

Batey, R. and Gill, J.H. 'Fact, Language and Hermeneutic', *SJT* 23/1 (1970), pp. 13-26.

Bauer, Walter *Orthodoxy and Heresy in Earliest Christianity* (ET) London: SCM, 1972.

Beasley-Murray, G.R. 'Demythologized Eschatology', *ThT* 14 (1957), pp. 61-79.

Betz, O. *What do we know about Jesus?* (ET) London: SCM, 1968.

Bousset, Wilhelm *Kyrios Christos* (ET) Nashville: Abingdon, 1970.

Bornkamm, G. *Jesus of Nazareth*, London: Hodder & Stoughton, 1960.

—'Die Theologie Rudolf Bultmanns in der neueren Diskussion', *ThR* 29 (1963-1964), pp. 33-141

Boutin, M. *Relationalität als Verstehensprinzip bei Rudolf Bultmann*, Beiträge zur evangelischen Theologie 67; Munich: Kaiser, 1974.

Braaten, Carl E. 'How New is the New Hermeneutic?', *ThT* 22 (1965), pp. 218-35.

—*History and Hermeneutics* (New Directions in Theology Today 2) London: Lutterworth Press, 1968.

Braaten, Carl E. and Harrisville, R.A. (eds.)*The Historical Jesus and the Kerygmatic Christ*, Nashville: Abingdon, 1964.

Bultmann, Rudolf (Fuller bibliographical details to 1966 are available in *The Theology of Rudolf Bultmann*, ed. C.W. Kegley, London: SCM, 1966. The following list of publications has been significant for this study. Titles are listed chronologically with republications and translations listed in brackets following the original publication.) 'Die Schriften des Neuen Testaments und der Hellenismus', *ChrW* 25 (1911), pp. 589-93.

—'Biblische Theologie', *ThR* 19 (1916), pp. 113-26.

—'Die Bedeutung der Eschatologie für die Religion des Neuen Testaments', *ZTK*, 27 (1917), pp. 76-87.

—'Vom geheimnisvollen und offenbaren Gott', *ChrW* (1917), pp. 572-79. ('Concerning the Hidden and Revealed God', *EF*, pp. 23-34.)

—Review of M. Dibelius, *Die Formgeschichte des Evangeliums*, *ThLZ* 44 (1919), pp. 173f.

—'Religion und Kultur', *ChrW* 34 (1920), pp. 417-21; 435-39; 450-53. (*Anfänge der dialektischen Theologie*, Jürgen Moltmann (ed.) München: Kaiser, 1963, II, pp. 11-29). ('Religion and Culture', *The Beginnings of Dialectic Theology*, James Robinson (ed.) Richmond: John Knox Press, 1968, pp. 205-20.)

—'Ethische und mystische Religion im Urchristentum', *ChrW* 34 (1920), pp. 725-31; 738–43. (*Anfänge der dialektischen Theologie*, II, pp. 29–47. 'Ethical and Mystical Religion in Primitive Christianity', *The Beginnings of Dialectic Theology*, pp. 221-35).

—*Die Geschichte der synoptischen Tradition*, Göttingen: Vandenhoeck & Ruprecht, 1921. (*The History of the Synoptic Tradition* [trans. John Marsh], New York: Harper & Row, 1963.)

—'Karl Barths Römerbrief in zweiter Auflage', *ChrW* 36 (1922), pp. 320-23; 330-34; 358-61; 369-73.

—'Der religionsgeschichtliche Hintergrund des Prologs zum Johannes-Evangelium', *Eucharisterion; Festschrift für H. Gunkel*, Göttingen: Vandenhoeck & Ruprecht, 1923.

—'Das Problem der Ethik bei Paulus', *ZNW* 30 (1924), pp. 123-40.

—'Die Bedeutung der neuerschlossenen mandäischen und manichäischen Quellen für das Verständnis des Johannesevangeliums', *ZNW* 24 (1925), pp. 100-46.

—'Das Problem einer theologischen Exegese des Neuen Testaments', *ZZ* 3 (1925), pp. 334-57. (*Anfänge der dialektischen Theologie*, II, pp. 47-72.)('The Problem of a Theological Exegesis of the New Testament', *The Beginnings of Dialectic Theology*, pp. 236-56.)

—'Welchen Sinn hat es, von Gott zu reden?', *ThBl* 4 (1925), pp. 129-35 (= *GV*, I, pp. 26-37). ('What Sense is there to Speak of God?' [trans. F.H. Littell], *Christian Scholar* 43 [1960], pp. 213–22. 'What Does it Mean to Speak of God?', *FU*, pp. 53–65.)

—*Jesus*, Berlin: Deutsche Bibliothek, 1926. (*Jesus and the Word* [trans. Louise Pettibone Smith and Erminie Huntress Lantero], New York: Charles Scribner's Sons, 1934.)

—'Geschichtliche und übergeschichtliche Religion im Christentum', *ZZ* 4 (1926), pp. 385-403 (= *GV*, I, pp. 65-84). ('Historical and Supra-historical Religion in Christianity', *FU*, pp. 66-95).

—'Wilhelm Heitmüller', *ChrW* 40 (1926), pp. 209-13.

—'Karl Barth: "Die Auferstehung der Toten"', *ThBl* 5 (1926), pp. 1-14 (= *GV*, I, pp. 38-64). ('Karl Barth, *The Resurrection of the Dead*', *FU*, pp. 66-94.)

—'Urchristliche Religion (1915-1925)', *AR* 24 (1926), pp. 83-164.

—Review of W. Bauer, *Das Johannesevangelium* (2nd edn), *ThLZ* 51 (1926), pp. 246f.

—'Das Johannesevangelium in der neuesten Forschung', *ChrW* 41 (1927), pp. 502-11.

—'Zur Frage der Christologie', *ZZ* (1927), pp. 41-69 (= *GV*, I, pp. 85-113). ('On the Question of Christology', *FU*, pp. 116-44.)
—'Die Eschatologie des Johannesevangeliums', *ZZ* 6 (1928), pp. 4-22 (= *GV*, I, pp. 134-52). ('The Eschatology of the Gospel of John', *FU*, pp. 165-83).
—*Der Begriff der Offenbarung im Neuen Testament*, Tübingen: Mohr, 1929 (= *GV*, III, pp. 1-34). ('The Concept of Revelation in the New Testament', *EF*, pp. 58-91.)
—'Zur Geschichte der Paulus-Forschung', *ThR* 1 (1929), pp. 26-59.
—'Das christliche Gebot der Nächstenliebe', *RHPh* (1930), pp. 222-41. ('To Love your Neighbour', *Scottish Periodical* 1 [1947], pp. 42-56.) (*GV*, I, 1933, pp. 229-44.)
—'Die Geschichtlichkeit des Daseins und der Glaube', *ZTK* n.s. 11 (1930), pp. 329-64. ('The Historicity of Man and Faith', *EF*, pp. 92-110.)
—'Mythus und Mythologie im Neuen Testament', *RGG*, 2nd edn, IV (1930), pp. 390-94.
—'Paulus', *RGG*, 2nd edn, IV (1930), pp. 1019-45. ('Paul', *EF*, pp. 111-46.)
—Review of H. Lietzmann, *Ein Beitrag zur Mandäerfrage*, *ThLZ* 56 (1931), pp. 577-80.
—'Urchristentum und Religionsgeschichte', *ThR* 4 (1932), pp. 1-21.
—Review of R. Reitzenstein, *Die hellenistischen Mysterienreligionen...* (3rd edn) and *Die Vorgeschichte der christlichen Taufe*, *HZ* 145 (1932), pp. 372-76.
—'Ginosko', *ThWB* (1933), pp. 688-719; = *TDNT*, I, (1964), pp. 689-719. ('Gnosis' [trans. J.R. Coates], New York: Harper, 1958.)
—'Zur Frage des Wunders', *GV* I (1933), pp. 214-28. ('The Question of Wonder', *FU*, pp. 247-62.)
—'Die Christologie des Neuen Testaments', *GV*, I (1933), pp. 245-67. ('The Christology of the New Testament', *FU*, pp. 313-31.)
—'Das Problem der "Natürlichen Theologie"', *GV* I (1933), pp. 294-312. ('The Problem of "Natural Theology"', *FU*, pp. 313-31.)
—*Glauben und Verstehen*, (4 vols.) Tübingen: Mohr, 1933-1965.
—'Die Bedeutung des Alten Testaments für den christlichen Glauben', *GV*, I (1933). ('The Significance of the Old Testament for Christian Faith', in *The Old Testament and Christian Faith*, ed. B.W. Anderson, London: SCM, 1964).
—'Vorwort', *Gnosis und spätantiker Geist*, by Hans Jonas, Göttingen: Vandenhoeck & Ruprecht, 1934.
—'Neueste Paulusforschung', *ThR* (1934), pp. 229-46.
—Review of E. Stauffer, *Grundbegriffe einer Morphologie des neutestamentlichen Denkens*, *ThLZ* 59 (1934), pp. 211-15.
—Review of H. Lietzmann, *Geschichte der alten Kirche*, I, *ZKG* 53 (1934), pp. 624-30.
—'Neueste Paulusforschung', *ThR* 8 (1936), pp. 1-22.
—'Reich Gottes und Menschensohn', *ThR* 9 (1937), pp. 1-35.
—Review of H. Lietzmann, *Geschichte der alten Kirche*, II, *ZKG* 58 (1939), pp. 260-66.
—Review of E. Hirsch, *Die Auferstehungsgeschichten und der christliche Glaube*, *ThLZ* 65 (1940), pp. 224-46.
—*Das Evangelium des Johannes*, Göttingen: Vandenhoeck & Ruprecht, 1941. (*Gospel of John*, Oxford: Blackwell, 1971.)
—*Offenbarung und Heilsgeschehen*, München: Lempp, 1941. ('Neues Testament und Mythologie', *KuM*, I, pp. 15-48.) ('New Testament and Mythology', *K&M*, I, pp. 1-44.) (Die Frage der natürlichen Offenbarung', *GV*, II, pp. 79-104.) ('The Question of Natural Revelation', *EPT*, pp. 90-118.)
—Review of W. Nestle, *Vom Mythos zum Logos*, *ThLZ* 67 (1942), pp. 146-48.

—'Antwort an H. Thielicke', *Deutsches Pfarrerblatt* 47 (1942), pp. 1-5. (*KuM*, I [3rd edn only], pp. 221-26.)
—'Zum Thema: Christentum und Antike', *ThR* 16 (1944), pp. 1-20.
—*Theologie des Neuen Testaments*, I, Tübingen: Mohr, (*Theology of the New Testament*, I [trans. Kendrick Grobel], New York: Charles Scribner's Sons, 1951.)
—'Zu Schniewinds Thesen', *KuM*, I (1948), pp. 122-38. ('A Reply to the Theses of J. Schniewind', *K&M*, I, pp. 102-23.)
—'Heilsgeschichte und Geschichte', *ThLZ* 73 (1948), pp. 659-66. ('History of Salvation and History', *EF*, pp. 226-40.)
—*Das Urchistentum im Rahmen der antiken Religionen*, Zurich: Artemis-Verlag, 1949. (*Primitive Christianity in its Contemporary Setting* [trans. R.H. Fuller] New York: Meridian Books, 1957.)
—'Das Problem der Hermeneutik', *ZTK* 47 (1950), pp. 47-69 (= *GV*, II, pp. 211-35). ('The Problem of Hermeneutics', *EPT*, pp. 234-61.)
—'Ursprung und Sinn der Typologie als hermeneutischer Methode', *ThLZ* 75 (1950), pp. 205-12.
—'Geleitwort', *Das Wesen des Christentums*, A. Harnack (ed.), Stuttgart: Ehernfried Klotz Verlag, 1950.
—*Theologie des Neuen Testaments*, II, Tübingen: Mohr, 1951. (*ThNT* II [trans. Kendrick Grobel], New York: Charles Scribner's Sons, 1955.)
—'Das christologische Bekenntnis des Ökumenischen Rates', *Schweizerische Theol. Umschau* 21 (1951), pp. 25-36. ('The Christological Confession of the World Council of Churches', *EPT*, pp. 273-304.)
—'Zum Problem der Entmythologisierung' (1952), *KuM*, II, pp. 177-208. ('Bultmann Replies to his Critics' [omitting first section of original], *K&M*, I, pp. 191-211) (= *GV*, IV, pp. 128-37.)
—'Die christliche Hoffnung und das Problem der Entmythologisierung', *Unterwegs* 7 (1953), pp. 257-64 (= *GV*, III, pp. 81-90). (*Die christliche Hoffnung und das Problem der Entmythologisierung*, Stuttgart: Evangelisches Verlagswerk, 1954.)
—'Antwort an Karl Jaspers', *Schweizerische Theologische Rundschau*, 3/4 (1953), pp. 74-106. (*KuM*, III, pp. 49-60.) (*Myth and Christianity: An Inquiry into the Possibility of Religion without Myth* by Karl Jaspers and R. Bultmann, New York: The Noonday Press, 1958.)
—'History and Eschatology in the New Testament', *NTS* 1 (1954), pp. 5-16.
—Review of C.H. Dodd, *The Interpretation of the Fourth Gospel*, *NTS* 1 (1954-1955), pp. 77-91. ('Rudolf Bultmann's Review of C.H. Dodd's *The Interpretation of the Fourth Gospel*', [trans. W.G. Robinson], *Harvard Divinity Bulletin* 27 (1963), pp. 9-22.)
—'Milestones in Modern Books', *ExpTim* 70 (1955). *Essays Philosophical and Theological* (ET of *GV* II, London: SCM, 1955).
—*Marburger Predigten*, Tübingen: Mohr, 1956. (*This World and the Beyond: Marburger Sermons*, London: Lutterworth, 1960.
—'Ist voraussetzungslose Exegese möglich?', *Theologische Zeitschrift* 54 (1957), pp. 409-17 (= *GV*, III, pp. 142-50).
—'Allgemeine Wahrheiten und christliche Verkündigung', *ZThK* 54 (1957), pp. 244-54 (= *GV*, III, pp. 166-77).
—*History and Eschatology*, Edinburgh: Edinburgh University Press, 1957.
—'Das Befremdliche des christlichen Glaubens', *ZTK* 55 (1958), pp. 185-200 (= *GV*, III, pp. 197-212).
—*Jesus Christ and Mythology*, New York: Charles Scribner's Sons, 1958.

—'Erziehung und christlicher Glaube', *Martin Heidegger zum siebzigsten Geburtstag*, Tübingen: H. Laupp, 1959 (= *GV*, IV, pp. 52-55).
—'Johannesevangelium', *RGG*, 3rd edn, III, Tübingen: Mohr, 1955, cols. 840-850.
—'Zum Problem der Entmythologisierung', *Il problema della demitizzazione* (ed. Enrico Castelli), Padova: A. Milani, 1961 (*KuM*, VI 1, pp. 20-27.) (On the Problem of Demythologizing', trans. S. Ogden, *JR* 42 (1962), pp. 96-102, and in *New Testament Issues of Today*, ed. R. Batey, London: SCM, 1970) (= *GV*, IV, pp. 128-37).
—*Das Verhältnis der urchristlichen Christusbotschaft zum historischen Jesus*, Heidelberg: Carl Winter, Universitätsverlag, 1962. ('The Primitive Christian Kerygma and the Historical Jesus', trans. Carl E. Braaten and Roy A. Harrisville, *The Historical Jesus and the Kerygmatic Christ*, New York: Abingdon Press, 1964.)
—'Anhang: Aus einem Briefwechsel zwischen Rudolf Bultmann und dem Verfasser anlässlich des Aufsatzes über die Unsterblichkeit', *Zwischen Nichts und Ewigkeit*, Hans Jonas, Göttingen: Vandenhoeck & Ruprecht, 1963.
—'Der Gottesgedanke und der moderne Mensch', *ZTK* 60 (1963), pp. 335-48. ('The Idea of God and Modern Man', *Translating Theology into the Modern Age* (ed. Robert W. Funk), New York: Harper & Row, 1965; and also in *World Come of Age*, ed. Gregor Smith, London: Collins, 1967) (= *GV*, IV, pp. 113-27).
—'Reflexionen zum Thema Geschichte und Tradition', *Weltbewohner und Weimaraner*, ed. by Refenberg, B., and Staiger, E., Zurich: Artemis, 1960.
—*Form Criticism* (ET) New York: Harper, 1962; with K. Kundsin.
—*Existence and Faith: Shorter Writings of Rudolf Bultmann* (ET) London: Collins, 1964.
—'General Truths and Christian Proclamation, in *History and Hermeneutic*, ed. by Funk, R., and Ebeling, G, Tübingen: Mohr, 1967.
—*The Old and the New Man in the Letters of Paul*, (ET) Atlanta: John Knox, 1967.
—*Faith and Understanding* (ET of *GV*, I) London: SCM, 1969.
—In the *Journal of Religion*
—1952 'Humanism and Christianity'
—1962 'On the Problem of Demythologizing'
—1972 'Protestant Theology and Atheism'
—*Karl Barth–Rudolf Bultmann Letters 1922/1966* (ed.) Berndt Jaspert, (ET) Michigan: Eerdmans, 1981.
—*The Second Letter to the Corinthians*, (ET), Augsburg, 1985.
Buri, F. *Wie können wir heute noch verantwortlich von Gott reden?*, Tübingen: Mohr, 1967.
Cairns, D. *A Gospel Without Myth. Bultmann's Challenge to the Preacher*, London: SCM, 1960.
Casey, R.P. 'Gnosis, Gnosticism and the New Testament' in *The Background of the New Testament and its Eschatology*, ed. Davies, W.D. and Daube, D., London: CUP, 1956.
Cassirer, Ernst *Language and Myth,* (ET) New York,Harper, 1946. *The Philosophy of Symbolic Forms II: Mythical Thought*, (ET) New Haven: Yale University Press, 1955.
Charlesworth, & Culpepper, R.A.J.H.'The Odes of Solomon and the Gospel of John', *CBQ* 35/3 (1973), pp. 298-321.
Clements, Keith 'Worldliness or Unworldliness? The Issue between Bonhoeffer and Bultmann as seen by Ronald Gregor Smith', *SJT* 34/6 (1981), pp. 531-49.
Collingwood, R.G. *The Idea of History*, 2nd edn, Oxford: Clarendon Press, 1946.

Colpe, C. 'New Testament and Gnostic Christology', in *Studies in the History of Religions XIV*, ed. J. Neusner, 1968.
—*Die religionsgeschichtliche Schule: Darstellung und Kritik ihres Bildes vom gnostischen Erlösermythus*, Göttingen: Vandenhoeck & Ruprecht, 1961.
Cupitt, Don *Taking Leave of God*, London: SCM, 1980.
Dart, John *The Laughing Saviour*, New York: Harper & Row, 1976.
Deegan, Daniel 'Wilhelm Herrmann: a Reassessment', *SJT* 19 (1966), pp. 188-203.
De Nys, M.J. 'Myth and Interpretation: Bultmann Revisited', *International Journal for the Philosophy of Religion* 2, (1980), pp. 27-41.
Dillenberger, John (ed.) *Martin Luther, Selections from his Writings*, New York: Doubleday, 1961.
Dillistone, F.W. *Myth and Symbol*, London: SPCK, 1966.
Dodd, C.H. *The Apostolic Preaching & Its Development*, London: Hodder & Stoughton, 1936.
—*The Interpretation of the Fourth Gospel*, London: CUP, 1953.
Drane, John *Paul: Libertine or Legalist*, London: SPCK, 1975.
Dudley, Guildford *Religion on Trial: Mircea Eliade & His Critics*, Philadelphia: Temple University Press, 1977.
Dunn, James D.G. *Unity and Diversity in the New Testament*, London: SCM, 1977.
—*Christology in the Making: An Inquiry into the Origins of the Doctrine of the Incarnation*, London: SCM, 1980.
Ebeling, Gerhard 'Hermeneutik' in *RGG*, 3rd edn, III, Tübingen: Mohr, (1959) cols. 242-262.
—*Word and Faith* (ET) London: SCM, 1963.
—*Theology and Proclamation: A Discussion with Rudolf Bultmann*, London: Collins, 1966.
—*Introduction to a Theological Theory of Language*, (ET) London: Collins, 1973.
Edwards, Paul (ed.) *Encyclopedia of Philosophy*, 8 vols., New York: Macmillan and Free Press, 1968.
Edwards, Rem. B. *Reason and Religion*, New York: Harcourt Brace Jovanovich Inc., 1972.
Eliade, Mircea *Myths, Dreams, and Mysteries: The Encounter between Contemporary Faiths and Archaic Reality*, (ET) London: Fontana, Collins, 1968; New York, Harper, 1960.
—*Patterns of Comparative Religion*, London: Sheed & Ward, 1958.
—*The Quest*, Chicago: Chicago University Press, 1969.
—*Images & Symbols*, New York: Sheed & Ward, 1969.
—*The Myth of the Eternal Return*, Princeton: Princeton University Press, 1954.
—*The Sacred & the Profane: The Nature of Religion*, New York: Harper, 1961.
Elliott, J.H. 'A Catholic Gospel: Reflections on "Early Catholicism" in the New Testament', *CBQ* 31 (1969), pp. 213-33.
Evans, C.F. 'The Gospel of John: A Commentary', Review Article of Bultmann's *GJ*, in *SJT* 26/3 (1973), pp. 360-64.
Fawcett, Thomas *The Symbolic Language of Religion*, London: SCM, 1970.
—*Hebrew Myth and Christian Gospel*, London: SCM, 1973.
Ferre, Frederick *Language, Logic and God*, London: Fontana, 1970.
Feuerbach, *The Essence of Christianity* (ET) London: John L.A. Chapman, 1854.
—*The Essence of Religion* (ET) New York: Harper & Row, 1967.
Flew, A. & MacIntyre, A. *New Essays in Philosophical Theology*, London: SCM, 1953.

Foerster, Werner *Gnosis: A Selection of Gnostic Texts* (2 vols.) Oxford: OUP, 1972, 1974.

Fortsman, J. *A Romantic Triangle: Schleiermacher and Early German Romanticism*, Missoula: Scholars Press, 1973.

Frank, Erich *Philosophical Understanding and Religious Truth*, Oxford: Oxford University Press, 1945.

Frei, Hans *The Eclipse of Biblical Narrative: A Study in Eighteenth and Nineteenth Century Hermeneutics*, New Haven: Yale University Press, 1974.

Fuchs, Ernst *Zum hermeneutischen Problem in der Theologie*, Tübingen: Mohr, 1959.

—*Zur Frage nach dem historischen Jesus*, Tübingen: Mohr, 1960. (Partly tr. in *Studies in the Historical Jesus*, London: SCM, 1964.)

—*Marburger Hermeneutik*, Tübingen: Mohr, 1968.

—*Hermeneutik*, Tübingen: Mohr, 1970.

Fuller, Daniel *Easter Faith and History*, London: Tyndale, 1968.

Fuller, R.H. *The New Testament in Current Study*, London: SCM, 1963.

—*The Formation of the Resurrection Narratives*, London: SPCK, 1965.

Funk, Robert W. 'Colloquium on Hermeneutics', *ThT*. 21 (1964), pp. 287-306.

—*Language, Hermeneutic and Word of God: The Problem of Language in the New Testament and Contemporary Theology*, New York: Harper & Row, 1966.

—(ed.) *Schleiermacher as Contemporary*, New York: Herder & Herder, 1970.

Funk, Robert W. & Ebeling, G. *History and Hermeneutic*, Tübingen: Mohr, 1967.

Gadamer, Hans-Georg 'Martin Heidegger und die Marburger Theologie', in E. Dinkler (ed.), *Zeit und Geschichte: Dankesgabe an Rudolf Bultmann zum 80. Geburtstag*. Tübingen: Mohr, 1964, pp. 479-90.

—'The Problem of Language in Schleiermacher's Hermeneutic', *JTC* 3 (1970), pp. 68-95

Galloway, A.D. 'Religious Symbols and Demythologizing', *SJT* 10/4 (1957), pp. 337-60.

Garish, A. 'Continuity and Change: Friedrich Schleiermacher on "The Task of Theology"', in *Tradition and the Modern World*, Chicago: Chicago University Press, 1978.

Geffre, Claude 'Bultmann on Kerygma and History' in T.F. O'Meara and D.M. Weisser (eds.) *Rudolf Bultmann in Catholic Thought*, New York: Herder and Herder, 1968.

Gibbs, G. 'Rudolf Bultmann and His Successors', *SJT* 18/4 (1965), pp. 396-410.

Gilkey, Langdon *Message and Existence*, New York: Seabury, 1979.

Gogarten, F. *Demythologizing and History* (ET) London: SCM, 1955.

Grant, R.M. *Gnosticism and Early Christianity*, New York: Columbia University Press, 1959.

—*Gnosticism: An Anthology*, London: Collins, 1961.

Gregor Smith, Ronald (ed.) *World Come of Age*, London: Collins, 1967.

Haardt, Robert *Gnosis: Character and Testimony*, Leiden: Brill, 1971.

Hanson, A.T. 'The Great Form Critic', *SJT* 22/3 (1969), pp. 296-304.

Hanson, R.P.C. *The Bible as a Norm of Faith*, Durham: Durham University Press, 1963.

Hartlich, Christian and Sachs, Walter *Der Ursprung des Mythosbegriffes in der modernen Bibelwissenschaft*, Tübingen: Mohr, 1952.

Harvey, Van Austin *The Historian and the Believer: The Morality of Historical Knowledge and Christian Belief*, London: SCM, 1967.

Heidegger, Martin *Being and Time* (ET) Oxford: Blackwell, 1962.

Henderson, Ian *Myth in the New Testament*, London: SCM, 1962.

—*Rudolf Bultmann*, London: Carey Kingsgate Press, 1965
Hengel, M. *The Son of God*, (ET) London: SCM, 1976.
—*Acts and the History of Earliest Christianity* (ET) London: SCM, 1979.
—*Judaism and Hellenism*, (ET) London: SCM.
Hepburn, R.W. 'Demythologizing and the Problem of Validity', in A. Flew and A. MacIntyre (eds.), *New Essays in Philosophical Theology*, London: SCM, 1955, pp. 227-42.
Herrman, Wilhelm *Die Religion im Verhältnis zum Welterkennen und zur Sittlichkeit*, Halle: Niemeyer, 1879.
—*Systematic Theology*, (ET) London: Allen & Unwin, 1927.
—*The Communion of the Christian with God Described on the Basis of Luther's Statements* (ET) London: SCM, 1972.
Heywood Thomas, John 'The Relevance of Kierkegaard to the Demythologizing Controversy', *SJT* 10/3, pp. 239-59.
Hick, John (ed.) *The Myth of God Incarnate*, London: SCM, 1977.
Hodges, H.A. *Wilhelm Dilthey: An Introduction*, Kegan Paul, London: French and Trubner, 1944.
—*The Philosophy of Wilhelm Dilthey*, London: Routledge & Kegan Paul, 1952.
Hopkins, Jasper 'Bultmann on Collingwood's Philosophy of History', *HTR* 58 (1965), pp. 227-33.
Hordern, Wm *Speaking of God: The Nature and Purpose of Theological Language*, London: Epworth Press, 1965.
Hübner, Hans *Politische Theologie und existentiale Interpretation*, Witten: Luther Verlag, 1973.
Johnson, Roger A. *The Origins of Demythologizing: Philosophy and Historiography in the Theology of Rudolf Bultmann*, Leiden: Brill, 1974.
Jonas, Hans *Gnosis und spätantiker Geist*, Göttingen: Vandenhoeck & Ruprecht, 1934 and 1954.
—*The Gnostic Religion*, Boston: Beacon Press, 2nd edn, 1963.
—'Heidegger and Theology', *RM* 18 (1964), pp. 207-33.
—'A Retrospective View', in *Proceedings of the International Colloquium on Gnosticism*, Leiden: Brill, 1977, pp. 1-15.
—*Augustin und das Freiheitsproblem. Ein philosophischer Beitrag zur Genesis der christlich-abendländischen Freiheitsidee*, Göttingen: Vandenhoeck & Ruprecht, 1930 and 2nd edition 1965.
—'Is Faith Still Possible? Memories of Rudolf Bultmann and Reflections on Philosophical Aspects of His Work', *HTR* 75 (1982), pp. 1-23.
Jung, C.G. *The Collected Works*, New York: Pantheon.
—*Memories Dreams Reflections*, New York: Random, 1961.
Jüngel, Eberhard *God as the Mystery of the World*, Grand Rapids: Eerdmans, 1983.
Kafka, Franz *The Great Wall of China: Stories and Reflections*, New York: Schocken Books, 1970.
Kähler, Martin *The So-Called Historical Jesus and the Historic Biblical Christ* (Eng. ed. by Carl E. Braaten) Philadelphia: Fortress, 1964.
Käsemann, Ernst *Essays on New Testament Themes* (ET) London: SCM, 1964.
—*New Testament Questions of Today* (ET) London: SCM, 1969.
Kegley, C.W. (ed.) *The Theology of Rudolf Bultmann*, London: SCM, 1966.
Kelsey, David H. *The Uses of Scripture in Recent Theology*, London: SCM, 1971.
Kierkegaard, S. *Concluding Unscientific Postcript to the Philosophical Fragments* (ET) Princeton: Princeton University Press, 1941.

—*Purity of Heart is to Will One Thing* (ET) London: Fontana, Collins, 1961.
Kimmerle, Heinz 'Hermeneutical Theory or Ontological Hermeneutics', *JTC* 4 (1967), pp. 107-21.
Kingsbury, J.D. 'The Gospel of Mark in Recent Research', *RSR* 5 (1979), pp. 101-107.
Kirk, G.S. *Myth, Its Meaning and Functions in Ancient and Other Cultures*, London: Cambridge University Press, 1970.
Klassen, W. and Snyder, G. (eds.) *Current Issues in New Testament Interpretation*, London: SCM, 1962.
Knauer, Peter *Okumenische Fundamental-Theologie*, Köln: Verlag Styra, 1978.
Küng, Hans *The Council in Action: Theological Reflections on the Second Vatican Council*, New York: Sheed and Ward, 1963.
—*Structures of the Church*, London: Burns & Oats, 1965.
—*On Being a Christian* (ET) London: Collins, 1977.
—*Does God Exist?* (ET) London: Collins, 1980.
Ladd, G.E. 'The Role of Jesus in Bultmann's Theology', *SJT* 18/4 (1965), pp. 396-410.
Laeuchli, S. *The Language of Faith: An Introduction to the Dilemma of the Early Church*, London: Epworth Press, 1965.
Lapointe, Roger 'Hermeneutics Today', *BTB* 2 (1972), pp. 107-54.
Mackintosh, H.R. *Types of Modern Theology*, Nisbet, 1937.
Macquarrie, John *An Existentialist Theology: A Comparison of Heidegger and Bultmann*, London: SCM, 1955; Pelican, London, 1973.
—*The Scope of Demythologizing: Bultmann and His Critics*, London: SCM, 1960.
—'Modern Issues in Biblical Studies: Christian Existentialism in the New Testament', *ExpTim* 71 (1960), pp. 177-80.
—*Studies in Christian Existentialism*, London: SCM, 1966.
—*God Talk: An Examination of the Language and Logic of Theology*, London: SCM, 1967.
—*Martin Heidegger*, London: Lutherworth Press, 1968.
—*Existentialism*, London: Pelican, 1973.
—(ed.) *Contemporary Religious Thinkers*, London: SCM, 1968.
Malet, A. *The Thought of Rudolf Bultmann* (ET) New York: Doubleday, 1971.
Malevez, L. *The Christian Message and Myth: The Theology of Rudolf Bultmann* (ET) London: SCM, 1958.
Marle, Rene *Introduction to Hermeneutics*, London: Burns & Oats, 1967.
Marshall, I.H. 'Palestinian and Hellenistic Christianity: Some Critical Comments', *NTS* 19/3 (1973), pp. 271-87.
—(ed.) *New Testament Interpretation*, Exeter: Paternoster Press, 1977.
Marxsen, Willi *Introduction to the New Testament, An Approach to its Problems* (ET) Philadelphia: Fortress, 1968.
—*Mark the Evangelist* (ET) Nashville: Abingdon, 1969.
McArthur, H.K. *In Search of the Historical Jesus*, London: SPCK, 1970.
McIntyre, J. 'Analogy', *SJT* 12/1 (1959), pp. 1-20.
McLelland, J.C.'Mythology and Theological Language', *SJT* 11/1 (1958), pp. 13-21.
Michaelson, Carl (ed.) *Christianity and the Existentialists*, New York: Scribner, 1956, especially Erich Dinkler, 'Martin Heidegger', pp. 97-127.
Miegge, G. *Gospel and Myth in the Thought of Rudolf Bultmann* (ET) London: Lutterworth Press, 1960.
Moule, C.F.D. *The Origins of Christology*, London: CUP, 1977.
Nethöfel, Wolfgang *Strukturen existentialer Interpretation: Bultmanns Johannes-*

kommentar im Wechsel theologischer Paradigmen, Göttingen: Vandenhoeck & Ruprecht, 1983.
Nicholls, Wm *The Pelican Guide to Modern Theology I: Systematic and Philosophical Theology*, London: Pelican, 1969.
Niebuhr, R.R. *Schleiermacher on Christ and Religion*, London: SCM, 1965.
Neill, S. *The Interpretation of the New Testament 1861-1961*, New York: Oxford University Press, 1966.
O'Collins, G. 'Karl Barth on Christ's Resurrection', *SJT* 26/1 (1973), pp. 85-99.
Oden, Thomas *Radical Obedience: The Ethics of Rudolf Bultmann*, Philadelphia: Westminster Press, 1964.
Ogden, Schubert 'Bultmann's Project of Demythologization and the Problem of Theology and Philosophy', *JR* 37 (1957), pp. 156-73.
—*Christ Without Myth: A Study Based on the Theology of Rudolf Bultmann*, London: Collins, 1962.
—*The Reality of God and other Essays*, London: SCM, 1967.
—'The Understanding of Theology in Ott and Bultmann', in *The Later Heidegger and Theology* (ed. by J.M. Robinson), New York: Harper & Row, 1963.
—'On Revelation' in *Our Common History as Christians*, ed. by Deschner, J., Howe, L.T., and Penzel, K.; New York: Oxford University Press, 1975.
—*The Point of Christology*, London: SCM, 1982.
Osborn, E.F., *The Beginning of Christian Philosophy*, Cambridge, 1981.
Ott, H. *Geschichte und Heilsgeschichte in der Theologie des Rudolf Bultmann* (Beiträge zur historischen Theologie 19), Tübingen: Mohr, 1955.
—*Denken und Sein. Der Weg Martin Heideggers und der Weg der Theologie*, Zurich: EVZ Verlag, 1959.
—'What is Systematic Theology?' in J.M. Robinson & Jn Cobb Jr (eds.) *New Frontiers in Theology: I The Later Heidegger and Theology*, New York: Harper & Row, 1963.
Otto, R. *The Idea of the Holy* (ET) London: OUP, 1923.
Painter, John *John: Witness and Theologian*, London: SPCK, 1975; second edition 1979; American edition entitled *Reading John's Gospel Today*, Atlanta: John Knox, 1980.
—'Rudolf Karl Bultmann', *JTSA* 17 (Dec. 1976), pp. 53-61.
—'Johannine Symbols: A Case Study in Epistemology', *JTSA* 27 (June, 1979), pp. 26-41.
—'A Note on the Hermeneutical Theology of Rudolf Bultmann', *ABR* 29 (October 1981), pp. 26-31.
—'The Origins of Demythologizing Revisited', *ABR* 33 (October 1985).
—'John 9 and the Interpretation of the Fourth Gospel', *JSNT* 28 (October 1986), pp. 31-61.
Palmer, R.E. *Hermeneutics: Interpretation Theory in Schleiermacher, Dilthey, Heidegger, and Gadamer*, Evanston: Northwestern University Press, 1969.
Pannenberg, Wolfhart 'The Revelation of God in Jesus of Nazareth', in Robinson, J.M., Cobb, J.B. (eds.) *New Frontiers in Theology* III *Revelation as History*, (ET) London: Sheed and Ward, 1969.
Pelikan, Jaroslav *Twentieth Century Theology in the Making*, Vols. I, II, III, (ET of a selection from the 2nd edition of *RGG*, Tübingen: Mohr, 1927-1932) London: Fontana, 1969.
Perrin, Norman *The Promise of Bultmann*, Philadelphia: Fortress, 1969.
—*Jesus and the Language of the Kingdom. Symbol and Metaphor in New Testament Interpretation*, London: SCM, 1976.

—*The Resurrection Narratives: A New Approach*, London: SCM, 1977.
Redeker, M. *Schleiermacher: Life and Thought*, Philadelphia: Fortress, 1973.
Richardson, A. *The Bible in the Age of Science*, London: SCM, 1961.
—*History Sacred and Profane*, London: SCM, 1964.
Richmond, James *Ritschl: A Reappraisal*, London: Collins, 1978.
Ricoeur, Paul *The Conflict of Interpretations. Essays in Hermeneutics*, Evanston: Northwestern University Press, 1974.
—'Biblical Hermeneutics', *Semeia* 4 (1975), pp. 29-145.
—*Essays on Biblical Interpretation*, Philadelphia: Fortress, 1980.
—*The Philosophy of Paul Ricoeur: An Anthology of His Work* (ed. by C.E. Reagan and D. Stewart), Boston: Beacon, 1978.
Riedl, J. *Das Heilswerk Jesu nach Johannes*, Freiburg: Herder, 1973.
Roberts, R.C. 'Rudolf Bultmann's View of Christian Ethics', *SJT* 29/2 (1976), pp. 115-36.
—*Rudolf Bultmann's Theology*, London: SPCK, 1977.
Robinson, J.A.T. *Honest to God*, London: SCM, 1963.
Robinson, J.A.T. and Edwards, D.L. (eds.) *The Honest to God Debate*, London: SCM, 1963.
Robinson, J.A.T. *The Human Face of God*, London: SCM, 1973.
Robinson, J.M. 'The Pre-history of Demythologization', *Interpretation* 20 (1966), pp. 65-77.
—(ed.) *The Future of Our Religious Past: Essays in Honour of Rudolf Bultmann*, London: SCM, 1971. (Part tr. of E. Dinkler *Zeit und Geschichte*.)
—(ed.) *The Beginnings of Dialectical Theology*, Atlanta: John Knox Press, 1968.
Robinson, J.M. &Cobb, J.B. (eds.) *New Frontiers in Theology I, The Later Heidegger and Theology*, New York: Harper & Row, 1963.
—*New Frontiers in Theology II, The New Hermeneutic*, New York: Harper & Row, 1964.
—*New Frontiers in Theology III, Theology as History*, New York: Harper & Row, 1967.
Robinson, J.M. 'The Coptic Gnostic Library Today', *NTS* 14 (1968), pp. 356-401.
—'Gnosticism and the New Testament' in *Gnosis: Festschrift für Hans Jonas*, Göttingen: Vandenhoeck & Ruprecht, 1978.
—(ed.) *The Nag Hammadi Library*, New York: Harper & Row, 1977.
Robinson, N.G.H. 'Barth or Bultmann?', *Religious Studies* 14 (1978), pp. 275-90.
Rordorf, W. 'The Theology of Rudolf Bultmann and Second Century Gnosis', *NTS* 13, pp. 351-62.
Rosenthall, K. 'Myth and Symbol', *SJT* 18/4 (1965), pp. 411-34.
Rudolf, Kurt *Gnosis*, Edinburgh: T. & T. Clark, 1983.
Rumscheidt, H.M. *Revelation and Theology*, London: Cambridge University Press, 1972.
Runzo, J. 'Relativism and Absolutism in Bultmann's Demythologizing Hermeneutic', *SJT* 32/5 (1979), pp. 401-20.
Sanders, E.P. *Paul and Palestinian Judaism*, London: SCM, 1977.
—*Jesus and Judaism*, Philadelphia: Fortress, 1985.
Sartre, Jean-Paul *Being and Nothingness* (ET) London: Methuen, 1957.
Schillebeeckx, Edward *Jesus: An Experiment in Christology*, London: Collins, 1979.
—*Christ: The Christian Experience in the Modern World*, London: SCM, 1980.
Schleiermacher, F.D.E. *The Christian Faith* (ET) Edinburgh: T. & T. Clark, 1928.
—*On Religion. Speeches to Its Cultured Despisers*. New York: Harper Torchbook, 1958.

—*Hermeneutik, nach den Handschriften neu herausgegeben und eingeleitet von Heinz Kimmerle*, Heidelberg: Carl Winter, 1959 (ET Missoula: Scholars Press, 1977).
Schmithals, W. *An Introduction to the Theology of Rudolf Bultmann*, (ET) London: SCM, 1968.
—*Gnosticism at Corinth* (ET) New York: Abingdon, 1971.
Schweitzer, A. *The Quest of the Historical Jesus*, (ET) London: Black, 1910.
Slater, P. 'The Kerygma and the Cuckoo's Nest', *SJT* 31/4 (1978), pp. 301-18.
Smith, D. Moody *The Composition and Order of the Fourth Gospel: Bultmann's Literary Theory*, New Haven: Yale University Press, 1965.
Smith, R.G. (ed.) *World Come of Age*, London: Collins, 1967.
Stuhlmacher, P. *Historical Criticism and Theological Interpretation of Scripture*, Philadephia: Fortress, 1977
Sykes, Stephen *Friedrich Schleiermacher*, London: Lutterworth, 1971.
Thielicke, H. 'Reflections on Bultmann's Hermeneutic', *ExpTim* 67 (1956), pp. 154-57.
Thiselton, A.C. *The Two Horizons*, Exeter: Paternoster, 1980.
Tillich, P. 'Existential Philosophy', *JHI* 5 (1944), pp. 44-68.
—*Theology and Culture*, New York: Galaxy Books, 1964.
—'The Religious Symbol' in *Myth and Symbol*, ed. by F.W. Dillistone; London: SPCK, 1961.
—'Myth and Mythology: The Concept and the Religious Psychology of Myth', from *RGG*, 2nd edn, (1927) (ET) in *Twentieth Century Theology in the Making*, II, ed. by Jaroslav Pelikan, London: Fontana, 1970.
—*The Protestant Era*, Chicago: Chicago University Press, 1948.
—*Ultimate Concern: Tillich in Dialogue* (ed. D. McKenzie Brown), New York: Harper, 1965.
—*What is Religion?*, New York: Harper & Row, 1969.
Torrance, J. 'Interpretation and Understanding in Schleiermacher's Theology: Some Critical Questions', *SJT* 21 (1968), pp. 268-82.
—'Hermeneutics according to F.D.E. Schleiermacher', *SJT* 21 (1968), pp. 257-67.
Torrance, T.F. *Theological Science*, London: OUP, 1969.
—*God and Rationality*, London: OUP, 1971.
—*Space, Time and Resurrection*
Troeltsch, Ernst *The Social Teaching of the Christian Churches*, (ET) London: Allen & Unwin, 1931.
Turner, Geoffrey 'Pre-understanding and New Testament Interpretation', *SJT* 28 (1975), pp. 227-42.
Tuttle, H.N. *Wilhelm Dilthey's Philosophy of Historical Understanding: A Critical Analysis*, Leiden: Brill, 1969.
Vermes, G. *Jesus the Jew*, London: Collins, 1973.
—*Jesus and the World of Judaism*, London: SCM, 1983.
Ward, K. 'Myth and Fact in Christianity', *SJT* 20/4 (1967), pp. 385-96.
Watson, Duncan 'Why Chalcedon?', *JTSA* 39 (1982), pp. 3-22.
Wilson, B.A. 'Bultmann's Hermeneutics: A Critical Examination', *International Journal for Philosophy of Religion* 8/3 (1977), pp. 169-89.
Wilson, S.G. *Luke and the Pastoral Epistles*, London: SPCK, 1979.
Wilson, R. McL. *The Gnostic Problem*, London: Mowbrays, 1958.
—*Gnosis and the New Testament*, Oxford: Blackwells, 1968.
Wink, W. *The Bible in Human Transformation: Towards a New Paradigm for Biblical Study*, Philadelphia: Fortress, 1973.

Yamauchi, Edwin *Pre-Christian Gnosticism*, London: Tyndale Press, 1973.
Young, N.J. *History and Existential Theology: The Role of History in the Thought of Rudolf Bultmann*, London: Epworth Press, 1969.
—*Creator, Creation and Faith*, London: Collins, 1976.
Zahrnt, Heinz *The Question of God: Protestant Theology in the Twentieth Century*, (ET) London: Collins, 1969.
Zuurdeeg, Wilhelm F. *An Analytical Philosophy of Religion*, London: Allen & Unwin, 1959.

INDEXES

INDEX OF BIBLICAL REFERENCES

INDEX OF AUTHORS